DIALOGUE AND DEMENTIA

This volume takes the positive view that conversation between persons with dementia and their interlocutors is a privileged site for ongoing cognitive engagement. The book aims to identify and describe specific linguistic devices or strategies at the level of turn-by-turn talk that promote and extend conversation, and to explore real-world engagements that reflect these strategies.

Final reflections tie these linguistic strategies and practices to wider issues of the "self" and "agency" in persons with dementia. Thematically, the volume fosters an integrated perspective on communication and cognition in terms of which communicative resources are recognized as cognitive resources, and communicative interaction is treated as reflecting cognitive engagement. This reflects perspectives in cognitive anthropology and cognitive science that regard human cognitive activity as distributed and culturally rooted.

This volume is intended for academic researchers and advanced students in applied linguistics, linguistic and medical anthropology, nursing, and social gerontology; and practice professionals in speech-language pathology and geropsychology.

Robert W. Schrauf is professor and head of the Department of Applied Linguistics at the Pennsylvania State University. He conducts both qualitative and quantitative research in cross-cultural gerontology, narrative gerontology, Alzheimer's disease, experimental and longitudinal approaches to multilingualism, and bilingual autobiographical memory. He is former president of the Association for Anthropology and Gerontology, a fellow of the Gerontological Society of America, and member of the editorial boards of the *Journal of Cross-Cultural Gerontology* and *Cross-Cultural Research*.

Nicole Müller is a professor of Communicative Disorders at the University of Louisiana at Lafayette, where she holds a Doris B. Hawthorne/BoRSF Endowed Professorship. Her areas of research interest include clinical linguistics, clinical discourse studies and pragmatics, age-related disorders of communication and cognition, multilingualism, and systemic functional linguistics. She is co-editor of the journal *Clinical Linguistics and Phonetics* and of the book series *Communication Disorders across Languages*.

LANGUAGE AND SPEECH DISORDERS
BOOK SERIES
Series Editors:
Martin J. Ball, University of Louisiana at Lafayette
Jack S. Damico, University of Louisiana at Lafayette

This new series brings together course material and new research for students, practitioners, and researchers in the various areas of language and speech disorders. Textbooks covering the basics of the discipline will be designed for courses within communication disorders programs in the English-speaking world, and monographs and edited collections will present cutting-edge research from leading scholars in the field.

PUBLISHED

Recovery from Stuttering, Howell
Handbook of Vowels and Vowel Disorders, Ball & Gibbon (Eds.)
Handbook of Qualitative Research in Communication Disorders, Ball, Müller, & Nelson (Eds.)
Dialogue and Dementia, Schrauf & Müller (Eds.)

FORTHCOMING

Applying English Grammatical Analysis: Clinical Language Assessment and Intervention, Jin & Cortazzi
Electropalatography for Speech Assessment and Intervention, McLeod, Wood, & Hardcastle

For continually updated information about published and forthcoming titles in the *Language and Speech Disorders* book series, please visit **www.psypress.com/language-and-speech-disorders**

CONTENTS

CONTRIBUTORS

Marta Baffy, Georgetown University, Washington DC, USA

Debra Crispin, St. Joseph's Healthcare, Hamilton ON, Canada

Michelle Daigneault, St. Joseph's Healthcare, Hamilton ON, Canada

Boyd Davis, University of North Carolina, Charlotte NC, USA

Jackie Guendouzi, Southeastern Louisiana University, Hammond LA, USA

Heidi E. Hamilton, Georgetown University, Washington DC, USA

Madelyn Iris, Leonard Schanfield Research Institute, Chicago IL, USA

Margaret Maclagan, University of Canterbury, Christchurch, New Zealand

Lisa Mikesell, Rutgers University, New Brunswick NJ, USA

Zaneta Mok, La Trobe University, Melbourne, Australia

Nicole Müller, University of Louisiana at Lafayette, Lafayette LA, USA

Anna Pate, Southeastern Louisiana University, Hammond LA, USA

Vaidehi Ramanathan, University of California Davis, Davis CA, USA

Ellen Bouchard Ryan, McMaster University, Hamilton ON, Canada

Robert W. Schrauf, The Pennsylvania State University, University Park PA, USA

Alison Wray, Cardiff University, Wales, UK

ACKNOWLEDGMENTS

Special thanks to the Pennsylvania State University Center for Language Acquisition, under the direction of Dr. James Lantolf, for providing funding for the Dialogue and Dementia Workshop in May 2011.

Part One

WHICH PARADIGM, WHOSE ENGAGEMENT, WHAT RESOURCES?

1

CONVERSATION AS COGNITION
Reframing Cognition in Dementia

Nicole Müller and Robert W. Schrauf

COGNITIVE ABILITIES IN NEUROCOGNITIVE PERSPECTIVE: THE ATOMISTIC VIEW

People who work with people with dementia and their caregivers often find themselves in a curious dilemma: We (that is, researchers, students, medical and rehabilitation professionals) learn about 'memory', 'cognition', 'brain disease', and so forth through the perspectives of medicine, neuropsychology, psychiatry, or cognitive science, depending on our pathways through education, and these perspectives tend to have certain elements in common: by and large, they are tidy, they are atomistic and focus on categorization and dissociation, and they seek to generalize. And then we have to explain to so-called 'lay' persons what it all means. What does the diagnosis of 'probable dementia of the Alzheimer's type' mean for my grandmother? What does it mean to have an MMSE score of 16? What does it mean when I'm told that I can expect that my father's procedural memory and motor learning skills are likely to remain more intact for longer than his word-finding, verbal fluency, and short term memory? How is this going to translate into 'real life'?

The atomistic, dissociation-focused view of cognitive and linguistic impairment (or skill, for that matter) is grounded in what Luria (1987a, b) referred to as 'classical science' (see also Sabat's [2001] discussion of 'classical' versus 'romantic' science as applied to Alzheimer's disease, with more detailed discussion of Luria's distinction). The 'classical' approach, which for centuries has dominated mainstream medical and psychological

3

research and practice, attempts to reconcile two basic strands of reasoning: one of generalization, and one of isolation. In terms of generalization, one attempts to isolate the common denominator in a category of people (defined by a complex of symptoms). Thus, people with recurring severe headaches, often confined to one side of the head, and in many individuals accompanied by one or several other symptoms, such as light aversion, nausea, and visual hallucinations (among others), might be diagnosed with recurring migraines, and thereby a category label is assigned to a symptom complex. Further investigation might reveal contributing causal factors: one individual may have allergic reactions to certain foods; in another, severe stress may be a trigger. The search for generalization is thus subserved by the search for isolable, and dissociable, factors or variables.

Dissociation of Memory Types

Students of dementia learn that memory impairment is a key impairment in dementing conditions. Further, we learn that memory is not a monolithic phenomenon, but rather that different subsystems of memory can be distinguished and experimentally verified and that separate memory subsystems are linked to specific neurological substrates and can be differentially impaired in different subtypes of memory disorder. The models developed by Baddeley, Squire, and colleagues have widespread currency in dementia studies (see, e.g., Squire, 1987, 2004; Squire & Kandel, 1999; Baddeley, 2002). A fundamental distinction is that between short term memory (STM) and long term memory (LTM). Two major components of STM are *immediate memory* and *working memory*. Immediate memory has a very limited storage capacity, both in terms of discrete units and time before information is lost (an upper limit of seven units, and less than 30 seconds unless information is rehearsed, are often cited; see, e.g., Squire & Kandel, 1999). The concept of working memory was established mainly through the work of Baddeley and colleagues (e.g., Baddeley, 2002, with earlier references). Working memory (WM) is understood as an information buffering center where information is held in conscious awareness, reviewed, and manipulated. Separate WM subsystems are distinguished: In the *phonological input store,* auditory traces are held active for a short time, and the *articulatory loop* serves as a subvocal rehearsal faculty. Visual and spatial information is kept active in the *visuospatial sketchpad.* The *episodic buffer* is an intermediary processor between WM and LTM. Further, Baddeley and colleagues distinguish a *central executive,* that is, a system that enables a person to focus attention, to access and retrieve information in long term storage, and to encode information and thus underlies the ability to make decisions and plans.

Researchers and diagnosticians distinguish two primary subsystems of LTM, namely *declarative* and *non-declarative,* or *explicit* and *implicit* memory systems. What the subsystems of non-declarative or implicit memory have in common is that they are generally considered not to be available for conscious, volitional review. Proverbial *procedural* skills are, for instance, those of swimming, or of riding a bicycle, that is, motor skill memories. These activities are learned by doing, rather than by conscious cognitive effort, reflection, or manipulation of information. They are also highly automatized, and once mastered, it is extremely unlikely that they are 'unlearned'; in other words, one doesn't 'forget' how to swim or ride a bicycle (what may become impaired, however, are other abilities that enable the execution of the skill, such as muscle function, balance, or vision). Other aspects of non-declarative memory are cognitive skills that are active without a person's conscious awareness, priming, habitual behaviors, and conditioned behaviors.

Declarative or *explicit* memory is knowledge about the world that is open to conscious review. Three distinct subsystems are distinguished: *Semantic* memory is memory for concepts and how they relate to each other, by way of propositions and schemata. *Episodic* memory is memory for events or episodes; one way to conceptualize it is as "semantic memory plus a context" (Bayles & Tomoeda, 2007, p. 42). *Lexical* memory is memory for words, their meanings, pronunciation, spelling, and cross-language equivalents or rough equivalents. Thus the *word* 'bicycle', and its German and Afrikaans counterparts 'Fahrrad' and 'fiets', respectively, are instances of lexical memory; these are of course closely related to the concept (an instance of semantic memory) of a two-wheeled vehicle powered by a pedal-and-chain transmission, with a handlebar and saddle, and prototypically built for single-person use. The memory of riding one's bicycle to work on a sunny day last week is an instance of an episode, or a concept with a context.

In the neuropsychology of memory and dementia, much research has been devoted to the discovery of which neural substrates support which memory system, and the breakdown of which neurological structures is responsible for which facet of memory impairment in dementing conditions. We shall not pursue this aspect of memory science further here; reference to specific brain lesions will be made in individual chapters of this collection where necessary (for overviews, see, e.g., Becker & Overmann, 2002; Bayles & Tomoeda, 2007).

Neurocognitive Assessment and Diagnostic Translation

Assessment of cognitive and language functions in the context of dementia pursues multiple aims. Examiners look for the presence of dementia as evidenced by the balance of cognitive and communicative deficits and preserved skills. This balance serves to establish a baseline of deficits and skills that informs the assignment of a diagnostic label, such as dementia, or a specific dementia subtype, such as dementia of the Alzheimer's type. Further, the baseline informs intervention, whether pharmacological or behavioral, as well as the measurement of intervention efficacy (which is of course tricky in progressive conditions). In addition, there also needs to be a counseling aspect, both for the individual (to be) diagnosed and those who will most closely be involved with (future) caregiving; this latter will typically involve questions on the part of the person with suspected dementia, and their caregivers, what the likely path of future decline will look like (see, e.g., Tomoeda, 2001; Bayles & Tomoeda, 2007).

In the absence of sudden onset of cognitive, memory, or language deficit that can be linked to a clear precipitating event, the diagnosis of dementia, and any one subtype of dementia is essentially one of elimination.[1] As well as a process of *elimination*, medical diagnosis of dementia is also a process of *decontextualization:* An individual may experience concerns about cognitive deterioration in daily life ('I keep forgetting appointments'; 'I can't seem to remember things I did or said a minute ago'; 'it's getting so hard to do sums in my head'). She may approach her primary care physician with these concerns, who may refer her to a neurologist. An examination involving brain scan comes back as normal, as do other physiological measures (e.g., screening for endocrine function, infections, or deficit states). At this stage, a case is made for thorough neuropsychological assessment, which in essence consists in the search for functional deficits of cognitive subsystems, such as short term memory, or executive function, which in turn have been established in the diagnostic literature as to be measured independently of contextual influence.

To the 'lay' mind, the cycle of assessment of cognitive skills and determination of functional consequences may appear somewhat circular: an individual may be concerned because she is finding it progressively more stressful and difficult to drive in busy traffic or unfamiliar surroundings, or because she finds she 'gets lost' when she attempts to prepare a complicated meal. Her concerns are duly taken note of and verified through neuropsychological examination, which reveals moderately severe deficits on measures of immediate and delayed recall, complex attention, and of processing speed and reaction time, and she is counseled that these deficits are likely to have an impact on complex tasks, for instance, driving or cooking.

An Example of Diagnostic Categorization and Labeling: The DSM

The standard reference work used in the US context for the diagnosis and classification of dementia and its subtypes is the Diagnostic and Statistical Manual of Mental Disorders, or DSM. The fourth edition, text revision (DSM-IV-TR; henceforth DSM-IV; American Psychiatric Association [APA], 2000) of this work was in current use at the time of chapter preparation, with the fifth edition (DSM-5, APA, 2013) just published before this volume went to press. DSM-5 introduced substantial revisions of several major diagnostic categories, among them dementia, and was published among a flurry of (at times very critical) discussion in various quarters, such as the US National Institutes of Mental Health.[2] In Table 1.1, we offer a brief side-by-side comparison of DSM-IV and DSM-5 diagnostic criteria. In DSM-IV, the superordinate category for dementia and its subtypes is "Delirium, Dementia, Amnestic, and Other Cognitive Disorders." DSM-5 introduces the superordinate category Neurocognitive Disorder (NCD), which includes delirium (which we don't discuss any further in this collection), major NCD and mild NCD, and their etiological subcategories. The defining difference between major and mild NCD is that the former involves "significant cognitive decline from a previous level of functioning" and the associated deficits "interfere with independence in everyday activities," whereas in the latter, cognitive decline is "modest" and does "not interfere with capacity for independence in everyday activities" (APA, 2013, p. 602, 605). DSM-5 makes the caveat that "the distinction between major and mild NCD is inherently arbitrary" and "the disorders exist along a continuum" (APA, 2013, p. 608).

The major categorical and terminological change in DSM-5 is obviously the removal of the term *dementia* as the label for the superordinate diagnostic category, although DSM-5 states that the "term *dementia* is retained in DSM-5 for continuity and may be used in settings where physicians and patients are accustomed to this term" (APA, 2013, p. 591). According to a report by the DSM-5 Neurocognitive Disorders Work Group, one motivation for this change was the "pejorative / stigmatizing connotation" associated with the term *dementia* (Jeste et al., 2010, p. 7).

While in earlier versions of DSM, memory impairment was treated as the core and defining symptom, DSM-5 removes memory impairment from the focal position and bases diagnostic criteria for the various subtypes of NCD around a set of six cognitive domains (see Table 1.1). While memory impairment is of course the hallmark symptom of dementia of the Alzheimer's type (NCD due to Alzheimer's disease, in DSM-5 terms), in other NCDs (such as frontotemporal degeneration), memory may be impaired relatively late in disease progression (or not at all), whereas other domains, for instance executive function or language, may be impaired much earlier (Jeste et al., 2010, p. 7).

DSM-5 criteria aim to be more specific than previously in terms of the evidence used to establish a diagnosis, requiring both observational evidence (patient, informant, and/or clinician concern) as well as

Table 1.1

Comparison of DSM-IV and DSM-5 Diagnostic Criteria for Dementia versus Major Neurocognitive Disorder

DSM-IV (from: American Psychiatric Association, 2000, p. 148–151)	DSM-5 (from: American Psychiatric Association, 2013, p. 602–603)
Criteria common to multiple dementia diagnoses:	Major Neurocognitive Disorder
A. The development of multiple cognitive deficits manifested by both	A. Evidence of significant cognitive decline from a previous level of performance in one or more cognitive domains (complex attention, executive function, learning and memory, language, perceptual-motor, or social cognition), based on:
(1) memory impairment (impaired ability to learn new information or to recall previously learned information)	(1) Concern of the individual, a knowledgeable informant, or the clinician that there has been a significant decline in cognitive function; and
(2) one (or more) of the following cognitive disturbances: (a) aphasia (language disturbance) (b) apraxia (impaired ability to carry out motor activities despite intact motor function) (c) agnosia (failure to recognize or identify objects despite intact sensory function) (d) disturbance in executive functioning (i.e., planning, organizing, sequencing, abstracting).	(2) A substantial impairment in cognitive performance, preferably documented by standardized neuropsychological testing, or, in its absence, another quantified clinical assessment.
B. The cognitive deficits in Criteria A1 and A2 each cause significant impairment in social or occupational functioning and represent a significant decline from a previous level of functioning.	B. The cognitive deficits interfere with independence in everyday activities (i.e., at a minimum, requiring assistance with complex instrumental activities of daily living such as paying bills or managing medications).
C. The deficits do not occur exclusively during a delirium.	C. The cognitive deficits do not occur exclusively during a delirium.
D. The disturbance is not better accounted for by another Axis 1 disorder, e.g., schizophrenia or major depressive disorder	D. The cognitive deficits are not better explained by another mental disorder (e.g., major depressive disorder, schizophrenia).

objective assessment (for major NCD defined as performance of > 2.0 SD below the mean, or 3rd percentile or below of an appropriate reference population, on a domain specific test; for minor NCD, defined as performance between 1–2 SD below appropriate norms, or between the 3rd and 16th percentiles).

Potentially the most far-reaching innovation in DSM-5 is the inclusion of the category of *mild* NCD, for which there is no direct equivalent in earlier DSM editions. This category is to apply to persons who present with identifiable levels of cognitive impairment that are, however, not sufficiently severe to warrant the diagnosis of *major* NCD; the change being "driven by the need of such individuals for care, and by clinical; epidemiological; and radiological, pathological and biomarker research data suggesting that such a syndrome is a valid clinical entity with prognostic and potentially therapeutic implications" (Jeste et al., 2010, p. 9). Table 1.2 illustrates how the differentiation between major and mild NCD is applied to the specific etiology of Alzheimer's disease, in comparison with the DSM-IV diagnostic criteria for dementia of the Alzheimer's type.

The category *mild* NCD due to Alzheimer's disease clearly looks to the future of biochemical brain research and imaging research to support reliable early diagnosis of AD. The NCD working group report acknowledges repeatedly that research into reliable early indicators of the presence of a dementing pathology, specifically Alzheimer's disease, is being pursued vigorously, and knowledge in this field is evolving rapidly. Among the avenues followed is research into biomarkers of the deposition of beta-amyloid protein, and of neuronal injury (see, e.g., Albert et al., 2011, for an overview). DSM-5 makes reference to diagnostic tests involving amyloid imaging on PET scans and reduced amyloid beta-42 levels in the cerebrospinal fluid, which "may have diagnostic value" (APA, 2013, p. 613). Early identification of *reliable* indicators may lead to early intervention and thus, possibly, the avoidance of severe cognitive symptoms associated with AD. It may also, in due course, remove some of the uncertainty currently associated with the presence of mild cognitive symptoms: Will they or won't they eventually develop into full-blown dementing conditions? In terms of the psycho-social consequences, the uncertainty represented by this question currently makes a diagnosis of mild cognitive impairment, or indeed minor NCD, a double-edged sword for those thus diagnosed, as well as their next of kin.

Assumptions about Cognition Enshrined in Diagnostic Processes, Tools, and Labels: The 'Cognitivist' Paradigm

Diagnostic labels such as 'dementia', 'dementia of the Alzheimer type (DAT)', and 'major NCD due to Alzheimer's disease' represent endpoints, as well as starting points. They represent the endpoints of diagnostic processes that rest on some strong and, we would argue, typically

Table 1.2

Diagnostic Criteria for DAT (DSM-IV), and Major or Mild NCD (DSM-5) Due to Alzheimer's Disease (AD)

DSM-IV (American Psychiatric Association, 2000, p. 157)	DSM-5 (American Psychiatric Association, 2013, p. 611)
A. (1) and (2), as in Table 1.1	A. Meets criteria for major or mild NCD.
B. As in Table 1.1	B. There is insidious onset and gradual progression of impairment in one or more cognitive domains (major: at least two domains must be impaired).

C. The course is characterized by gradual onset and continuing cognitive decline.	C. **Major** NCD: Probable AD is diagnosed if either of the following is present; otherwise, probable Alzheimer's disease should be diagnosed:
	1. Evidence of a causative AD genetic mutation from family history or genetic testing
	2. All three of the following are present:
	  a. Clear evidence of decline in memory and learning and at least one other cognitive domain …
	  b. Steadily progressive, gradual decline in cognition, without extended plateaus
	  c. No evidence of mixed etiology (…).
	
	Mild NCD: Probable AD is diagnosed if there is evidence of a causative AD genetic mutation from either genetic testing or family history. Possible AD is diagnosed if there is no evidence of causative AD genetic mutation … and all three of the following are present:
	1. Clear evidence of decline in memory and aging
	2. Steadily progressive, gradual decline in cognition, without extended plateaus
	3. No evidence of mixed etiology (…).

D. The cognitive deficits in criteria A1 and A2 are not due to any of the following: (1) other central nervous system conditions that cause progressive deficits in memory and cognition (…) (2) systemic conditions that are known to cause dementia (…) (3) substance-induced conditions	D. The disturbance is not better explained by cerebrovascular disease, another neurodegenerative disease, the effects of a substance, or another mental, neurological, or systemic disorder.
E. As in point C, Table 1.1	
F. As in point D, Table 1.1[1]	

[1] DSM-5 removes distinction of early versus late onset Alzheimer's disease (thus far defined as onset at age 65 years or below, or after age 65 years, respectively).

unquestioned assumptions, among them the following: (a) that cognition can be modeled as a set of dissociable deficits and skills, (b) that these deficits and skills reside in an individual brain and can be meaningfully accessed and measured in a decontextualized fashion, and (c) that the sum of these skills and deficits adds up to a 'whole' cognitive apparatus. Diagnostic criteria are thus framed as dissociable component deficits (a good example here is early significant memory loss, generally accepted as a highly reliable criterion for Alzheimer's dementia). These diagnostic criteria in turn define not only the dividing line between what constitutes normal functioning, as contrasted with deviant, or deficient functioning, but also the categories of deficiency, such as dementia.

We use the term *cognitivist* paradigm to refer to a construct of dementia that is grounded in biomedical and neuropsychological models (see Hughes, 2011, for a more extensive discussion of such models) and that results from a medical diagnostic process that attempts to be objective and reliable, and therefore uses diagnostic criteria that in turn rest on (purportedly) measurable and (theoretically) isolable constructs of what makes up human cognition. This approach to cognition is grounded in classical reductionist science and attempts to capture skills and deficits in context-free terms. An illustration of this atomistic approach is represented by the identification, in DSM-5, of six separate cognitive domains (see Table 1.1) that are used to identify and anchor component cognitive skills and deficits (APA, 2013, p. 593–595). There is of course a gap between 'real-life' behaviors or difficulties that may motivate an individual to seek out a diagnostic evaluation, and context free, 'objective' assessment of cognitive subskills. DSM-5 attempts to address this gap by making specific recommendations for which types of tests would tap into the skills and deficits underlying specific symptoms. For instance, the cognitive domain of 'complex attention' is further subdivided into sustained attention, divided attention, selective attention, and processing speed. An example of an observation in the major NCD category would be that an individual has "increased difficulty in environments with multiple stimuli (TV, radio, conversation); is easily distracted by competing events in the environment" (APA, 2013, p. 593). Examples of assessments listed to probe subsystems of attention are pressing a button every time a tone is heard over a period of time (sustained attention), hearing numbers and letters read but being asked to count only letters (selective attention), or rapidly tapping while learning a story being read (divided attention). This can be seen as an earnest and honest attempt to bridge the gap between observations in a person's life that give rise to concern, and replicable measurements that can be used in experimental or quasi-experimental (i.e., context-free assessment) settings. However, it does not address the underlying problem, namely, that difficulties arise and therefore should be observed in context. Further, the attempted mapping of a contextualized difficulty ('I'm finding it harder to follow a conversation when the TV is on') onto domain-specific tests cements the decontextualization that is part of the diagnostic process, which in turn may also mean that the diagnostic label resulting from this process, and any measurement of severity that comes with it, may only be a poor reflection of a person's contextualized functioning.

Much of the research into dementia from the cognitivist perspective centers around memory and its components, given that memory impairment is a key component of the symptom complex of Alzheimer's disease (or major NCD due to Alzheimer's disease), which is the most commonly diagnosed form of dementia (or NCD). In the cognitivist perspective, memory is modeled primarily in terms of storage (encoding and preservation) and retrieval of mental representations, which are subdivided into various types along the dimensions of duration (short term and working memory versus long term memory) and type of representation (declarative versus procedural; episodic versus semantic and lexical; see our discussion of dissociation of memory types earlier in this chapter, also Parkin, 2000). Further, memory research from this perspective attempts to capture memory in an individual, understood as dissociable abilities, or splinter skills, that can be detected in the clinical interview or the laboratory via decontextualized tasks employing standardized stimuli (words, pictures, puzzles) that are designed to target specific kinds of memory tasks (immediate or delayed recall, for example).

Thus, perhaps the most powerful, and potentially most problematic assumption inherent in the cognitivist account, an assumption that is typically entirely implicit and taken for granted, is that 'cognition' resides and happens in an individual brain. This approach is also inherently 'defectological', in that it emphasizes the identification and tracking of progressive decrements of an individual's cognitive functioning, mirroring (however imperfectly) the progressive pathological processes within that individual's brain.

As we mentioned previously, diagnostic labels and categories are results, but they are also starting points: Diagnostic labels create categories of people. A diagnosis of probable DAT or major NCD due to Alzheimer's disease confers the status of 'dementia patient' on a person who has increased difficulties thinking. Diagnostic labeling can of course have a number of positive consequences. For example, in many countries, an accepted medical diagnosis is necessary in order to make a person eligible to receive certain medical, nursing care, or hospice care services. On the other hand, labeling can also have negative consequences; among such detrimental consequences is the circumstance that assumptions inherent in a label create expectations. In the case of AD, for instance, in what we have labeled the cognitivist perspective, the expectations are of increasing deterioration of cognitive skills, specifically memory, caused by an incurable brain disease that leads to dissolution of individuality and personality (by way of increasing loss of memory capacity) and, eventually, death. These are not unrealistic expectations, but they are far from the whole picture. As mentioned already, the diagnostic label, and any attending measurement of severity, does little to illuminate how a person functions in daily life and what affordances or hindrances in their life contexts impact their functioning and quality of life. In order to gain a perspective on this complex picture, an alternative perspective on dementia is necessary.

SHIFTING PARADIGMS: THE DISCURSIVIST APPROACH

As applied linguists, clinical linguists, and language scholars, the contributors to this book subscribe generally to an alternate paradigm concerning dementia, which differs point for point from the cognitivist (as defined previously) view. This *discursivist* perspective is variously shaped by an emphasis on

- social constructionist vs. biomedical approaches to the disease,
- preserved abilities vs. irreversible losses,
- attention to complex (holistic) cognitive functioning in meaningful social contexts vs. measurement of splinter skills with artificial tasks, and
- cognition as co-constructed in dyadic, triadic, and group conversation vs. cognition as information processing that takes place within individuals.

From the social constructionist perspective, dementia, and specifically Alzheimer's disease as both a disease entity and a diagnostic category, emerged under particular historical and cultural circumstances and continues to evolve as circumstances change (Ballenger, 2006; George, Qualls, Camp, & Whitehouse, 2013; Gubrium, 1986; Whitehouse, Maurer, & Ballenger, 2000). Notable moments in this history include the transformation of the diagnostic category from a young-onset and rare form of dementing process in the early 1900s—Alois Alzheimer's landmark case—to the medicalization, in the 1970s and 1980s, of the 'senility' experienced by a considerable proportion of the elderly (Ballenger, 2000; Holstein, 2000; Katzman & Bick, 2000), the emergence of a vigorous advocacy movement and massive outlays of public funding for biomedical research from the 1980s to the present (Fox, 2000), and the more recent revisions of the diagnosis, for research purposes, by both the National Institute on Aging and the Alzheimer's Association (McKhann et al., 2011), and for diagnostic purposes, by the DSM-5 (Jeste et al., 2010; APA, 2013). These shifts in diagnostic paradigms point up the ongoing 'construction' of Alzheimer's in both the research and medical communities.

A social constructionist view of the disease also has distinct *linguistic* implications in two particular senses. First, linguists ask, who is doing the social constructing and for what purpose? At the beginning of this chapter, we mentioned that researchers, students, and medical and rehabilitation professionals learn about memory, cognition, brain disease, and so forth through the perspectives of medicine, neuropsychology, psychiatry, or cognitive science, and that these perspectives tend to have something in common. As Schrauf (chapter 2) points out, the medical and care professionals in these various areas share a specific discourse about the disease, and consequently, they may be said to constitute a particular 'discourse community' around research, diagnosis, and treatment. This is the 'professional world' of health care. Alternately, older adults—who are actually at greater risk for the disease because of their age—share a different, but related, discourse about the disease around the existential concerns of being susceptible to or being patients with the disease. As Schrauf explains, this latter discourse is shaped by the 'lifeworld' (Mishler, 1984). In this sense, dementia is discursively constructed in different but overlapping ways across communities of discourse. Contributors to this volume gather data—generally conversational (interview) data, but also written texts produced by persons with dementia—from within a lifeworld context of everyday speech.

A second, explicitly discursivist concern for linguists with a social constructionist bent is their understanding of language itself, not as a store of lexical units (words) and a system of syntactic structures (grammar), but rather as real-life communicative activity, and especially talk-in-interaction where meanings are co-constructed or achieved in successive turns between speakers. In this view, cognition itself is something that takes place between interlocutors (rather than within them) as together people share views, react to events, make plans, do projects, complain, rue, satirize, fantasize, joke, pray, *and* remember, and do all the other things embraced by everyday *talk*. This approach shifts the question of cognition away from information processing within individual minds to a focus on co-constructed, interactive acts of cognition unfolding over time between interlocutors. This focus on dyadic, triadic, and group cognition sets the stage for looking at the preserved abilities of persons with Alzheimer's disease, or at least the efficacious cognitive and linguistic compensations of persons with Alzheimer's, as they engage in everyday conversation with other people. In consequence, the book addresses these kinds of questions:

1. What are the real-world conversational and discursive tasks that prove challenging for persons with Alzheimer's disease?
2. What are the linguistic and cognitive resources—abilities, strategies, devices—available to persons with Alzheimer's for 'doing' successful social cognition in talk or other discourse?

Cognitive and Communicative Devices

In the second part of this volume, each contributor works from empirical, conversational data, first, to address the question of specific real-world interactional tasks and, second, to demonstrate the particular discursive devices used by persons with dementia in meeting those challenges. Three of the chapters concern persons with Alzheimer's disease, and the final chapter in the section expands our view to include frontotemporal dementia.

One of the most common and intriguing challenges facing conversation partners who are strangers to one another is figuring out who the 'other' is and hence what the parameters of the conversation might be: How should I address you? What are acceptable and promising topics? What issues should I avoid? What threads might I pursue if conversation falters? What will you find funny, entertaining, or interesting? and so on. Müller and Mok (chapter 3) point out that this conversational task requires that a person elicit and evaluate information appropriately, situate the known relative to the unknown, and distribute the task across interlocutors and across time. Thus, a person with Alzheimer's disease might use repetition (in part) as a means of "active learning management and conversation based rehearsal" (chapter 3)—a way of tracking and rehearsing information. Further, as interlocutors acquire information about the other, they integrate this new information into their existing cultural and social schemata and successively update these from moment to moment. Obviously, this is a delicate cognitive dance, and Müller and Mok point out that as an individual with Alzheimer's disease experiences progressive memory loss, his or her recognition of the interlocutor may be restricted to the moment of conversation and need to be re-established with each encounter. This mundane conversational task requires rather complex cognitive processing, the coding and retention of information in working memory, the retrieval of information from long term memory, and continual updating of the situation model.

From a discursivist perspective, this cognitive task is in fact a social, distributed achievement, requiring from all speakers the careful coordination of self-revelation, appropriate contributions, ongoing uptake of information, and a concern for maintaining the flow of conversation.

In a kind of bottom-up approach to conversational requirements, Davis and Maclagan (chapter 4) examine the conversations of one individual—"Maureen Littlejohn"—across multiple conversations to uncover her strategic deployment of certain micro-features of talk. In particular, the authors look at formulaic language, including extenders (e.g., 'and so on', 'all that stuff', 'you know'), colloquial phrases (e.g., 'grow like weeds', 'dog eat dog'), and other placeholders. They note that extenders, for instance, "provide a way for the speaker with DAT to have little islands in the stream of discourse, upon which she can perch while planning the next part of an utterance, and to create or simulate shared understandings with the conversation partner" (chapter 4). One advantage of fixed expressions is that they may be recalled as multiword wholes, rather than constructed bit by bit, and in producing them, speakers come across as fluent and engaged. At more molar levels, Davis and Maclagan demonstrate the sensitivity of Maureen to the responses of her interlocutor as signals of attunement, alignment, and affiliation with her, and to the ways in which she either elaborates, diminishes, or terminates her contributions accordingly. Again, these conversational strategies reflect exquisite coordination and activation of cognitive abilities in the maintenance of the seemingly simple activity of conversation, and they draw our attention to how an individual with Alzheimer's disease capitalizes on preserved abilities in social functioning.

Undeniably, of course, Alzheimer's disease involves the gradual degeneration of cognitive abilities over time, and as Guendouzi and Pate (chapter 5) point out, these losses become noticeable and often constitute very real losses of 'face'. Where conversation partners expect one another to keep track of the thread of conversation or to remember crucial personal details from past experiences, the person with Alzheimer's disease may not be able to do so, and from the perspective of politeness theory, these conversational missteps become face-threatening acts, which interlocutors must work to repair. In one sense, persons with Alzheimer's disease fall afoul of a conversational cooperative principle (Leech, 1983, drawing on Grice, 1975)—that interlocutors work to seamlessly co-construct their conversation. As compensatory strategies, both formulaic phrases and nonverbal behaviors may be used by persons with AD to signal their active engagement in the conversation and thus maintain identity and agency. However, as Guendouzi and Pate discuss, use of these strategies, or indeed their conversational effects, may not be either volitional or conscious for the individual. Nevertheless, these strategies can be quite effective in preserving the flow of conversation. Or, for instance, whereas lexical retrieval may fail for the target lexical entry, the semantic system may automatically supply another exemplar within the target category, and the production of that related (but inexact) item serves to preserve—albeit imperfectly—the flow of conversation. As interlocutors accommodate to these non-target-like productions, they allow the individual to save face and (interestingly) comply with the cooperative principle. An interesting implication of this work is that 'preserved abilities' may be seen to include those ways in which the underlying cognitive system compensates for potentially infelicitous conversational contributions.

In the final chapter in this section, Mikesell (chapter 6) expands our view beyond dementia of the Alzheimer's type to frontotemporal dementia (FTD), an executive disorder that affects interpersonal behavior and social functioning but that does not include the memory deficits seen in Alzheimer's disease. Conversationally, individuals with FTD are seen to be adept at dealing with immediate prior turns, and hence would not show the kinds of short term or working memory deficits seen in AD, but they often have trouble orienting to the goals and purposes governing whole series of turns.

Mikesell looks in particular at how three persons with FTD signal their uptake of prior turns. Drawing on Sacks's (1992) empirical work on how interlocutors signal understanding in second turns, she modifies his original distinction between *claims* of understanding (a response that repeats or rephrases some portion of the immediate turn) and *demonstrations* of understanding (a response that provides additional evidence not present in the previous turn) by refining the typology to include *displays* of understanding. Thus, Mikesell proposes that Sacks's demonstrations are in fact displays. These provide additional material, and perhaps an interpretation of the prior turn. While it is easy for a speaker to feign a claim of understanding, it is more difficult (though possible) to feign a display of understanding. In a *demonstration* of understanding, on the other hand, the interlocutor must show an 'embodied understanding' or clear orientation to the larger ongoing activity. Crucially, the attempt to feign a demonstration of understanding will fail. Logically then, as critically related to the larger ongoing activity of the conversation, demonstrations of understanding are more often co-constructed. This is precisely where individuals with FTD have difficulties, and on balance these difficulties seem to have more to do with executive rather than memory abilities.

Interestingly, Mikesell notes that this way of looking at executive deficits may be outside the reach of current laboratory (and possibly clinical?) paradigms. Mikesell's observation could lead one to conclude either that clinical instruments should target conversation itself as an appropriate assessment task *or* that the parsing of executive versus memory abilities is inherently problematic, since the executive ability to track the relation between micro-turns and macro-activities also includes a memory component.

Enriching Engagement

The third section of this volume examines particular contexts of engagement designed to enrich the communicative activity of persons with dementia. Again, using empirical data gathered from these various activities, the contributors address the strategies and devices used by individuals to 'do' meaningful and successful conversation. The chapters address a variety of abilities that may ultimately depend on underlying cognitive components, but that are experienced as basic human abilities at more molar levels. All three chapters, for instance, address issues of personhood, identity, and agency. All three chapters also focus on preserved abilities, or the enhancement of preserved abilities.

A number of years ago, Ryan proposed the Communication Predicament of Aging (Ryan, 1992), which suggests that people speaking with older adults often adjust their speech and expectations according to negative stereotypes about what older adults are capable of, and in the process, trigger either passivity or subpar conversational contributions on the part of the older adult. These responses seemingly confirm the interlocutor's negative stereotypes and perpetuate the cycle. The same model applies to individuals with Alzheimer's disease in the sense that cognitively healthy adults often approach conversations with persons with dementia with predictable stereotypes about memory loss and (naturally) aging. Of course, the experience of memory loss is a fact for persons with dementia, and such losses have very real consequences for their autobiographical remembering and conversational storytelling. Given that storytelling is so common in everyday talk, and of paramount importance in establishing and maintaining a social identity, persons with dementia are in a double bind: their ability to remember is compromised, and interlocutors may expect them not to remember. As conversation grinds to a halt or slips into banalities, so a critical avenue for preserving one's social identity also fades away.

In chapter 7, Ryan, Crispin, and Daigneault present the results of a series of interventions designed to assist persons with dementia in remembering their life stories and to assist caregivers in revising and overcoming their often unconscious biases about conversation with them. These methods involve the "collaborative elicitation of life story fragments in conversation and the use of written recordings of these stories as triggers for future conversations in long term care settings" (chapter 7). From a cognitivist perspective, the transcribed stories, along with items and pictures in a Memory Box or collected in Memory Binders, provide cues for the retrieval and possibly elaboration of autobiographical memories, but from the discursivist perspective, they in fact do much more. As Ryan et al. point out, the very activity of personal storytelling in a conversational setting adds meaning to life, facilitates social engagement, and quite simply gives pleasure to participants. "In terms of models, this person-centered approach creates a prepared, enhanced communication environment enabling persons with dementia to assert their identities and connect with others on their terms (Elliot, 2011; Lubinski, 2011; Ryan, 2010)" (chapter 7). Again, from a discursivist perspective, it is the holism of this project that is of special note. It is not simply the re-invigoration of failing memory that is important. Rather, in the interventions of Ryan et al., it is the consequences of re-invigorating memory in a social situation and in interactive talk that count: the re-affirmation of social persona, the sense of participation, and the joy of doing so.

In conversation, and particularly in storytelling, individuals claim an identity, exercise agency within their social worlds, and shape and occupy differing roles within their real and storied worlds. The diagnosis of Alzheimer's, as well as the slowly manifesting cognitive deficits, place identity at risk and pose very real challenges to a person's sense of agency. As Kitwood (1997) and Sabat and Harré (1992, 1994) have discussed, individuals with Alzheimer's disease can be socially positioned as less than full partners in conversation (and in life!), robbing them of contexts in which they can reasonably exercise their abilities. In chapter 8, Hamilton and Baffy present interactive data from a fascinating project in which older individuals with Alzheimer's disease in a senior center produce a theatrical production in which they read letters that they have collaboratively written about their experiences. Ultimately, in the final production the participants read their letters to an audience, which creates a social context in which memory is not an issue and in which the participants can bond around their shared experience. The data, however, come from an early moment in the project when the group was composing a letter of complaint to a local paratransit service. In their analysis, Hamilton and Baffy adroitly show how individuals use 'power-claiming' discourse strategies (e.g., interruptions, questions, directives) to enhance their agency (see Ainsworth-Vaughan, 1998) in both the conversations that they narrate in their stories, as well as in the context of collaborative storytelling. Interestingly, as the authors point out, the agency claimed by participants either in the storyworld or even within the group may not stand outside these 'safer' contexts. Nevertheless, these contexts provide a space in which preserved abilities may be demonstrated and in fact *enjoyed.*

In chapter 9, Ramanathan takes up the analysis of six 'pathographies,' autobiographical accounts of the illness experience, written by individuals who have been diagnosed with Alzheimer's disease and their next of kin. Because the authors of these personal memoirs essentially engage in a 'memory exercise', their writings lend themselves to the consideration of what the experience of memory loss is like. Ramanathan draws on Derrida's (1978) notion of memories as 'traces'—fragments of scenes, images, conversations, and on the individual fragment as a *recit,* which carries with it the expectation of being able to repeat the remembered experience in some way in the future. This brings home in striking fashion how much of life is built on the ability to do-again, say-again, feel-again, and ultimately *be-again* (to re-deploy the remembered) and how much our familial and social worlds are founded on mutual expectations about such repetition. Such memory fragments and the ability to recall them, this *ability to repeat,* amounts to what Ramanathan refers to as "one's sure signs that define oneself," and it is the loss of these traces that poses the existential threat. "The dread of loosening the grip on meaning for people with Alzheimer's and their caregivers suggests that there is a slow erasure of that initial moment of the signification process, that gramme in the arche-memory that enables meaning to be constructed on the basis of difference" (chapter 9). This is an analysis far from the cognitivist's talk of working memory, long term memory, executive functions, and the rest, but Ramanathan's accomplishment is *not* the re-mapping of existential dynamics onto cognitivist mechanisms. Rather, by allowing us to read the writings for ourselves, she shows us how individuals who are experiencing the losses of Alzheimer's disease themselves struggle to maintain a sense of continuity of self and world by inscribing their experiences into written forms. Her sensitive and moving analysis shows us the acts of self-preservation by very real people.

Following on her seminal work on formulaic language (Wray, 2002, 2008), Wray has been exploring the ways such language figures in the speech of persons with Alzheimer's disease (2010, 2011). In chapter 10, she provides a brief summary of the cognitive and conversational benefits of formulaic language for normal interaction and then moves on to show how such speech may affect conversations with caregivers of persons with AD. Clearly, it is cognitively efficient for a speaker to retrieve a pre-stored word string with phrasal, idiomatic, or metaphoric meaning, but the enunciation of such a phrase reduces the cognitive effort of the hearer as well and provides subtle reassurance that meanings are being exchanged in appropriate and expectable ways. Further, Wray points out that when a speaker introduces new information into ongoing talk, he or she does so by combining both formulaic and innovative elements, and hearers can concentrate their processing resources on the new information. The person with Alzheimer's disease can 'cash in' on the benefits of using pre-stored word strings, but if his or her speech becomes overly reliant on formulaic phrases, then caregivers may experience it as rude, disengaged, self-aggrandizing, or a sign of inattention. This exposes the caregiver to a distasteful dilemma: either to assume that the person with AD is in fact being rude, disengaged, etc., and to respond accordingly, or to disengage from the conversation and produce the same kinds of superficial and inconsequential talk. Neither of these responses is helpful to the person with Alzheimer's, and Wray considers the benefits to be gained from explicit training in compassion—particularly in the practice of empathy, or entering into another's world. Indeed, if the caregiver can learn to read the formulaic and repetitive language of the person with Alzheimer's as the attempt to achieve his or her goals, communicate meaning, and share experience, then the dilemma may be moot.

> When cognition is compromised, formulaic language may not be a marker of *lack* of attention, as it would be in normal circumstances. Rather it may be the very evidence of attention. Formulaic language may become the carrier of the main message, rather than background information. Thus, it needs to be taken seriously, not necessarily for its *direct* content meaning, but for its functional purpose in the discourse. (Chapter 10)

In the end, this chapter points up in dramatic fashion the notion that cognition is essentially a shared social activity because it refocuses our attention on the interlocutor who actively co-constructs meaning with the person who has dementia. Perhaps in testament to the commitment on the part of all of this volume's contributors to an emphasis on preserved abilities, this chapter demonstrates that preserving abilities is itself a shared, social activity.

THE PATH FORWARD

This chapter began with a sustained reflection on the nature and underlying assumptions of neurocognitive assessment, detailing the current taxonomy of memory types and cognitive functions that are principally affected by the progressive neurodegeneration that marks dementia. We suggested that this approach focuses on dissociable 'splinter-skills' and loses some of the holism inherent in everyday cognitive (and human) functioning. Along the way, we described the recent shifts in diagnostic nosology, from DSM-IV to DSM-5, and the re-conceptualizations of the disease implicit in these recent developments. We applied the label 'cognitivist' to the dominant model of cognition, and, by extension, dementia, a model that assumes that cognition takes place within individual minds and may be assessed, and even understood, using experimental tasks that address specific sub-domains of cognition, divorced from any social context. As an antidote to this individualistic view of human cognition, we advanced an alternate *discursivist* paradigm that assumes that cognition is in fact something that takes place between people. Consequently, we suggested that the examination of the cognitive challenges involved in everyday conversation and the linguistic, discursive, and narrative devices used by people in meeting those challenges would give a different view of dementia.

Readers of the chapters will decide for themselves whether the analysis of empirical data provides sufficient support for adopting this alternate view. However, it is useful to consider at this point whether the discursivist paradigm substitutes for or complements the cognitivist paradigm. Further, explicitly addressing this seemingly academic question may in fact reveal what can be done in practical terms for improving our diagnostic abilities and connecting them to real-world patients, for the creative development of new and non-pharmacological interventions, and the training of caregivers for the emotionally taxing task of caring for their loved ones. Let's take a brief look at the question of whether either of these paradigms reduces to the other. Interestingly, this too is an empirical question that begs for data collection and analysis from both sides.

From within the cognitivist paradigm, it is obvious that much research supports the disociability of the sub-components of cognition that comprise the current neurocognitive taxonomy. Without losing sight of this valuable work, one could propose the new empirical challenge of identifying the more meso- or macro-level emergent combinations of abilities that allow individuals to engage in meaningful conversation. So, for instance, where Müller and Mok describe 'getting-to-know-you' as a necessary skill, or where Davis and Maclagan demonstrate the ability to keenly sense and adroitly respond to signals of interlocutor alignment, it would be interesting to figure out whether these conversational abilities could be described and tested as stable, interpersonal (emergent, combined), cognitive abilities in and of themselves. This portends an extended taxonomy beyond the traditional splinter skills, as well as a considerable psychometric challenge. Nevertheless, the effort would very likely pay off in ecological validity and provide more intuitively obvious paths for caregiver training. This move does not reduce the discursivist view to the cognitive view, but incorporates it. In fact, there is a comparatively recent, but growing body of research in cognitive science that explicitly addresses the embodied, distributed, and culturally grounded nature of human cognition (see, e.g., Hutchins, 1995; Clark, 1997; Rogers, 2006). To date, relatively little of this work has spilled over into applied and/or clinical contexts (but see, e.g., Duff, Mutlu, Byom, & Turkstra, 2012; Dahlbäck, Kristiansson, & Stjernberg, 2013; also Müller & Mok, this volume), but this is a promising avenue for future interdisciplinary research.

From within the discursivist paradigm, the neurocognitive approach essentially embodies another discourse, produced by an identifiable discourse community: the professionals in medicine, neuropsychology, psychiatry, or cognitive science mentioned in the first paragraph of the chapter. The clinical linguists, applied linguists, and linguistic anthropologists who authored these chapters constitute another discourse community, as 'lay' people from within the lifeworld constitute a third discourse community. As noted previously, these various discourses about dementia overlap to varying degrees, and from the discursivist's view, the coordination of that overlap may well be the best way to make a difference in diagnosis and real-world care. Thus, where the cognitivist view is short on holism and focused on decrements and deficits, the discursivist view is long on ecological validity and focused on preserved abilities. These emphases are inherently comforting and motivating in the world of treatment and caregiving. Whereas the discursivist view is short on questions of etiology and cure, the neurocognitive view is moving ever more relentlessly toward identifying and assessing pathological processes in prodromal stages of the disease. The combined strengths of these different discourses may well offer the best path forward. It is in that spirit that we offer the studies in this volume.

NOTES

1. In fact, while the presence of a trigger event such as a closed head injury focuses the diagnostic effort, individuals with diffuse brain damage tend to present with a broad spectrum of deficits. Thus, while a medical diagnosis in such a case would be 'traumatic brain injury', the cognitive-behavioral symptoms may be very wide-ranging in type and severity.
2. We shall not pursue this discussion any further in this chapter. Thomas Insel's blog entry on "Transforming Diagnosis" (April 29, 2013; http://www .nimh.nih.gov/about/director/2013/transforming-diagnosis.shtml) provides a useful starting point for interested readers.

REFERENCES

Ainsworth-Vaughn, N. (1998). *Claiming power in doctor patient talk.* New York: Oxford University Press.

Albert, M. S., DeKosky, S. T., Dickson, D., Dubois, B., Feldman, H. H., Fox, N. C., . . . Phelps, C. H. (2011). The diagnosis of mild cognitive impairment due to Alzheimer's disease: Recommendations from the National Institute on Aging-Alzheimer's Association workgroups on diagnostic guidelines for Alzheimer's disease. *Alzheimer's & Dementia, 7,* 270–279.

American Psychiatric Association. (2000). *Diagnostic and statistical manual of mental disorders. Fourth edition, text revision.* Washington, DC: APA.

American Psychiatric Association. (2013). *Diagnostic and statistical manual of mental disorders. Fifth edition.* Washington, DC: APA.

Baddeley, A. D. (2002). The psychology of memory. In A. D. Baddeley, M. D. Kopelman, & B. A. Wilson (Eds.), *The handbook of memory disorders* (pp. 3–15). New York: Wiley.

Ballenger, J. (2000). Beyond the characteristics plaques and tangles: Mid-twentieth century U.S. psychiatry and the fight against senility. In P. J. Whitehouse, K. Maurer, & J. Ballenger (Eds.), *Concepts of Alzheimer's disease: Biological, clinical, and cultural perspectives* (pp. 83–103). Baltimore: Johns Hopkins.

Ballenger, J. F. (2006). *Self, senility, and Alzheimer's disease in modern America.* Baltimore: Johns Hopkins.

Bayles, K., & Tomoeda, C. (2007). *Cognitive-communication disorders of dementia.* San Diego: Plural.

Becker, J. T., & Overman, A. A. (2002). The memory deficit in Alzheimer's disease. In A. Baddeley, M. D. Kopelman, & B. A. Wilson (Eds.), *The handbook of memory disorders* (pp. 569–589). New York: Wiley.

Clark, A. (1997). *Being there. Putting brain, body and world together again.* Cambridge, MA: MIT Press.

Dahlbäck, N., Kristiansson, M., & Stjernberg, F. (2013). Distributed remembering through active structuring of activities and environments. *Review of Philosophy and Psychology, 4,* 153–165.

Derrida, J. (1978). *Writing and difference* (trans. A. Bass). Chicago: Chicago University Press.

Duff, M. C., Mutlu, B., Byom, L., & Turkstra, L. (2012). Beyond utterances: Distributed cognition as a framework for studying discourse in adults with acquired brain injury. *Seminars in Speech and Language, 33,* 44–54.

Elliot, G. (2011). *Montessori methods for Dementia: Focusing on the person and the prepared environment.* Hamilton, ON: McMaster University.

Fox, P. J. (2000). The role of the concept of Alzheimer's disease in the development of the Alzheimer's Association in the United States. In P. J. Whitehouse, K. Maurer, & J. F. Ballenger (Eds.), *Concepts of Alzheimer's disease: Biological, clinical, and cultural perspectives.* Baltimore: Johns Hopkins.

George, D. R., Qualls, S. H., Camp, C. J., & Whitehouse, P. J. (2013). Renovating Alzheimer's: "Constructive" reflections on the new clinical and research diagnostic guidelines. *The Gerontologist, 53*(3), 378–387.

Grice, H. P. (1975). Logic and Conversation. In P. Cole & J. Morgan (Eds.), *Syntax and Semantics 3: Speech Acts* (pp. 41–58). New York: Academic Press.

Gubrium, J. F. (1986). *Oldtimers and Alzheimer's: The descriptive organization of senility.* Greenwich, CT: JAI Press.

Holstein, M. (2000). Aging, culture, and the framing of Alzheimer's disease. In P. J. Whitehouse, K. Maurer, & J. Ballenger (Eds.), *Concepts of Alzheimer's disease: Biological, clinical, and cultural perspectives* (pp. 158–180). Baltimore: Johns Hopkins.

Hughes, J. C. (2011). *Thinking through dementia.* Oxford: Oxford University Press.

Hutchins, E. (1995). *Cognition in the wild.* Cambridge, MA: MIT Press.

Jeste, D., Blacker, D., Blazer, D., Ganguli, M., Grant, I., Paulsen, J., . . . Sachdev, P. (2010). *Neurocognitive disorders: A proposal from the DSM-5 Neurocognitive Disorders Work Group.* Washington, DC: American Psychiatric Association.

Katzman, R., & Bick, K. L. (2000). The rediscovery of Alzheimer's disease during the 1960s and 1970s. In P. J. Whitehouse, K. Maurer, & J. Ballenger (Eds.), *Concepts of Alzheimer's disease: Biological, clinical, and cultural perspectives* (pp. 104–114). Baltimore: Johns Hopkins.

Kitwood, T. (1997). *Dementia reconsidered: The person comes first.* Milton Keynes, England: Open University Press.

Leech, G. (1983). *Principles of pragmatics.* London: Longman.

Lubinski, R. (2011). Creating a positive communication environment in long-term care. In P. Backhaus (Ed.), *Communication in elderly care* (pp. 4–61). London: Continuum Press.

Luria, A. R. (1987a). *The man with a shattered world.* Cambridge, MA: Harvard University Press.

Luria, A. R. (1987b). *The mind of a mnemonist.* Cambridge, MA: Harvard University Press.

McKhann, G. M., Knopman, D. S., Chertkow, H., Hyman, B. T., Jack Jr., C. R., Kawas, C. H., . . . Phelps, C. H. (2011). The diagnosis of dementia due to Alzheimer's disease: Recommendations from the National Institute on Aging-Alzheimer's disease workgroups on diagnostic guidelines for Alzheimer's disease. *Alzheimer's and Dementia, 7*(3), 263–269.

Mishler, E. (1984). *The discourse of medicine: Dialectics of medical interviews.* Norwood, NJ: Ablex.

Parkin, A. J. (2000). The structure and mechanisms of memory. In B. Rapp (Ed.), *The handbook of cognitive neuropsychology: What deficits reveal about the human mind* (pp. 399–422). Philadelphia, PA: Psychology Press.

Rogers, Y. (2006). Distributed cognition and communication. In K. Brown (Ed.), *The encyclopedia of language and linguistics* (pp. 181–202). Oxford, UK: Elsevier.

Ryan, E. B. (1992). Beliefs about memory changes across the adult lifespan. *Journal of Gerontology: Psychological Sciences, 47,* pp. 41–46.

Ryan, E. B. (2010). Overcoming communication predicaments in later life. In L. Hickson (Ed.), *Hearing care for older adults 2009: Proceedings of the Second International Adult Conference* (pp. 77–86). Staefa, Switzerland: Phonak.

Sabat, S. R. (2001). *The experience of Alzheimer's disease: Life through a tangled veil.* Oxford: Blackwell.

Sabat, S. R., & Harré, R. (1992). The construction and deconstruction of self in Alzheimer's disease. *Aging and Society, 12,* 443–461.

Sabat, S. R., & Harré, R. (1994). The Alzheimer's disease sufferer as semiotic subject. *Philosophy, Psychiatry, and Psychology, 1*(3), 145–160.

Sacks, H. (1992). *Lectures on conversation* (2 volumes). Oxford: Basil Blackwell.

Squire, L. R. (1987). *Memory and brain.* New York: Oxford University Press.

Squire, L. R. (2004). Memory systems of the brain: A brief history and current perspectives. *Neurobiology of learning and memory, 82,* 171–177.

Squire, L. R., & Kandel, E. R. (1999). *Memory: From mind to molecules.* New York: Scientific American Library.

Tomoeda, C. (2001). Comprehensive assessment for dementia: A necessity for differential diagnosis and management. *Seminars in Speech and Language, 22,* 275–289.

Whitehouse, P. J., Maurer, K., & Ballenger, J. F. (Eds.). (2000). *Concepts of Alzheimer's disease: Biological, clinical, and cultural perspectives.* Baltimore, MD: Johns Hopkins University Press.

Wray, A. (2002). *Formulaic language and the lexicon.* Cambridge: Cambridge University Press.

Wray, A. (2008). *Formulaic language: Pushing the boundaries.* Oxford: Oxford University Press.

Wray, A. (2010). We've had a wonderful, wonderful thing: Formulaic interaction when an expert has dementia. *Dementia: The International Journal of Social Research and Practice, 9*(4), 517–534.

Wray, A. (2011). Formulaic language as a barrier to effective communication with people with Alzheimer's disease. *Canadian Modern Language Review, 67*(4), 429–458.

2

"WHAT THEY'RE SAID TO SAY"
The Discursive Construction of Alzheimer's Disease by Older Adults

Robert W. Schrauf and Madelyn Iris

INTRODUCTION

Alzheimer's disease is at once an irreversible neurodegenerative disorder, a pathological process in the brain, a shifting diagnostic category, a public policy challenge, a scientific conundrum, an illness experience for millions of older adults, and a threatening possibility for millions more. In each of these guises, "Alzheimer's" is also a whole set of overlapping, but not coterminous, *discursive constructions* by specific discourse communities with particular interests, motives, goals, and interests (for the notion of discourse community, see Swales, 1990). The scientific community constructs a pathological process, the medical community constructs a clinical disease, advocacy groups construct a public health challenge, the social service community constructs a behavior-to-be-managed, and so on. From a discourse perspective, the insiders in each of these discursive communities (scientists, clinicians, lobbyists, social workers, etc.) share a patterned style of speaking, perhaps a formal register, with particular genres, indexed to accepted social hierarchies, across an identifiable array of informal and formal institutional contexts. Although there is considerable overlap in an interlocking hierarchy of concerns, Alzheimer's disease is constructed differently across these communities.

The primary risk factor for Alzheimer's disease is age, and, not surprisingly, older adults talk, joke, quip, complain, tell stories, and worry about the disease more than young people. Whether or not "older adults" comprise a discourse community in the same sense as do the clinical, public health, or social service communities seems questionable. (Are "they" sufficiently homogenous to constitute a community of discourse? Is there a style of speaking—certainly not a register—that marks older adults?). Rather, it seems more productive to think of older adults as occupying the "lifeworld" in contradistinction to the "institutional" worlds of science, medicine, social work, and so on (see Mishler, 1984). Nevertheless, within this lifeworld, older adults do participate in a particular discursive construction of Alzheimer's disease, driven not by the institutional concerns of scientists, clinicians, and social workers, but rather by existential concerns about the difference between the normal forgetfulness associated with aging and dementia and what the experience of dementia is like. In other words, the discourse of older adults is focused on the phenomenology of the illness experience. Further, the symptoms of Alzheimer's disease are not physically manifest in bodily disorder, but rather they are primarily manifest in behavior and more specifically *in talk*. Thus, probing the phenomenology of the disease largely entails representing talk—by, with, and about the person who has the disease (Davis, 2005; Guendouzi & Müller, 2006). Thus, the research question that drives this chapter is, *how do older adults discursively construct Alzheimer's disease?*

One way of addressing this question is to examine the stories that people tell about their experiences with people who have the disease—family members, friends, neighbors, co-workers, and others. These narratives provide a particularly powerful means of plumbing lived reality, in part because, unlike descriptions, which are perhaps like snapshots of symptoms and stages, narratives are more like a video clip of experience. Telling a story more closely approaches what it's like because our fundamental experience of life is episodic (Bruner, 1991; Sarbin, 1986). Interestingly, in telling stories about family and friends with Alzheimer's disease, narrators frequently relate *what they're said to say* in "reported speech." These renderings in reported speech are essentially dramatizations of speech (and not verbatim accounts), and an examination of the discourse devices that people use in performing the speech of individuals with Alzheimer's offers important clues to how Alzheimer's is understood.

Why might this be an interesting question in a book about communicative and cognitive engagement with persons who have the disease? In conversational interchanges between persons with dementia and noncognitively impaired interlocutors, both parties bring to their talk multiple assumptions and expectations that shape both their speaking and their hearing. These form the cultural context of talk. From a discourse perspective, we might ask how the speech of older adults who have the disease is represented, quoted, or reported by those who do not have the disease. Narratives offer a rich site for such dramatizations, and this chapter is based on stories told by people about their family members and neighbors who have the disease. At the micro-level of talk, such stories may be approached either in terms of their content—*what* they report— or in terms of their telling—*how* they are told (Ochs & Capps, 2001; Riessman, 2008). To a large extent the persuasive power of a story lies precisely in how it is told (Goffman, 1974), and this is where narrators' "doing" reported speech is most revealing. In this chapter, the narratives about Alzheimer's disease that we examine come from a research study conducted in the United States among African Americans and Mexican Americans. Topics in the study ranged from normal aging to memory loss and Alzheimer's disease, and although participants were not explicitly asked to tell stories about family members and friends, they often did so.

LAYERED SETTINGS, SCRIPTS, AND REPORTED SPEECH

As component parts of oral conversations, stories are told in specific contexts for specific purposes and against a background of shared knowledge and assumptions about how the world works (De Fina, 2012; Ochs, 2004). In storytelling, contexts (or settings) are multiple and layered or nested. At the minimum, there are the context of the telling and the context of the storyworld.

First, there is the *context of the telling,* the social setting in which the narrator tells the story. Concretely, this includes the physical place where the narrator tells the story, the interlocutor(s) who hear or even share in the construction of the story, and the ongoing conversation in which the story presumably has some relevance. Regarding the latter, it is important to emphasize that people tell stories at particular moments in a conversation to accomplish specific interactional goals (to entertain, inform, argue, defame, distract, etc.) and that, therefore, stories do some "work" in the conversation.

As noted previously, the stories that form the data for this chapter come from research interviews. The participants in an interview occupy fairly well-understood roles as interviewer (research professional) and interviewee (local expert), and they follow a fairly standard conversational protocol in which the interviewer asks the questions and the interviewee provides answers and makes comments (Sarangi, 2003). In that sense, there is a schema or script to which both participants orient themselves as the conversation unfolds turn-after-turn. In research interviews in particular, interviewees know what the topic of the interview is, and generally they orient their talk to that overall topic (for a discussion of the interviewee's "stake" in interviews, see Potter & Hepburn, 2005). Nevertheless, despite their orientation to their interview roles, either the interviewee or the interviewer is in principle free to shift his or her footing within the interview and to cast him or herself in another role (e.g., friend, accomplice, expert-in-another-area, victim, etc.; Sarangi, 2003). This is particularly evident when one of the participants introduces a first-person story in which they cast themselves in another role (beyond that of interviewee) as someone with a particular identity in the lifeworld (beyond the institutional world of the interview).

When a participant launches a story (Ochs & Capps, 2001), he or she cues the *setting of the storyworld*. A good narrative must provide sufficient background information to set up the action of the story. In the case of stories about persons with Alzheimer's disease, narrators often construct *scripts* of patterned behavior against which, or within which, to portray the behaviors of their characters. Readers of this chapter with roots in the institutional worlds of science, medicine, clinical linguistics, social work, etc., will be tempted to see in these scripts the "standard symptoms" of Alzheimer's disease (e.g., cognitive deficits, behavioral and psychiatric symptoms, etc.), but the analytic goal is to suspend these professional schemata in favor of detecting how lay-persons script the disease in the lifeworld. Thus, a key focus of the chapter is to attend to the processes of *script formulation* by narrators in their stories (Edwards, 1995, 1997).

Not infrequently, in telling such stories, narrators often recount conversations or other forms of *reported speech* in which they (the narrators) take on the voice of the individual with dementia (Clark & Gerrig, 1990; Holt, 1996, 2000). By doing so, narrators effectively perform their stories and thus provide a dramatic rendition of the experience of the disease (Schrauf & Iris, in press). How they do this, or more precisely, the devices that they use to accomplish these performances, tell us a great deal about how they understand the disease. In this sense, the analytic focus of this chapter is not so much on the content or themes of the stories themselves, but rather on how these themes or reported speech are worked up in the telling. These two discursive foci—script formulation and reported speech—are the principle analytic lens through which we will interpret the narrative data of the chapter.

SCRIPTING DEMENTIA

According to the classic version of schema theory in cognitive and social psychology, people construct mental outlines of common objects, places, and events on the basis of repeated exposure to them (Johnson-Laird, 1983; Neisser, 1976; Schank, 1982). These *schemata* or *scripts* then serve to guide perception, cognition, and action. Similarly, anthropologists speak of group-level schemata as cultural models that structure social experience and cultural activity (Holland & Quinn, 1987). Scripts and schemata are implicitly understood to be mental resources for talk: frames of experiences that are available both to speakers, who provide instantiations of selected slots, and to hearers, who mentally supply information in the empty slots according to the shared script. In this theory, storytelling is *about* script-deviations—noticeable exceptions to the predictable, taken-for-granted, ordinary schema—because they render an otherwise scripted event *tellable* (Ochs, 2004; Ochs & Capps, 2001). For example, in a prior study, we reported the story of a person who asked her coworkers for the time in order to check the accuracy of her watch (Schrauf & Iris, in press), which is an ordinary event that fits a well-understood social script. However, the person in question asked the same question every day, over and over again. This is an odd practice, and this script deviation makes the story tellable.

Script and culture model theory have been criticized for their inability to account for which script is actually operative at any given time, given the realities of script interruption and higher order goals—a kind of "granularity" problem. For example, a person may return home to check that the oven is off and purportedly activate a "check the oven script," but upon arriving at the door find that she has lost her keys to the house. She might then initiate a second script: "look for the keys" (with predictable components: "check the ignition (again)," "check all pockets," "check the floor of the car," etc.). If the person suspects that she locked the keys in the trunk, this may trigger another script, and so on. Presumably, however, the "check the oven script" is operative (suspended?) throughout. Further, there is the question of script hierarchy. For example, does the "check the oven" script differ from "turn off all of the appliances" script, and does the "turn off all the appliances" script differ from a larger "leave the house for the day" script and so on (Holland, 1992)? For the analyst, it is difficult to know what script is activated at any one time. Nevertheless, the basic insight of script theory retains its force: we do seem to approach the social world with the expectation of predictable regularities about common events.

From a discursive perspective, a more empirical, bottom-up approach begins with actual talk and asks how the notion of a script functions as a resource in ongoing interaction (Edwards, 1997). That is, scripts are built by interactants for some purpose in a conversation, and the questions are how and why? In this approach to scripts, the analyst begins with a stretch of talk and looks for how speakers invoke social regularities (about events, social roles, personal dispositions, etc.), what specific details they articulate or point to, and how these are relevant to the ongoing conversation. In essence, what drives the subject of talk is not precisely deviations-from-scripts (as the canonical theory would have it), but rather what is interactionally relevant to the interlocutors at any one moment (Edwards, 1994, 1995)—and this may be a script element, a deviation from the script, or a seemingly minor detail. This analytic approach shifts the emphasis *from* scripts as readily available, pre-existing, mentally represented outlines for perceiving the world *to* scripts as on-the-fly, conversational constructions of social regularities for constructing particular descriptions at a particular moment. Thus, interlocutors both invoke cultural knowledge about social regularities but rework these scripts in an ongoing "bricolage" according to their immediate interactional needs and goals.

Therefore, in analyzing talk for scripts, we are asking two questions. First, what discursive devices do narrators use to construct scripts? This is the *how* question. Edwards (1995) provides a partial list, of which several items are recruited in the following analyses: (a) the casting of an event as an instance of, or exception to, a more generalized pattern; (b) continuous or progressive verbs, or modals indicating iteration; and (c) extreme formulations. The second question is, what is the work these scripts do in the narration? This is the *why* question.

Casting an Event as an Instance or Exception

In one sense, stories are shot through with scripts because stories are told against a background of shared knowledge (expected regularities of the world) that is entirely necessary to understanding them. Further, scripts figure prominently as a discursive means of establishing the dispositions of individuals (another form of regularity). Nevertheless, stories themselves can be script-like in that they are designed by interlocutors to be heard as a one-off event, an instance of a larger generalized pattern (a script), or an exception to such a pattern (Edwards, 1994, 1995). In this sense, stories and scripts are mutually conditioning because stories may either demonstrate the content of scripts or challenge the normativity of scripts. For instance, given that forgetfulness may be normal and age-related, a story about being forgetful is not itself an indication of cognitive impairment, but if a narrator casts the story as part of an ongoing, scripted pattern of forgetfulness, then he or she may be "building a case" of dementia (Schrauf & Iris, in press).

Progressive Past Tenses and Modal Verbs

In English the past progressive tense (or past continuous) can indicate either an action that occurred once over a period of time in the past that provides the context for another action that occurred within the bounds of that first action (e.g., "I *was going back* to check the oven when I realized that I had lost my keys"), or to indicate an action that occurred in the past on a regular basis (e.g., I *was going back* to check the oven every time I left the house"). Note that in the latter case, the repeated action is modified by the adverbial "every time." Repetitiveness can also be expressed by the modal auxiliary verb "would," as in "I *would go back and check* the oven every day." Similarly, speakers of Spanish use imperfect forms to indicate either type of continuous action. Imperfect aspect may be marked either on the main verb, as for example, *planeaba* ("I planned") or via the use of past progressive forms of *to be* (*estar*) plus the gerundive form of the verb (*-ndo*), as in *estaba planeando* ("I was planning"). Narrators build scripts by using past progressive tenses to suggest that events are not one-off occurrences but part of larger and repeated patterns.

Extreme Case Formulations (ECFs)

These "are descriptions or assessments that deploy extreme expressions such as *every, all, none, best, least, as good as it gets, always, perfectly, brand new,* and *absolutely*" (Edwards, 2000, pp. 347–348; see Pomerantz, 1986). Edwards notes that ECFs are "factually brittle" in that the absolutism implied is always open to challenge by hearers, and hence that they are sometimes softened (Edwards, 2000). Nevertheless, ECFs provide an important resource for claiming scriptedness. If I say, for instance, "I was going back to check the oven *every time* I left the house," the adverbial "every time" serves as an ECF that claims unfailing regularity—a script. What counts is the indexicality of the ECF—the interactional situation in which the extreme claim has particular relevance. Thus, Edwards argues that the lexical descriptor is not in fact necessary because "any unqualified statement can be considered logically absolute" (2000, p. 349). Extending this example, in a particular context (e.g., talking about all the components of my daily routine) I could say, "I went back to check the oven" and still *be heard* as claiming scriptedness for my actions.

Extreme formulations are also important for establishing personal dispositions—again as interactionally relevant to the situation of the talk (Edwards, 2000). For instance, I might say, "Mom never could remember anything, so I was used to going back to check on the oven all the time." The ECFs *never* and *anything* are not meant as literal descriptions of mom. (Surely, she wasn't so densely amnesic throughout her life that she forgot everything!) Rather, these words serve to characterize mom as a habitually forgetful person, and perhaps (in the context) to allay the suspicion that her current forgetfulness has anything to do with dementia. Thus, the speaker may be cuing a script to bolster an *account* of mom's current behavior.

The "Work" of Scripts

As a final note, script formulations and disposition work are ultimately not about making, testing, or denying descriptions of the world, but rather they are about accounting for the world in specific interactional situations. Script and disposition formulations are powerful means of giving reasons for what goes on in the world, and interactants very often construct them—temporarily, on the fly, ad hoc—to accomplish this end (Edwards, 1994, 1997).

PERFORMING DEMENTIA IN REPORTED SPEECH

Reported speech offers narrators a particularly powerful means of moving beyond the description of story events to the "performance" of those events. In a seminal piece, Clark and Gerrig (1990) argue that in reported speech, a speaker depicts or demonstrates (versus describes) an action in a highly selective manner by selecting for linguistic and paralinguistic portrayal just those elements that suit his or her desired ends. Thus, far from attempting a pristine reproduction of the exact wording of what another person said in precisely the way he or she said it, interlocutors produce a paraphrase adapted to their own intentions, strategically performing aspects of voice (pitch, quality, tenor), speech defects, emotional state, gestural accompaniment, accent, "foreign language," dialect, and register *as these are relevant to the interlocutor's intentions in producing the "quote"* (Clark & Gerrig, 1990, pp. 775–780). Thus, because reported speech is a selective performance of what someone else has said, it is as much a commentary on what another person said as it is a report about what that person said.

As a demonstration or performance, reported speech gives a story the ring of authenticity, because it functions as evidence. In Schrauf and Iris (in press) we argue that people construct narratives of persons-with-dementia as a way of doing case-based reasoning about the disease, and that "doing" the reported speech of persons-with-dementia serves to show the interlocutor "what it's like." Linguistically, this is accomplished by a subtle shift in deictic center whereby the speaker assumes the position of another person. Thus, the pronouns, spatial and temporal references, and verb tenses of the reported speech do not reflect the social, psychological, or physical position of the speaker but those of the person that he or she is quoting (Holt, 1996, 2000). By shifting the deictic center to someone else, the speaker suggests that, "These are not my words, but those of so-and-so," and thus makes them available for independent inspection and evaluation by his or her hearers. As Holt notes, "It is clear that by reproducing the 'original' utterance or utterances speakers can provide access to the interaction being discussed, enabling the recipient to assess it for himself or herself" (1996, p. 229).

In analyzing talk for reported speech, we attend particularly to the discursive devices that narrators use to construct and characterize such speech. In this chapter, the following are particularly important: prosody, the presence and absence of quotatives, and adjacency pairs.

Prosody

Changes in sound and voicing are subtle yet powerful resources available to speakers for signaling that they are doing reported speech and for commenting on the speech that they produce. Thus, speakers often use shifts in prosody to signal a shift in deictic center, effectively "giving the floor" to another speaker (the story character). Whereas the pitch, loudness, timing, rhythm, and speed of speech are usually those of the speaker, by changing one or all of these, speakers indicate a shift in footing to another speaker—or to oneself in other circumstances (Couper-Kuhlen, 1998, 2004). In this sense, the vocal alteration (in pitch, loudness, timing, etc.) can function in the same way as quotation marks in written speech, with the exception that the vocal alteration can be maintained across the entire "quote" (Klewitz & Couper-Kuhlen, 1999). In addition to introducing reported speech, Clark and Gerrig (1990) note that people

> often mark: (1) voice pitch, e.g. speaking in a higher voice for women than men, (2) voice age, e.g. using a tremulous voice and slower rate for older speakers; (3) voice quality, e.g. stuttering; (4) emotion, e.g. speaking in an angry, excited, or contemptuous tone of voice; and many other things. (p. 776)

Effectively, by strategically combining changes in pitch, volume, timing, rhythm, and speed of speech, along with changes in voice quality, speakers demonstrate *how* the reported speech should be heard by recipients. As will be evident in the following transcripts, narrators skillfully use a variety of prosodic features to portray or model whole (but short) conversations—normal, disoriented, agitated—between themselves and persons in their families who are experiencing memory loss and possibly dementia.

Presence and Absence of Quotatives

Interlocutors signal direct reported speech via verbs of report: "said," "whispered," "claimed," "shouted," "goes," etc. However, in reported speech the quality of the quotative is often left to the prosodic accompaniment rather than lexical choice. That is, for example, the speaker who wants to say that someone whispered may actually whisper rather than employ the quotative "He whispered." In this sense, the common quotatives "said," "goes," "is like," may be qualified by changes in pitch, volume, and register to indicate the manner of speaking. Further, the absence of quotatives is an interesting topic in its own right. As noted, shifts in prosody can effectively signal the inception of reported speech without an explicit reporting verb. These are termed *zero quotatives* (Mathis & Yule, 1994) and may be used to achieve a dramatic effect. Thus, the elimination of the introductory quotative gives to the reported speech a sense of urgency or importunity. For instance, in reporting the turns of a heated argument between two or more people, a speaker can "perform" the interruptions or intrusiveness of speakers by dispensing with the quotative at each turn (Schrauf & Iris, in press).

Adjacency Pairs

Originally described in research in conversation analysis (Schegloff & Sacks, 1973), adjacency pairs are sequentially organized utterances in which the first pair part occasions a preferred second pair part. This is particularly true of conventionalized formulae, such as "How are you?" / "Fine," but applies as well to broader forms, as, for instance, asking a question is a first pair part that assumes an answer as a second pair part. Of course, as Schegloff (1972) points out, the second pair part is not obligatory, and an interlocutor can choose not to supply it. This in turn requires either some repair or an accounting for proffering the dispreferred response (Edwards, 1997). In stories about Alzheimer's disease, narrators may place dispreferred responses in the mouths of persons-with-dementia as signs of their loss of conversational fluency, or (as we will see later), a narrator may relate a series of perfect adjacency pairs to demonstrate cognitive lucidity.

PARTICIPANTS, INTERVIEWS, TRANSCRIPTION

The narratives presented in this chapter were taken from a larger study titled "The Alzheimer's Beliefs Study" (Schrauf & Iris, 2011a, 2011b, in press) conducted in Chicago, Illinois, among English-speaking African Americans, bilingual Spanish-English Mexican Americans, and bilingual Russian-English speaking immigrants and refugees from the

Former Soviet Union (FSU). In the first phase of this project, 10 individuals from each of these groups (30 total) participated in structured interviews about aging, memory loss, and Alzheimer's disease. Following a *reputational case selection* methodology (Miles & Huberman, 1994), we selected individuals for participation who had a reputation (by word of mouth) in their local communities as "being knowledgeable about aging." To ensure a diversity of opinion, we asked each participant to name another potential participant who was known to hold different opinions than him- or herself (*maximum variation sampling*; Guba & Lincoln, 1989). In general, these participants were middle-aged, with African Americans and FSU refugees having some college and Mexican Americans having high school educations. Most participants either knew someone with Alzheimer's disease or in fact had a family member with the disease (for additional details, see Schrauf & Iris, in press). These interviews were conducted in the language of the participant's choice, and each lasted about one hour.

We transcribed all interviews verbatim (Powers, 2005) and coded them in Atlas.ti (Muhr, 2004) using a combination of a priori codes—concerning aging, memory loss, Alzheimer's disease, and community opinions—and inductive codes drawn from the interviews themselves. For this chapter we extracted all texts coded as "cases" and re-transcribed them in the original languages using conversation analytic conventions (Table 2.1). Of the 34 cases in the data, three were chosen for this chapter because they offered rich examples of the scripting and reported

Table 2.1
Transcription Conventions*

Convention	Description
(0.5)	Silent gap in tenths of a second
(.)	Silent gap less than one-tenth of a second
° °	Enclosed talk is spoken more quietly than the surrounding talk
> <	Enclosed talk is spoken more quickly than surrounding talk
:	Preceding sound or letter has been stretched; more colons indicate greater stretching
↑↓	Falling or rising intonational shift in what follows
=	Spoken sounds follow immediately on one another
underline	Greater emphasis than surrounding talk
.hh	In-breath; more h's indicate longer in-breath
hh	Out-breath; more h's indicate longer out-breath
CAPS	Speech noticeably louder than surrounding speech

*adapted from Hutchby & Wooffitt (1988).

speech found throughout the cases. The project was approved by the Institutional Review Board of the Leonard Schanfield Research Institute, Chicago, Illinois.

EXCERPTS AND ANALYSIS

Each of the following three excerpts has been drawn from a portion of interview talk in which the participant was answering the interviewer's question about what happens to individuals with memory loss and what might cause such memory loss. The analysis of each excerpt focuses first on the narrators' construction of scripts and second on the discursive devices that narrators use to "perform" the symptoms of their family members or friends. In the first two excerpts the narrators construct their stories as generalized patterns and instances of behaviors associated with Alzheimer's disease, and in the third excerpt, the narrator tells his story as an exception to a script that he constructs about the irreversibility of memory loss. All three stories revolve around the reported speech constructed by narrators between themselves and the characters in their stories.

Excerpt 1: "It Was All About His Work in The Building"

In Excerpt 1, the participant is a 70-year-old African American woman with 18 years of education who works in the regulatory policy area of the health field. The interviewer is a 38-year-old white woman who is an applied anthropologist and research coordinator for the study. The following transcription begins with the participant (PAR = participant) responding to the interviewer's (INT = interviewer) request, "Tell me about memory loss." After some comments about her own failing memory, the narrator relates that no one in her biological family has been diagnosed with Alzheimer's disease but that her stepfather did in fact have Alzheimer's. In the following transcript, the narrator tells of visits to her stepfather in the nursing home.

Excerpt 1

1	PAR:	<u>Now</u> (.) my ↑stepfather .h I went to see him
2		usually once a week=twice a week in the nursing home (.)
3		at that time he wasn't on any medication (.)
4		at all .h I <u>imagine</u> they had Aricept=this is in the 80s
5		they had Aricept=I don't know Memantine

6		=I don't know whether they had those tho:se drugs
7		prob [ably] they ↓didn't
8	INT:	[uh-uh]
9	PAR:	<u>okay</u> so therefore he was on no medication
...		
15	PAR:	his <u>thinking</u> was ↑very ↓fluid (.) ↑<u>very</u>
16		↑<u>but</u> it was (.) in the 70s (laughs) it was (laughs)
17		.hhh he used to be a janitor (.)
18	INT:	mmm hmmm
19		of uh >I don't know how many flats<
20		that was a <u>biggie</u>
21		thirty-six flat building, [I think]
22	INT:	[wow]
23	PAR:	it was a biggie .h he was a janitor=
24		one of the janitors
25		.h and uh when I'd go to the nursing home
26		.h he would say,↑Juna-bug,
27		↓my middle name is [Jeanne]
28	INT:	[uh huh]
29	PAR:	and I drove a ↑Volkswagen .h
30		so he started calling me the lady <u>with the bug</u>
31		so he called me <u>Juna</u>-bug.
32		He was sitting (breathy voice)°in the nursing home°
33		and he'd say Juna-bug?
34		how's everything going? How's mamma?
35		(regular voice) Mother's ↓dead okay?
36		<u>been</u> gone
37	INT:	yeah
38	PAR:	(breathy voice) He says how's mamma?
39		I say (breathy voice) oh: she's fi:ne.
40		(regular voice) Yeah well I fired up my boilers today
41		Lord have mercy hh and then you know
42		(strident voice) that ↑<u>ignorant</u> so and so and so and so
43		and that <u>apartment</u> blah blah blah .h
44		he just went through the who:le thing
45		<u>every</u> single time I went to °visit him
46		it was all about his work in [the buildin'°]
47	INT:	[mmm hmmm]
48	PAR:	and I jiss (.) went along with it
49	INT:	uh-huh yeah
50	PAR:	.h There was no need for me to

51   <u>make</u> (.) my stay <u>a:dver</u>sarial .h
52 INT: yeah
53 PAR: by ↑arguing with ↑him (2.0)
54   ↑<u>he</u> is the ↓one that's in the nursing home because(3.0)
55   <u>he</u> has a memory ↓problem
56 INT: mmm hmmm.

Scripting Dementia: A Generalized Pattern of Dysfunctional Conversation

There are at least three script formulations of particular interest in this excerpt. First, although the narrator reports a specific conversation with her stepfather, she represents this conversation as an instance of many similar conversations. Thus, in lines 1 and 2, she says "I went to visit him once, twice a week in the nursing home." Also, her verb tenses are past progressive: "when I'd go to the nursing home, he *would* say . . ." (lines 25–26). Second, she establishes their long and easy relationship by giving an origin story for his nickname for her (lines 26–31), again using the past continuous: "he started calling me the lady with the bug he'd say, Juna-Bug" (lines 32–33). Third, she characterizes the conversation with him as itself a generalized pattern via the extreme case formulation in lines 45–46, "*every single time* I went to visit him it was all about his work in the buildin." In essence, the narrator is summarizing over a number of occasions and constructing a script of which this one conversation is an instance.

Finally at the level of the interaction between interviewer and narrator, it is interesting to note that the interviewer's back-channeled interjections serve largely to signal acceptance or understanding of the narrator's statements. For instance, in line 18 ("mm hmm"), line 28 ("uh huh"), line 37 ("yeah"), line 47 ("mmm hmm"), line 52 ("yeah"), and line 56 ("mmm hmmm"), the narrator simply registers recognition of what the narrator has said. Only in line 22 does the interviewer's "wow" communicate some surprise. In short, the interviewer shows her attentive listening but does not engage in active co-tellership (Ochs, 2004).

Performing the Experience: Speech Accommodation

Interestingly, the narrator represents her stepfather as a competent conversationalist. In reported speech in lines 26 and 33, she shows him appropriately taking the floor ("securing the listener's attention," Ochs & Capps, 2001, pp. 114–117) by addressing her by name ("Juna Bug?"), and then in line 34 and 38 she quotes him as enunciating the first half of a common adjacency pair ("How's mamma") to which she supplies the second half ("She's fine") in line 39.

She signals her accommodating to him by shifting back and forth from her interviewee voice to a breathy voicing of both him and herself in this adjacency pair. For instance, when she first reports his addressing her in line 26 ("He would say Juna Bug"), she voices him in her interviewee voice, and continues with an explanation of that nickname, again in her interviewee voice. However, when she returns to reporting their conversation (lines 32–33), she repeats the same line ("He'd say Juna Bug") in a breathy voice and maintains that voice in reporting his question: "How's everything going? How's mama?" (line 34). This is the first pair part of a common adjacency pair and requires an answer. However, before continuing, she shifts back to her interviewee voice to explain to the interviewer that "Mother's dead, okay? been gone" (lines 35–36), and then immediately shifts back to a breathy voice to supply her response to him ("Oh she's fine") in the second half of the adjacency pair. Thus, she accommodates her voice to his (matching his breathy voice with hers), and she accommodates to him by playing along with his assumption that his wife (her mother) is alive.

Having demonstrated her accommodation to him in this breathy voicing, she shifts to her regular (interview) voice to depict his appropriate use of a turn initial ("yeah well," line 40; Holt, 1996) to change his topic and launch a "troubles telling" narrative (Brenneis, 1988) about "firing up his boilers" (line 40). Within his narrative, she again shifts to a higher, more intense intonation, suggesting a strident voice, as she represents his telling about a problematic tenant ("that ignorant so and so," line 42).

Thus, by skillfully alternating between tones of voice, she portrays her accommodating, not only to his speech, but to his disorientation in time and place. In her coda to the story (lines 48–55), she explicitly articulates this ("I jiss went along with it" etc.). At the same time, she portrays him as a competent narrator in his own right. Via reported speech, she shows him taking the floor (Ochs & Capps, 2001), initiating an appropriate adjacency pair (Schegloff & Sacks, 1973), and then telling troubles (Brenneis, 1988). Nevertheless, she implicitly signals that his disorientation in place and time was a recurrent feature by reporting the quotation without propositional content ("blah blah blah," line 43; Clark & Gerrig, 1990, p. 780) and by explicitly saying, "Every single time I went to see him it was all about his work in the buildin'," lines 45–46). With these summaries she signals that this conversation represents a generalized pattern, itself a new and ongoing way of her relating to her stepfather. In the end, the narrator has responded to the interviewer's question about memory loss by characterizing her stepfather's disorientation as explicitly memory-related: "He is the one that's in the nursing home because he has a memory problem" (lines 54–55).

Excerpt 2: "He Didn't Recognize Us as His Children"

In Excerpt 2, the same research interviewer as in Excerpt 1 (INT = interviewer) speaks about memory loss with a 60-year-old Hispanic man with 18 years of education (PAR = participant). Specifically, the interviewer begins by asking him what causes memory loss, and he responds by offering a story about his own father who was ultimately diagnosed as having Alzheimer's disease.

Excerpt 2

1	INT:	.h que opina usted de lo que (.) <u>causa</u> (.)
		.h what's your opinion about the (.) cause
2		la pérdida de la memoria o-
		of memory loss?
3	PAR:	(clears throat) no sé exáctamente no sé=
		(clears throat) I don't know exactly I don't know=
4		pero una de las cosas que me tiene muy intrigado
		but one of the things that intrigues me
5		.h acerca de: de lo de mi papa (3.0)
		.h about: all that about my father (3.0)
6		.h es que: si salimos a un ↑lado (.)
		.h is that if we go ↑somewhere
7		en el ↑día anda: (1.0) °muy contento° (2.0)
		during the ↑day he's (1.0) °very happy° (2.0)
8		>estémos donde [estémos]<
		>wherever [we are]<
9	INT:	[mmm hmm]
		[mmm hmm]
10	PAR:	en el día está muy bien en todo
		during the day he's just fine
11		h. pero llega la noche (3.0) y (2.0)
		h. but come nighttime (3.0) and (2.0)
12		ya no se siente bién ya::
		then he doesn't feel well then::
13	INT:	hmmm
		hmmm
14	PAR:	busca: su casa y todo eso (1.0)
		he searches his house and all (1.0)
15		.h una vez estuvimos en un lado y este::
		.h one time we were somewhere and uh::
16		dice bueno dice bueno este:
		he says well he says well um::

17		bue:no:s vamos a dormirnos=
		okay: let's go to bed=
18		estábamos en un hotel (1.0)
		we were in a hotel (1.0)
19		=vamos a dormirnos
		=let's go to bed
20		y dice mi papá mi: este: mi papa (1.0)
		and he says my: uh: my father says (1.0)
21		(plaintive) ↑no (1.0) ustedes quiénes son? (1.0)
		(plaintive) no! (1.0) who are you people? (1.0)
22	INT:	hmmm
		hmmm
23		y: AUX↑ILIO POR FAVOR SE↑ÑORES AY↑ÚDENME
		and ↑HELP! PLEASE! ↑SOMEONE ↑HELP ME
24	INT:	mmmm
		mmmm
25	PAR:	QUE ME QUIEREN RAP↑TA:R
		THEY WANT TO ↑KIDNAP ME
26		y que no sé que que no sé cuánto
		and on and on
27		y gritó y gritó y todo eso .h
		he yelled and yelled and everything .h
28		(clears throat) y no durmió toda la noche=
		(clears throat) and he didn't sleep the whole night=
29		decía por favor suéltenme
		he kept saying please let me go
30		yo no tengo dinero mira
		Look I don't have any money
31	INT:	ah:: ↓no
		Ah:: ↓no
32	PAR:	no tengo dinero tú sabe que (.)
		I don't have any money you know so
33		y no nos [reconocía]
		and he didn't [recognize] us
34	INT:	(softly) [yeah]
		(softly) [yeah]
35	PAR:	como sus hijos para ↑na:da
		as his children at ↑all
36		sino que nada mas estaba con esa y toda la cosa
		but he just kept up with that and everything
37	INT:	que era como secuestrado él pensó yeah
		that he thought he was being kidnapped yeah

Scripting Dementia: An Instance of Dramatic Agitation at Night

In Excerpt 2, the interviewer has asked what causes memory loss (lines 1–2), but the participant says he doesn't know and indicates a change of topic with the disjunctive marker *pero* ("but") and the initiation of a narrative about his father (lines 4–5). First, the narrator constructs a script according to which during the day his father is *muy contento* ("very happy," line 7) and *muy bien en todo* ("just fine," line 10), but that at night (lines 11–14) *pero llega la noche* ("but come nightfall"), his father *no se siente bien* ("doesn't feel well") and *busca su casa* (searches his house and all). The narrator then sets up his story as an instance of this script in line 15: *una vez estuvimos en un lado* ("one time we were somewhere"). The events that follow constitute an example of the father's particularly dramatic agitation at night.

From the viewpoint of script theory in discourse analysis, it is interesting to note that the narrator has made a strategic selection from among at least two possibilities in giving the background for the story. The script that he has chosen is "peaceful-by-day/agitated-at-night," but another possible script would be "peaceful-at-home/agitated-when-away" construction. For one reason or another, the narrator selected the former but not the latter move. Obviously, the night/day construction fits better with the details of the story, "We were going to bed. . ."

Performing the Experience: A Struggle for Meaning

In the setting of the story, the family is staying at a hotel (line 18), and the narrator uses the quotative *dice* ("he says") in line 16 to report his father's suggestion that they go to bed: *vamos a dormirnos* ("let's go to bed," lines 17 and 19). Prefaced again by the quotative *dice mi papá mi este papá* ("and he says my uh my father says," line 20), he reports his father's confusion *no! ustedes quiénes son* ("who are you people?" line 21). The narrator raises his intonation on *no!* and maintains that rise through a softly voiced *ustedes quiénes son,* which makes his father's inability to recognize his own children sound like innocent wonderment. The interviewer signals that she has understood this with a back channeled *hmm* (line 22).

Maintaining the raised intonation but much more loudly and perhaps stridently, the narrator voices his father yelling AUXILIO POR FAVOR, SEÑORES AYUDENME ("help please someone help me," line 23) and continues that tone with the next line: QUE ME QUIEREN RAPTAR ("they want to kidnap me," line 25). The relative pronoun *que* here might be taken to indicate indirect reported speech, but the prosody clearly signals the continuation of the former line. Again, the interviewer marks her having heard this with another back channeled *hmm* (line 24).

Perhaps in response to these affirmations from the interviewer, the narrator extends the father's reported speech, first indirectly, *y gritó y gritó y todo eso* ("he yelled and yelled and everything," line 27) and then directly, *decía por favor suéltenme yo no tengo dinero mira* ("he kept saying please let me go look I don't have any money," lines 29–30), now with raised intonation but more softly. Note that the narrator uses the imperfect form of the verb 'to say' (*decía*) to indicate the repetition. Again, the interviewer voices her sympathy with *ah no*, with falling intonation (line 31).

Several features of this transcript are particularly interesting. First, the narrator's use of prosodic features such as raised intonation, loud volume, and a vocabulary of abduction ("help," "let me go," "they want to kidnap me") effectively dramatize the father's sense of being victimized by total strangers, who are tragically in fact his own children. As noted previously, direct reported speech amounts to a demonstration, rather than a description (Clark & Gerrig, 1990). In essence, the narrator *performs* the behavior in a specific speech act, and by doing so in just this way he performs a "symptom" of a disease process rather than simply an odd or idiosyncratic behavior (Schrauf & Iris, in press).

Second, the effect of this performance is to give the interviewer perceptual access to the experience of such speech, and in that sense provide evidence for his claims (Holt 1996, 2000). By backchanneling at four crucial junctures, the interviewer signals that she has captured the significance of his performances. That is, she responds with a sympathetic *hmm* after he performs his father's mistaking his children for criminal strangers (lines 21–22), and again after he performs his father yelling for help (lines 23–24). After he voices his father's pleading that the "strangers" release him (lines 29–30), she clearly sympathizes in line 31 with a falling *ah: no*. Finally, as the narrator voices his father's saying *no tengo dinero* ("I don't have any money," line 30) and summarizes the situation with *no nos reconocía* ("he didn't recognize us," line 33), the interviewer sympathetically overlaps in line 34 with a soft *yeah*. Far from challenging or even interrupting the narrative, these vocalizations seem to signal acceptance of the "evidence."

Third, and relatedly, it is arguable that the narrator elaborates and extends the father's reported speech *in response to* the affirmations of the interviewer. That is, three times the narrator provides additional reported speech *after* the interviewer inserts backchanneled responses to the narrator's reported speech. More importantly, in contrast to the flat interjections by the interviewer in Excerpt 1, these back-channeled responses are given prosodic contours signaling sympathy and possibly commiseration. Thus, by responding to some elements of the narrative and remaining silent on others, and by prosodically signaling fellow-feeling, the interviewer participates in shaping the narrative performance (Goodwin, 1984, 1986).

Excerpt 3: "Two Months Before She Died, She Recovered Her Memory"

Excerpt 3 is taken from an interview between the same research interviewer (INT = interviewer) as in Excerpt 1, a 38-year-old white woman, applied anthropologist, who is a fluent, second-language speaker of Spanish, and the participant (PAR = participant), who is a 54-year-old Hispanic man, now retired. In this stretch of talk, the interviewer has asked, "What do you think makes people lose their memory?" and the participant responds by talking about Alzheimer's as something that affects the brain but that may leave other bodily systems and organs untouched so that a person may seem quite healthy. He then talks about a woman who towards the end of her life had moments of seemingly perfect lucidity. He had introduced this woman earlier in the interview as a neighbor and "leader in her church" who was placed in a nursing home during her fifties as a result of severe memory problems. He recounted that they would visit her there, but that she "didn't know who we were."

Excerpt 3

1	PAR:	pero la señora ya murió
		but the lady has died
2		y lo lo (.)otras cosas de las
		and (.) something else
3		antes que muriera como dos meses antes
		before she died like two months before
4		reco↓bró el conocimiento
		she rec↓overed her consciousness
5	INT:	↑hmmm (3.0)
		↑hmmm (3.0)
6	PAR:	y fuimos a ↑verla
		and we went to ↑see her
7		y sabía quién ↓era
		and she knew who it ↓was
8	INT:	↑hmmm
		↑hmmm
9	PAR:	pero ya se iba a morir
		but she was about to die
10	INT:	↑hmmm
		↑hmmm
11	PAR:	Pero es triste porque a veces
		but it's sad because sometimes
12		<u>nunca</u> vuelven a recono-de [conocer] a uno (.)
		they never again recogni- [know] you (.)

13 INT: [↑hmmm]
      [↑hmmm]
14 PAR: ella sí se nos accord[ó y nos] habló
      she did rememb[er us and] talked to us
15 INT: [↑hmmm]
      [↑hmmm]
16 PAR: y estaba a lecho de muerte
      and was on her deathbed
17   y fuimos a verla (2.0)
      and we went to see her (2.0)
18   y como están?
      How are you?
19   Bien °dice° porqué no me han venido a ver? (1.0)
      Fine °she says° why haven't you come to see me? (1.0)
20   °y entonces° si vemimos a ↑verla
      °And so° we did come to see ↑you
21   pero uste::d no se a↑cuerda
      but you:: didn't re↑member
22   si: que pasó así así
      yes what happened and so on and so on
23 INT: ↑hmmm
      ↑hmmm
24 PAR: No me acuerdo pero: (2.0)
      I don't remember bu:t (2.0)
25   y otra vez empezó así
      and she started again like that
26   (unintellible) que murió
      (unintelligible) she died
27   pero (.) hay otras personas a los cincuenta años
      but (.) there are other persons fifty years of age
28   tienen Alheimer y nu:nca >recobran la memoria< (.)
      have Alzheimer's disease and never >regain their memory<

Scripting Dementia: An Exception to Unrelenting Decline

Over a series of turns the narrator has told about a woman in his community who was diagnosed with Alzheimer's disease in her fifties and who, despite having not recognized her neighbors for a long period, experienced momentary lucidity shortly before her death. The narrator's precise words were that she *recobró el conocimiento* (line 4). Roughly this may be translated as "recovered her knowledge /or/ understanding /or/ cognition /or/ consciousness," (and the very elasticity here is interesting), but he certainly means "recovered her memory" because that is the phrase he repeats in line 28. In fact, the evidence that he gives for this recovery is her recognizing him and engaging in meaningful conversation with him. He constructs a brief conversation in which he performs perfectly normal, friendly speech between himself and his friends (*nosotros,* "us") and the woman. He represents these moments of lucidity as remarkable because they occur late in the disease progression and very near the end of her life, a fact that he mentions three times (lines 1, 9, and 16), dramatically placing her *a lecho de muerte* ("on her deathbed," line 16) with the final mention.

He also repeats three times that she briefly recovered her mental faculties (lines 3–4, 7, 14), and he repeats twice that this is wholly unexpected: first, at the beginning of the story, *es triste porque a veces nunca vuelven a reconocer a uno* ("it's sad because sometimes they never again recognize you," lines 11–12), and again as a coda at the end, *pero hay otras personas a los cincuenta años tienen Alzheimer's y nunca recobran la memoria* ("but there are other persons fifty years of age have Alzheimer's and never regain their memory," lines 27–28). Since we know that variation in forgetting from day to day is fairly common in Alzheimer's disease, his use of *nunca* (never) in both of these lines (12, 28) signals an extreme case formulation that serves to construct a script of unrelenting decline to which this narrative is an exception.

Performing the Experience: Fluid Conversation

The narrator begins the first line of their reported speech (his own and that of his friends) in line 18, *y como están* ("And how are you?"), without a quotative, a slight rise in register, and the first pair part of an adjacency pair. The rise in register, in comparison to the surrounding speech, serves here as a kind of prosodic quotation mark (Couper-Kuhlen, 1998; Klewitz & Couper-Kuhlen, 1999). He maintains the slight rise in register to show the continuation of reported speech, and he reports her immediate response, *bien* ("fine") in line 19. Although he employs no quotative to show that the lady now has the floor, he clearly signals that she is speaking because *bien* is clearly the second pair part of the adjacency pair and clearly indicates a change in speaker (Mathis & Yule, 1994). After her *bien,* he inserts the quotative *dice* ("she says"), spoken almost inaudibly, and immediately returns to louder volume and the raised register of the reported speech: *porqué no me han venido a ver* ("Why haven't you come to see me?" line 19). This phrase constitutes the first pair part of another adjacency pair, with which she again maintains the floor.

He signals the shift in speaker (from her, to him and his friends) in line 20 by pausing for one second and beginning with *entonces* ("so"), spoken again at very low, almost inaudible volume, and then rising again to the higher register and louder volume of his reported speech, *y enton-ces si venimos a verla pero usted no se acuerda* ("we did come to see you but you didn't remember," lines 20–21). He drops his pitch on the final sylla-ble of *acuerda* ("remember") at the end of line 21, which signals the end of his (their) turn. In line 22, he signals her taking up her turn (but with no quotative) by raising the pitch of her first word *sí* ("yes"), followed by her asking *que pasó* ("what happened?"). He implies that their talk con-tinued by having her say *así así* ("and so on and so on")—maintaining the intonation of reported speech but without propositional content (Clark & Gerrig, 1990). The interviewer signals her uptake of this by back chan-neling *hmm* (line 23), and the narrator continues the woman's reported speech (again at the higher register) in line 24, *no me acuerdo pero* ("I don't remember but"), trailing off on the *pero,* which may again indicate her continuing her turn. The narrator allows a two second pause, returns to lower register—his "narrator's voice"—and comments *y otra vez em-pezó así* ("and she started again like that") in line 25.

Four linguistic devices allow the narrator to represent a smooth, highly "normal," conventional conversation. First, by dispensing with the initial quotatives that would serve to indicate shifts in turns and speaker, and by using prosodic information to signals shifts in speaker, he effectively performs nearly seamless speech. Mathis and Yule (1994) report that the explicit use of the quotative to signal turn-taking "tends to occur when a conversation with a stranger is being reported and is much less in evidence when the conversation reported was with someone familiar to the interlocutors" (p. 65). Further, Mathis and Yule (1994) note that zero-quotatives may be used to achieve dramatic effect, such as urgency. In this case, however, the narrator's use of a second linguistic device—prosodic shifts in register and volume (Couper-Kuhlen, 1998; Klewitz & Couper-Kuhlen, 1999)—support rather the notion that the conversation flowed easily and reflected none of the memory difficulties that seem to have affected her talk prior to this instance. In essence, the narrator gives a sense of restored, easy intimacy between the lady and himself and his friends. Note, too, that when he interrupts the talk to include a quotative, as in line 22, he drops into nearly inaudible speech. The contrast between her previous state and this current state is in fact that topic of conversa-tion that he puts in their mouths.

DISCUSSION

The research question of this chapter is, *How do older adults discursively construct Alzheimer's disease?* Given that all talk is necessarily situated, it is important to point out that these transcripts derive from research interviews. Thus, whatever "discursive constructing" these participants were up to was necessarily keyed to the purposes and protocol of a semi-structured, social science interview. In establishing the relevance of these results for a volume that is otherwise focused on dialogue with persons who actually have the disease, it will be important to attend to how this context shapes the stories from cognitively healthy narrators. In brief, we argue that both narrators and the interviewer exit their roles as questioner and respondent in the institutional world of the interview and that both enter the lifeworld to wrestle with, and to co-construct, the phenomenology and meaning of the disease as a social phenomenon and not simply a disease condition belonging to a patient.

Let us return for a moment to the distinction between the institutional world and lifeworld of Alzheimer's disease. Across the institutional world, Alzheimer's is associated with progressive memory loss—its primary and criterial feature—reflected variously in discursive "objects" such as neurodegeneration, cortical atrophy, below-threshold scores in delayed recall, word-finding difficulties, inability to remember new information, and so on. Interestingly, the narrators exemplified previously do not orient to memory loss in the sense of "forgetting things." Rather, their stories seem eminently *social,* and the forgetting seems far more "fundamental" than merely mental. These are stories about *disorientation in time and place,* as in Excerpt 1 where the stepfather in the nursing home talks as if he is still employed as a janitor in an apartment building; *the inability to recognize intimately familiar faces,* as in Excerpt 2 where the father does not recognize his own adult children; and the *seemingly miraculous return to lucidity* after a long period of apparently dense amnesia, as in Excerpt 3 where the lady in the nursing home suddenly recognizes her friends and neighbors after years of non-recognition.

What is common across all three of these stories is that narrators are attempting within the context of an institutionally framed, research interview to make sense of Alzheimer's disease as they personally experience it. First of all, they each exit the world of the institutional interview, along with their roles as "respondents" and "local experts," and they *cue another identity in the lifeworld* in which they have some personal experience of the disease. Second, the narrators skillfully employ reported speech to show, demonstrate, or *perform the symptomatic speech* of their loved ones or friends who have Alzheimer's disease. Third, their stories evince the *social co-construction of the disease in talk.*

Cuing an Identity in the Lifeworld

In each case, the narrators signal a shift away from their roles as respondents in the interview to another role in the lifeworld. In Excerpt 1, the narrator uses a disjunctive marker ("Now") and cues her identity as "stepdaughter": "Now my stepfather, I went to see him twice a week in the nursing home." In Excerpt 2, the narrator uses a story preface ("One of the things that intrigues me about all that about my father . . ." to cue his identity as a son (on story prefaces, see Ochs & Capps, 2001). The narrator of Excerpt 3 introduced his main character as "a neighbor of ours" earlier in his interview, and thus cast himself as "neighbor."

Performing Symptoms

In previous work (Schrauf & Iris, in press), we argued that narrators often strategically render the reported speech of individuals with Alzheimer's disease to perform or dramatize symptoms, effectively saying, "This is what Alzheimer's disease looks like." In this chapter, we hone that observation to "This is how persons with Alzheimer's disease sometimes talk"—effectively reporting *what they're said to say*. Indeed, as is frequently the case with this disease, symptoms are not categorically evident, but rather must be construed as such in context. Thus, in Excerpt 1 the older man's stories of his years as a janitor are not hearable as symptoms simply because he repeats the stories over and over. After all, repeating one's stories may be annoying, but it is not necessarily suggestive of cognitive disorder. Rather, his repeated tellings are hearable as symptoms because he seems to believe that the events occurred just *now*. In a sense, the context creates the symptomatic speech. More dramatically in Excerpt 2, the narrator intensifies in successive turns his father's insistence that his children are in fact strangers set on assaulting him. It is interesting to note that the narrator offers little commentary or interpretation of his father's behavior *as symptomatic*. Rather his prosodic renderings of his father's speech are hearable as symptoms. As noted in the introduction, such reported speech is offered as evidence for independent inspection by the interlocutor (Holt, 1996), or, as we argued previously, narrators present them as "eye-witness" reports about their experience (Schrauf & Iris, in press).

Co-constructing Alzheimer's in Talk

This discursive co-construction has two senses. On the one hand, narrators often perform (quote, report, cite) conversations between themselves and individuals who have the disease and effectively dramatize the co-construction of the disease in reported speech. On the other hand, in the context of the interview, the interviewer may actively co-construct talk about the disease with the narrator by commenting on, adding to, correcting, or simply backchanneling about the narrator's story. Participation by the interviewer is an act of "co-tellership" (Ochs & Capps,

2001) that may affect the direction, quality, length, or purpose of the story-as-told. The notion of co-tellership makes the point that interviewers are often drawn into the lifeworld stories of narrators, as themselves participants in the broader lifeworld, and not impassive, neutral, disinterested observers of that world.

In Excerpt 1, in reported conversation with her stepfather, the narrator dramatizes *her perduring collusion in co-constructing an unreal world* in which he is still the janitor of a large apartment building. She does this by speech accommodation in which she skillfully matches his prosody (i.e., using a breathy voice for him, "how's mama?" and a breathy voice for herself in answering him, "She's fine," when she knows that mama has been dead for some time), and she explicitly draws the lesson about this accommodation when she says, "I jiss went along with it . . . every time I went to visit him." She shapes her story, which is certainly not the veridical report of any one conversation with her stepfather, as a generalized pattern reflecting the social world that she shares with him.

In essence, she constructs a script. The approach to scripts taken in this chapter has been to emphasize their ad hoc construction during ongoing talk, serving the situation-specific interactional goals during that talk. When a narrator constructs a script, he or she makes relevant (or even creates from scratch) regularities that inform or qualify the topic at hand. What is particularly interesting in Excerpt 1 is that the narrator's story is itself about constructing a new social pattern, *a new regularity,* or perhaps a new script for talking with her stepfather. Having established at first the regularity of their talk ("I'd visit him twice a week in the nursing home"), she concludes with a new regularity ("I went along with it . . . every time I went to visit him"). At the core of the discourse world of Alzheimer's disease is the fact of irreversible cognitive decline over time refracted in changing social roles, patterns of interaction, and conversational routines. The "regularities" of today will slowly morph into new regularities in three months, six months, a year, etc. For this reason, script formulation is an especially interesting feature of talk about Alzheimer's in the lifeworld, where script formulation is a crucial strategy for constructing dispositions—of persons who have the disease, of caregivers, of sympathetic friends, of clinicians, etc. It is also an interesting reflection of what ongoing discourse is like with an individual who has the disease and arguably forms one of the expectations that interlocutors develop in subsequent visits with family and friends who have the disease.

Excerpt 2 is an example of co-tellership in the interview itself in which the interviewer and interviewee engage in the *co-construction of the stunning inability of a father to recognize his children.* In this story, the narrator does not simply describe the incident, but rather he demonstrates his father's inability to recognize them in reported speech. The narrator voices the father in progressively strident tones, and his performances are systematically met by the interviewer's backchanneled responses of recognition and reinforcement. Given that reported speech is not a verbatim representation but a strategic dramatization, via selected lexical, prosodic, and discursive devices, and given that the interlocutor's backchanneled responses have an effect on the ongoing telling (Schegloff, 1982), it is arguable that the narrator is expanding on his father's speech and not simply recalling additional things that his father said.

What might be the purpose of this co-constructed amplification of the story? In fact, the data do not offer an answer to this question. The narrator articulates neither an evaluation of the story nor a coda that would situate the story in the interview, and the interviewer goes on to change the topic after the narrator has finished. Further, although the narrator has constructed a script of nighttime agitation as background to the story, the actual story seems to be too powerful in its implications to function simply as an "instance" of that script. Nor is the narrator imparting information about *prosopagnosia* (the inability to recall familiar faces, Mendez, Martin, Smyth, & Whitehouse, 1992), which is often seen in the disease. Indeed, it would seem that the narrator's goal is not primarily about imparting information. ("I don't know but one of the things that intrigues me about all that about my father is . . ."). Rather, having shifted the footing of the interview from "research" to "lifeworld," the narrator is sharing his experience with a sympathetic listener, and they effectively co-construct a disquieting, strange, and ultimately heart-wrenching account of the real-world implications of the disease.

In Excerpt 3, the narrator uses various prosodic devices, articulates adjacency pairs, and eliminates quotatives to perform a perfectly normal, fluid conversation between himself and his friends and the lady who had not recognized them for years. Thus, he does not describe, but *constructs her momentary lucidity in a reported conversation.* The variation in behaviors (symptoms) from day to day, month to month, and year to year within the same individual is a commonly remarked feature of Alzheimer's disease, and momentary flashes of lucidity can be both thrilling and deeply troubling to family members and caregivers. Although there is little research on this phenomenon, it is a frequent topic on caregiver websites, in the caregiver literature, and in caregiver conversation.

The story in Excerpt 3 points up again that these moments of lucidity are most often experienced *in talk.* It is the return of meaningful interaction that marks the "moment of lucidity." This is not a question of suddenly producing correct morphosyntactic forms and appropriate lexical expressions, nor even of taking appropriate conversational turns. Rather the return to competence is tantamount to being conversant again with a seemingly lost world of daily concerns, histories of intimate relationships, and immediate and (daringly) future concerns.

In the end, all three of these narratives point up the essentially discursive nature of the lifeworld and the experience of Alzheimer's disease as a fundamental challenge to the taken-for-granted-ness of the lifeworld. In the introductory paragraphs of this chapter, we suggested that the discursive construction of Alzheimer's disease from within the lifeworld differed from such constructions from within the institutional world, in part because the latter is motivated by existential vs. medical, clinical, public health concerns. In one way or another, the behaviors at issue in these stories may be recast discursively in the institutional world (as retrograde amnesia, prosopagnosia, etc.), but these lifeworld narrators do not talk about memory but rather about people whom they know and who are acting in unexpected, strange, and sometimes threatening ways.

CONCLUSION

Alzheimer's disease from within the lifeworld is more than a medical disease, illness condition, or abnormal mental state. Rather it is a social experience in which a loved one, friend, or acquaintance talks and acts more and more abnormally, challenging over time the taken-for-granted-ness (scriptedness) of daily life and requiring the construction of ever new—hopefully workable, but always temporary—patterns (scripts) for social interaction, marked confusingly, thrillingly, but ultimately deceptively, by moments in which all the symptoms seem to disappear and their loved one, friend, or acquaintance is his or her old self all over again. Poised between the "normal and the pathological" (Canguilhem, 1991), people need to make sense of such an experience, and narrative becomes a prime vehicle for doing this (Schrauf & Iris, in press). Put simply, one powerful reason for telling stories about Alzheimer's disease is to try to make sense of the disease. In the lifeworld, narrating is an act of meaning-making.

This chapter has focused on talk *about* Alzheimer's disease, which may seem an odd contribution to a book about dialogue with individuals who *have* the disease. Nevertheless, research in the ethnography of communication (as well as common sense) shows that interlocutors come to concrete speech situations with their own ideas, beliefs, assumptions, and biases about how conversation will unfold, and this is as true in speech with persons with Alzheimer's disease as anywhere else (see chapter 3 in Guendouzi & Müller, 2006). By looking at how older adults use the discursive devices of narrative as a specific genre, script formulations as a means for developing accounts, and reported speech as a means of performing (vs. reporting) experience, we have tried to shine a light on how ideas, beliefs, assumptions, and biases about talk with people who have the disease are actualized in talk. When told, stories take on a life of their own, and particularly good stories become part of the stock of "common wisdom." In the end, all talk involves meaning-making, and the narratives that circulate about Alzheimer's very likely form the expectations and framings that cognitively healthy interlocutors bring to their dialogue with persons who have the disease.

REFERENCES

Brenneis, D. (1988). Telling troubles: Narrative, conflict and experience. *Anthropological Linguistics, 30*(3/4), 279–291.

Bruner, J. (1991). The narrative construction of reality. *Critical Inquiry, 18*, 1–21.

Canguilhem, G. (1991). *The normal and the pathological* (Trans. C. R. Fawcett & R. S. Cohen). New York: Zone Books.

Clark, H. H., & Gerrig, R. T. (1990). Quotations as demonstrations. *Language, 66*(4), 764–805.

Couper-Kuhlen, E. (1998). Coherent voicing: On prosody in conversational reported speech. *InLiSt: Interaction and Linguistic Structures, 1*, 1–28.

Couper-Kuhlen, E. (2004). Prosody and sequence organization in English conversation: The case of new beginnings. In E. Couper-Kuhlen & C. F. Ford (Eds.), *Sound patterns in interaction: Cross-linguistics studies from conversation* (pp. 335–376). Philadelphia: John Benjamins.

Davis, B. (Ed.). (2005). *Alzheimer talk, text and context*. New York: Palgrave MacMillan.

De Fina, A. (2012). *Analyzing narrative: Discourse and sociolinguistic perspectives*. New York: Cambridge University Press.

Edwards, D. (1994). Script formulations: An analysis of event descriptions in conversation. *Journal of Language and Social Psychology, 13*(3), 211–247.

Edwards, D. (1995). Two to tango: Script formulations, dispositions, and rhetorical symmetry in relationship troubles talk. *Research on Language and Social Interaction, 28*(4), 319–350.

Edwards, D. (1997). *Discourse and cognition*. Thousand Oaks, CA: Sage.

Edwards, D. (2000). Extreme case formulations: Softeners, investment, and doing nonliteral. *Research on Language and Social Interaction, 33*(4), 347–373.

Goffman, E. (1974). *Frame analysis: An essay on the organization of experience*. New York: Harper and Row.

Goodwin, C. (1984). Notes on story structure and the organization of participation. In M. Atkinson & J. Heritage (Eds.), *Structures of social action* (pp. 225–246). Cambridge: Cambridge University Press.

Goodwin, C. (1986). Audience diversity, participation and interpretation. *Text, 6*(3), 283–316.

Guba, E., & Lincoln, Y. (1989). *Fourth generation evaluation.* Newbury Park, CA: Sage.

Guendouzi, J., & Müller, N. (2006). *Approaches to discourse in dementia.* Mahway, NJ: LEA.

Holland, D. (1992). The woman who climbed up the house: Some limitations of schema theory. In T. Schwartz, G. M. White, & C. Lutz (Eds.), *New directions in psychological anthropology* (pp. 68–79). Cambridge: Cambridge University Press.

Holland, D., & Quinn, N. (Eds.). (1987). *Cultural models in language and thought.* Cambridge: Cambridge University Press.

Holt, E. (1996). Reporting on talk: The use of direct reported speech in conversation. *Research on Language and Social Interaction, 29*(3), 219–245.

Holt, E. (2000). Reporting and reacting: Concurrent responses to reported speech. *Research on Language and Social Interaction, 33*(4), 425–454.

Hutchby, I., & Wooffitt, R. (1988). *Conversation analysis: Principles, practices, and applications.* Malden, MA: Blackwell Publishers.

Johnson-Laird, P. N. (1983). *Mental models: Toward a cognitive science of language, inference, and consciousness.* Cambridge, MA: Harvard University Press.

Klewtitz, G., & Couper-Kuhlen, E. (1999). Quote-unquote: The role of prosody in the contextualization of reported speech sequences. *Pragmatics, 9*(4), 459–485.

Mathis, T., & Yule, G. (1994). Zero quotatives. *Discourse Processes, 18,* 63–76.

Mendez, M. F., Martin, R. J., Smyth, K. A., & Whitehouse, P. J. (1992). Disturbances of person identification in Alzheimer's disease: A retrospective study. *Journal of Nervous and Mental Diseases, 180,* 94–96.

Miles, M., & Huberman, A. (1994). *Qualitative data analysis: An expanded sourcebook* (2nd edition). Thousand Oaks, CA: Sage.

Mishler, E. (1984). *The discourse of medicine: Dialectics of medical interviews.* Norwood, NJ: Ablex.

Muhr, T. (2004). *Atlas.ti: The knowledge workbench (Version 5.0).* Berlin: Scientific Software Development.

Neisser, U. (1976). *Cognition and Reality.* San Francisco: Freeman.

Ochs, E. (2004). Narrative lessons. In A. Duranti (Ed.), *A companion to linguistic anthropology* (pp. 269–289). Malden, MA: Blackwell.

Ochs, E., & Capps, L. (2001). *Living narrative: Creating lives in storytelling.* Cambridge, MA: Harvard University Press.

Pomerantz, A. (1986). Extreme case formulations: A way of legitimating claims. *Human Studies, 9,* 219–229.

Potter, J., & Hepburn, A. (2005). Qualitative interviews in psychology: Problems and possibilities. *Qualitative Research in Psychology, 2,* 281–307.

Powers, W. R. (2005). *Transcription techniques for the spoken word.* Lanham, MD: Altamira Press.

Riessman, C. K. (2008). *Narrative methods for the human sciences.* Thousand Oaks, CA: Sage.

Sarangi, S. (2003). Institutional, professional, and lifeworld frames in interview talk. In H. van den Berg & H. Houtkoup-Steenstra (Eds.), *Analyzing race talk: Multidisciplinary perspectives on the research interview* (pp. 64–84). New York: Cambridge University Press.

Sarbin, T. R. (1986). The narrative as a root metaphor for psychology. In T. R. Sarbin (Ed.), *Narrative psychology: The storied nature of human conduct* (pp. 3–21). New York: Praeger.

Schank, R. C. (1982). *Dynamic memory: A theory of reminding and learning in computers and people.* Cambridge: Cambridge University Press.

Schegloff, E. A. (1972). Notes on a conversational practice: Formulating place. In D. Sudnow (Ed.), *Studies in social interaction* (pp. 75–119). Glencoe, IL: Free Press.

Schegloff, E. A. (1982). Discourse as an interactional achievement: Some uses of "uh huh" and other things that come between sentences. In D. Tannen (Ed.), *Georgetown University Roundtable on Languages and Linguistics* (pp. 71–93). Washington, D.C.: Georgetown University Press.

Schegloff, E. A., & Sacks, H. (1973). Opening up closings. *Semiotica, 7,* 289–327.

Schrauf, R. W., & Iris, M. (2011a). A direct comparison of popular models of normal memory loss and Alzheimer's disease in samples of African Americans, Mexican Americans, and refugees and immigrants from the Former Soviet Union. *Journal of The American Geriatrics Society, 59*(4), 628–636.

Schrauf, R. W., & Iris, M. (2011b). Using consensus analysis to investigate cultural models of Alzheimer's disease. In D. Kronenfeld, G. Bennardo, V. de Munck, & M. D. Fischer (Eds.), *A companion to cognitive anthropology* (pp. 548–568). Malden, MA: Wiley-Blackwell.

Schrauf, R. W., & Iris, M. (in press). How to construct a case of Alzheimer's disease in three languages: Case-based reasoning in narrative gerontology. *Ageing and Society.* Advance online publication. doi: http://dx.doi.org/10.1017/S0144686X12000979

Swales, J. M. (1990). *Genre analysis: English in academic and research settings.* Cambridge: Cambridge University Press.

Part Two

COGNITIVE AND COMMUNICATIVE RESOURCES FOR ENGAGEMENT

3

"GETTING TO KNOW YOU"
Situated and Distributed Cognitive Effort in Conversations with Dementia

Nicole Müller and Zaneta Mok

It's not the having, it's the getting.
(*Garfield*, Jim Davis, Feb. 24, 1980)

INTRODUCTION

Conversation and Dementia: Looking for Skill in the Deficit

Conversations in the context of dementia have been analyzed from a variety of angles (see, e.g., Guendouzi & Müller, 2006). What we are attempting to do here is tease out some aspects of what makes conversation a suitable site for identifying and analyzing cognition as it happens. Success in this endeavor will have implications for the applied analysis of conversations in the context of dementia, specifically the assessment of, and following from this, intervention for, conversational-cognitive skills of persons with dementia and their conversation partners. The ultimate goal is to establish ecologically valid tools for the evaluation of the skills and needs of persons with dementia and those interacting with them on a daily basis.

The dominant discourse of dementia, in the medical as well as the behavioral sciences, is (still) one of deficit. Evaluation of cognitive skills is interpreted in terms of progressing deficit, and context-free assessments essentially test decontextualized skills. This makes sense in a medical perspective: the aim of medicine is to identify illness or damage (level of cholesterol, location, size and type of a tumor, blood pressure, for instance) and to administer a cure, or ringfence the source of damage in order to minimize its effect on non-damaged body systems. The perspective in the rehabilitation sciences, including speech-language pathology and its underlying research base, is somewhat different, in that the starting point for any intervention (in the widest sense) most usefully is the set of skills a person brings to the rehabilitation process. Therefore, our perspective is one of looking for the skills amid the deficit: While we are of course not blind to the cognitive-communicative deficits we encounter in our participants with dementia, we deliberately foreground what a person with dementia *can do*. In addition, for present purposes, we focus more on the moment of interaction than on long-term effects. In other words, and as hopefully shall become clearer as we proceed, we are looking at the person with dementia as a learner, explorer, and hypothesis tester *in the moment of interaction.*

Cognition and Conversation

Given that this chapter is part of a book about conversation as cognitive activity, a (tentative) definition of what we mean by 'cognition' is in order. For the purposes of what we are trying to achieve here, we look at cognition as the system of operations that goes into the completion of a task that involves knowledge, and hasten to add that such a system of operations is not conceptualized as exclusively centered in one individual, but rather is contextually distributed. Conceptually, we draw on approaches that focus on the distributed, embodied, and cultural nature of cognition, such as those developed by Clark (1997) and Hutchins (1995; Hutchins & Palen, 1997; see also Duff, Mutlu, Byom, & Turkstra, 2012). In these approaches, cognitive activity is not isolated within any one individual brain but distributed in an extended cognitive system situated within a sociocultural environment. This extended system includes other individuals, as well as artifacts, and also extends to the interchange of cognitive representations between individuals and external artifacts. According to Hutchins and Palen (1997, p. 24), "communicative behaviours are the representations by which a socially distributed cognitive system does its work."

Our discussion in this chapter is couched in terms of systemic functional linguistics (SFL). SFL was developed by Michael Halliday and colleagues first and foremost as a theory of language use in context and has, over the course of the past few decades, become an increasingly popular framework in clinical applied linguistics (see, e.g., Ferguson & Thomson, 2008; Müller, Mok, & Keegan, in press). The name of the theory encapsulates its basic tenets: language is envisioned as a network of *systems,* or alternatives among which language users choose for *functional* purposes, that is, in order to create meaning. The current standard reference work in SFL theory is Halliday and Matthiessen (2004); Eggins (2004) is a somewhat more user-friendly introduction to the theory and its analytical tools. Eggins and Slade (2005) specifically deals with casual conversation from an SFL perspective. We shall introduce the analytical tools and concepts we use later, in the methods section.

Halliday and Matthiessen (1999, p. ix) formulated the point of departure of the SFL endeavor as follows: "Language evolved, in the human species, in two complementary functions: construing experience, and enacting social processes." The former function, or in SFL terminology *metafunction,* is typically referred to as the *ideational,* and the latter as the *interpersonal* function. In addition, linguists in the SFL tradition distinguish a *textual* metafunction, which refers to the building of complex meanings out of simpler building blocks through the creation of texts. Thus, language use as well as the architecture of language is viewed not only as inherently functional, but as multifunctional. In addition, SFL incorporates the role of context in the creation of meaning and analyzes language use as a situated activity. In the context of multi-party interactions, situated activity by definition becomes multiply distributed. Linguists in the SFL tradition have, in the main, had a preference for the analysis of texts (essentially defined as contextually situated instances of language use) as a window on how language enables meaning creation, without second-guessing the cognitive, mental, or psychological processes involved, or without making claims as to the nature of the neural distribution or representation of such processes. There is, however, also work in SFL that is explicitly cognitive-linguistic in orientation (see, for instance, Halliday & Matthiessen, 1999), in that it attempts to model cognition in terms of meaning-making through language.

Our working definition of cognition, provided previously, to an extent overlaps with Halliday and Matthiessen's (1999) meaning- and language-based perspective on cognition, but we confess to (at the present time) being agnostic in regards to their claim that cognition is (that is, can most profitably be modeled as) "not thinking but meaning: the 'mental' map is in fact a semiotic map, and 'cognition' is just a way of talking about language. In modeling knowledge as meaning, we are treating it as a linguistic construct: hence, as something that is construed in the lexicogrammar. Instead of explaining language by reference to cognitive processes, we explain cognition by reference to linguistic processes" (p. x). At present, we feel that a discussion of what comes first, language or cognition, and whether language is a cognitive resource and artifact (see, e.g., Clark, 1997), or whether cognition and cognitive processes originate in language, would lead us to a 'chicken-and-egg' debate that would distract from the purpose at hand, namely to examine conversational interaction as a cognitive event. However, no matter whether language is chicken or egg, Halliday and Matthiessen's insistence on meaning as *jointly constructed*, that is "a shared resource which is the public enterprise of a collective" (1999, p. x) is an important facet of our thinking about cognition and language.

As mentioned earlier, we draw on Hutchins's (1995) work, and we are borrowing his concept of 'cognition in the wild' in order to underline our stance that cognitive activity is not only distributed (that is, not isolated in any one individual brain), but also culturally situated. Conversation is surely one of the most robust cognitive and cultural events in human life (both individually and collectively). Not only is conversation one of the premier sites for learning, as well as for the building and cementing of social relations across the human lifespan, but it is also an activity that is governed by powerful cultural conventions, that is, accepted routines and procedures, values, and norms shared by members of a community (see, e.g., Hymes, 1972). Conversations have long been a privileged data source for the analysis of human interaction and, in recent years, have increasingly become a focus of interest in the context of disorders of communication and cognition. There is some controversy as to what actually represents a 'conversation', as opposed to two or more people talking in the same situational context (see, e.g., Goffman, 1974; Atkinson & Heritage, 1984). In this chapter, we specifically deal with *casual* conversation. Eggins and Slade (2005) use the label *casual conversation* (which they contrast with *pragmatic* conversation) to refer to informal interactions during which participants talk for the sake of talking and interacting; in other words, there is no specific pragmatic goal that has to be achieved (as would be the case, for instance, in a service encounter, where the participants' goal is to purchase and sell, respectively). However, while casual conversation does not have specific transactional goals, it is a far from pointless endeavor. In the SFL tradition, various researchers have explored the interpersonal work accomplished in casual conversation (see, e.g., Eggins & Slade, 2005; Mok, 2011; Müller & Mok, 2012; Mok & Müller, in press), as well as the vital role conversation plays in the acquisition of language (see, e.g., Halliday's [1975] classic study on *learning how to mean*).

Our goal is to examine how participants with dementia use linguistic tools to 'do cognition' in casual conversation. Specifically, we shall focus on how one person with dementia of the Alzheimer's type (DAT) negotiates the cognitive task of 'getting to know' unknown visitors, that is, how she uses language to situate the unknown relative to the known; to elicit, rehearse, and establish information; and to distribute the cognitive effort involved in these tasks in her environment. As a progressive dementing condition, such as DAT, becomes more severe, the process of 'getting to know you' becomes more and more rooted in the moment of negotiation, as well as more confined to the moment of negotiation: casual encounters, especially brief ones, or ones that are separated by considerable time intervals, tend to not be remembered in the moderate to severe stages of DAT, which in turn means that common ground in terms of factual knowledge has to be established fresh at every meeting. It is this juncture that we are specifically interested in; that is, what is of interest is not only *how* a person with dementia negotiates the process of who someone is, and what they are doing, why they are there, in other words, *how* she tries to make sense of an encounter in the moment of the encounter, but also, *that* she uses language to make sense of the encounter, that she has the drive, the will to know.

The circumstance that learning involves more effort does of course not mean that persons with DAT do not have the ability to establish new episodic or semantic content; however, it does mean that in order for long-term storage to be established, exposure to information has to be more intensive, prolonged and repetitive than for cognitively unimpaired individuals (see, e.g., Camp, Foss, O'Hanlon, & Stevens, 1996; Camp & Stevens, 1990; Cherry, Simmons, & Camp, 1999; Vanhalle, Van der Linden, Belleville, & Gilbert, 1998). The same appears not entirely to be true for emotional content, that is, for emotional responses such as a positive predisposition towards an individual (such as a visitor), who for all intents and purposes otherwise has remained a stranger even after repeated encounters (Blessing, Keil, Linden, Heim, & Ray, 2006; Evans-Roberts & Turnbull, 2010).

METHOD

Participants

The conversation that forms the basis of this chapter involves four participants. Two of them, here referred to as Mary and Rose (all names used are pseudonyms), were graduate students at the time of recording and were doing fieldwork under the direction of the first author of this chapter. In addition, both had a special interest in dementia and its impact on cognition and communication. Both were in their twenties, with Mary somewhat younger than Rose. Mary was a native of South Louisiana, where the conversation took place, while Rose had come to Louisiana in order to pursue her doctoral studies (this circumstance features in the later conversation).

The two other participants, Ms Beatrice and Ms Frances, both had a diagnosis of dementia of the Alzheimer's type (DAT). However, there were no recent formal assessment data available for either. Both resided in a nursing home in South Louisiana. Ms Frances used a wheelchair, while Ms Beatrice was independently mobile. Ms Frances also wore corrective glasses, and both ladies were, based on our observations, somewhat hard of hearing, but neither wore hearing aids, or found casual conversation, on the whole, hard to follow. The circumstance that no independent, formal assessment data are at our disposal for these participants is in some sense a limitation in that it precludes a 'compare and contrast' approach between their behavioral indicators of cognitive processes and results from tests probing specific cognitive or linguistic skills (for instance, short-term memory or word finding). On the other hand, the lack of formal test data also prevents the a priori labeling of a participant as 'moderately' or 'severely impaired', which in turn may lead to a certain level of expectations of failure and success in conversation and, indeed, to the (again, possibly unconscious) adaptation of conversation partners' language use to the expected level of impairment.

Staging and Recording Casual Conversations, and the Data in this Chapter

The very fact that a casual conversation is recorded and subsequently transcribed makes it into something not-quite-casual; in Eggins and Slade's term, this "problematizes" (2005, p. 18) a casual conversation in the sense of drawing attention to something that is typically not monitored or preserved for posterity. One may only partially agree with Eggins and Slade's statement that "[w]hen we engage in casual conversation, we assume that anything we say will not be held against us"; however, the emergent, spontaneous, and collaborative nature of casual conversation is central to what we try to achieve in this chapter, and it is these characteristics that are potentially put at risk by 'staging' conversations and by overtly recording them.

The staging of conversations between residents in dementia care facilities for the purposes of investigating interpersonal relationships, and as a facilitative context for the development and maintenance of such relationships (and by implication a reduction in social isolation), has been discussed in some detail by Mok (2011). The data under investigation in this chapter also represent a staged conversation in that two participants, Mary and Rose, deliberately seek out a third, Ms Frances, in order to spend time with her and chat. Thus the overt goal of the conversation is just that: to visit and to have a conversation. There is also a covert goal, in that Mary and Rose are graduate students doing fieldwork under the direction of the first author and have volunteered to do so because they wish to learn about interactions with persons with dementia. Ms Frances does not question Mary's and Rose's presence, but expresses her appreciation of having both Mary and Rose, as well as Ms Beatrice, visiting her: (turn 40) "come make a round to see me, I'm glad to have a little company." By the time the conversation examined here took place, Mary and Rose had visited Ms Frances and Ms Beatrice several times, and this was the second conversation they recorded. The presence of a recording device can potentially have a deleterious effect on the casualness of a conversation. However, neither Ms Frances nor Ms Beatrice ever remarked on the small digital recorder and microphone that was used and appeared to not pay attention to it once they had given verbal permission to switch the recorder on. The setting for this conversation is Ms Frances's room in the nursing home where she resided at that time. Ms Beatrice occupied a room across the hall from Ms Frances and was in the habit of dropping in for a chat; she did so on this occasion, and enters the room, after knocking on the open door, 32 turns after the recording starts.

Table 3.1 gives a brief quantificational overview of the conversation. Ms Frances (F) and Ms Beatrice (B) are the more active conversationalists. Ms Beatrice is present for a total of 292 turns out of a total of 471 turns. Rose, by comparison with the other participants, stays somewhat in the conversational background. The circumstance that the two students are doing fieldwork, and are at the same time learning from and about persons with dementia, may very well have impacted the distribution of the conversational load here, in that the students may deliberately have chosen to not take the lead, but rather leave the running of the conversation to Ms Beatrice and Ms Frances.

Analytical Tools

We use SFL as a theoretical and analytical framework, and we shall throughout make reference to tools provided by this approach. A detailed

Table 3.1
Participants' contributions to the conversation

	F	B	M	R
turns	169	108	107	87
words	1,124	958	568	229
different words	269	284	199	85
MLU (words / turn)	6.6	8.87	5.3	2.6

introduction to both framework and tools would go beyond the scope of this chapter; background and detail may be found in Eggins (2004), and Halliday and Matthiessen (2004). We trust that our brief sketch here will suffice to orient readers to the concepts and categories used. As mentioned previously, SFL practitioners consider the function of language to make sense of, or construe, human experience as one of the two basic functions of language. Within this *ideational* (meta)function, SFL further distinguishes the *experiential* and the *logical* function. Experiential meanings are expressed (and hence analyzed) at the level of the clause. Thus, in terms of experiential meaning, a clause represents a *figure,* or a configuration of a *process,* and its attending *participants,* plus (typically optionally) any prevailing *circumstances.* A process is something that happens: an action, event, a state of being, in English and related languages prototypically expressed by means of a lexical verb. Participants are entities directly involved in or affected by a process, such as an actor (active agent), a goal (the entity most directly affected by a process carried out by an actor), a scope (denoting the extent of an action); participants are typically expressed by means of noun groups. Circumstantial elements (often prepositional phrases or other adjuncts, such as adverbs) add information concerning, for instance, causality, location, or time. The major process types distinguished in SFL are illustrated in Table 3.2 (see Eggins, 2004, for subcategories of process types and detailed discussion of associated participant types).

Table 3.2
Process and Participant types (summarized from Eggins, 2004)

Process type	Definition	Example
Material	Process of doing or happening	She *wrote* a chapter. The ice *melted* in the sun.
Mental	Processes of sensing— perceiving, thinking, desiring, and feeling	She could *see* the cat. She *thought* it was a bad idea. She *wants* a vacation.
Relational	Processes of characterization (identifying, attributing)	She *is* a professor. She *has* a new bicycle.
Verbal	Process of saying	She *said* she was sick. She *told* her friend that she was sick.
Existential	Process of existing	*There is* a cat in the yard.
Behavioral	Physiological and psychological processes	She *coughs* a lot. She *laughed* out loud.

In SFL parlance, the term TRANSITIVITY refers to the system of process types. Choices made in the TRANSITIVITY system reflect how speakers use language to construe events in the world. To illustrate, the configuration 'I have a headache' relates the speaker to the headache by way of a relational process of possession (expressed by the verb 'have'), where the speaker ('I') is the carrier/possessor of an attribute, namely the headache. Thus the headache is construed as something that characterizes the speaker. The configuration 'this headache is killing me', on the other hand, places the headache in the position of the actor and controlling agent in a material process ('killing'), whereas the speaker ('me') is portrayed as the goal, that is, the participant most directly affected by the process, without agency, and the least powerful participant in this configuration.

An analysis of experiential configurations allows insight into *what* speakers say about how they experience the world; how they choose to configure participants, processes, and circumstances. However in a conversation, speakers don't simply 'mean', they 'mean for each other', that is, they exchange meanings and offer and elicit meanings to and from each other. In doing so, they adopt roles and enact relationships. This level of meaning, how language users relate to each other (and to the messages they are exchanging), is referred to as *interpersonal meanings* in SFL. The roles that conversation participants adopt, and how they negotiate meanings, can be captured by investigating the sequence and distribution of *speech function moves* used. A *move* is a unit of discourse, and may be coextensive with a clause, but can also be expressed by other means (for example, a single word may represent a move, or even a nonverbal signal). *Moves* are also distinguished from *turns*: a *turn* is defined as all the talk a speaker produces before another speaker takes over; a turn may realize more than one move.

SFL views dialogue as a process of exchange; the two fundamental roles in this process are those of *demanding* and of *giving*, and what is exchanged is either information, or goods and services. Cross-referencing these two categories results in four basic speech functions that can be used to open an exchange: a statement (giving information), an offer (of goods and services), a question (demanding information), and a command (demanding goods and services) (see, e.g., Halliday & Matthiessen, 2004; Eggins, 2004). Eggins and Slade (2005), using these four basic speech functions as a point of departure, developed a comprehensive categorization of speech function moves. We shall draw on their classification in our analysis, but pursue fewer levels of subcategorization (or, in SFL terminology, 'delicacy'). Table 3.3 briefly summarizes speech function moves and their definitions.

Table 3.3
Speech function moves, definitions and illustrations (summary based on Eggins &
Slade, 2005)

Move type	Definition	Examples bold (contextualizing items in parentheses)
Open: Attend	An attention-getting device	**Hey Bob!**
Open: Initiate	Speaker introduces content, typically a proposition, for negotiation, by either adopting a demanding or giving role	**What's for lunch?** **We went to that new Chinese restaurant last week.**
Sustain	A move that continues negotiation of the content introduced in an opening move	
Sustain: Continue	A sustaining move contributed by the same speaker	(We went to that new Chinese restaurant last week). **i) I had their smoked duck. ii) It was delicious, kind of expensive, though.**
Sustain: React	A sustaining move contributed by another speaker	
React: Respond	A reacting move that contributes to the completion of the current exchange	(A: What's for lunch?) B: **I could make scrambled eggs.**
React: Rejoin	A reacting move that prolongs the negotiation of the current exchange, for instance, a tracking move, which serves to check or clarify a previous move	(A: What's for lunch?) B: **Say what?** (A: We went to that new Chinese restaurant last week) B: **Which one would that be?**

IDENTIFYING 'COGNITION IN THE WILD' IN CONVERSATIONS WITH DEMENTIA

For the remainder of this chapter, we shall focus on how Ms Beatrice navigates the process of getting to know the visitors she encounters in Ms Frances's room, particularly Rose. In other words, what is of interest is how she uses conversation, and language, to establish a shared cognitive space with others, or, in Clark's (1996) terms, common ground. As we mentioned earlier, no results of formal cognitive or language assessments were available for the two participants with DAT, Ms Beatrice and

Ms Frances. However, we may note that over the course of roughly two years, during which the first author was a regular visitor (approximately once every two weeks), neither Ms Beatrice nor Ms Frances appeared to retain factual information, such as the visitor's name, job, marital status, and the like, and these contents were negotiated repeatedly during conversations with both Ms Beatrice and Ms Frances, and both ladies always showed interest in their visitors.

Opening a Cognitive (and Social) Space for Negotiation, and Initial Hypothesis Testing

Ms Beatrice enters the conversation at turn 33 of the transcript, a few minutes after Mary and Rose arrive at Ms Frances's room. (Comments regarding aspects of this conversation not captured in the transcript are derived from discussion with one of the graduate students.) Ms Beatrice knocks on Ms Frances's open door, and the conversation proceeds as follows (transcript conventions are explained in the appendix to this chapter):

Example 1

33	Mary:	hi Miss B. ((R's voice in background; greeting))
34.1	Beatrice:	hello? (4.0)
34.2		how y'all doin.
35	Mary:	fine? =
36	Rose:	= good thank you,
37	Beatrice:	y'all come visit?
38	Mary:	[yeah,* ((laughs))
39	Rose:	[mhm,*
40.1	Frances:	come make a round to see me,
40.2		I'm glad to have a little company.
41	Beatrice:	she's your grandma?
42	Mary:	no. =
43	Rose:	= no,
44	Mary:	no we're just visiting, (2.0) ((chuckles))
45	Beatrice:	well y'all must know her then,
46.1	Mary:	huh? (3.0)
46.2		you wanna sit- you want me to get you a chair or do you wanna sit on on the bed, ((3 sec. unintelligible; several voices overlap))
47	Frances:	(xx) she could- (.) sit on the bed.

Ms Beatrice's first move (34.1) is a response to Mary's opening attending move (33). She follows this up, after a four-second pause, with another opening move (34.2), a conventional greeting. We may assume that during those four seconds, she is likely to attempt to situate the two visitors relative to Ms Frances, whom she knows. Mary's and Rose's responses (35–36) are likewise conventional, and Ms Beatrice proceeds to elicit information (37) relating the visitors to Ms Frances, by choosing the material process 'come visit'; thus, she opens up negotiation of 'what are you doing here' (rather than, for example, 'who are you'). The active negotiation of the visitors' relation with Ms Frances continues with another opening move from Ms Beatrice (41). She invokes a possible kinship relation, using a relational process, and using perceptual information as well as cultural knowledge to inform her choice of attribute ('your grandma'): the two visitors are obviously far younger than Ms Frances, and one of the social conventions of kinship is to visit relatives. Mary's extension (44) of the two students' disagreement with Ms Beatrice's opening move prompts her to revise her assessment of the constellation in front of her (45); if the two young women aren't Ms Frances' kin, they 'must know her', offering familiarity as a possible reason for why the students are present. The use of the interpersonal theme 'well', of modality ('must'), and the adjunct 'then' express how Ms Beatrice changes tack, as it were, stating her revised assessment as fact, after the students disagree with her. It is interesting to note that Ms Beatrice's initiative to unambiguously place the visitors in relation to Ms Frances is collaboratively derailed, as it were: Mary (46.1) makes a tracking move (a non-specific request for clarification) that is not resolved, and then offers an opening question (46.2), which concerns the arrangement of the physical space, i.e., where Ms Beatrice should sit, which is first met with simultaneous talk by several participants, after which Ms Frances contributes a response (47) to Mary's opening move, thus leaving Ms Beatrice's avenue of investigation.

This brief exchange would appear to give insight into the way in which Ms Beatrice divides up the cognitive space that opens up by her entering the conversation. Rather than negotiating the identities of the visitors independently or in their own right, she draws on her existing understanding of her social environment and links the unknown (the visitors) to the known (Ms Frances) by way of investigating the possible relationship between the two. The declarative mood configuration of her opening moves puts her in the role of offering information for discussion, rather than requesting it. However, she acknowledges her inquiry and uncertainty by pairing the declaratives with rising intonation.

As mentioned previously, opening moves offer content for negotiation, and thereby steer the conversation in a certain direction. Looked at from a social-interactive angle, the use of opening moves signals the adoption of an assertive role: the speaker is in a position (in terms of the role relations between participants) to "claim a degree of control over the conversation" (Eggins & Slade, 2005, p. 194). Exercising control over what is negotiated involves the selection of transitivity configurations, that is, processes and the participants involved in them, as well as (typically optionally) the circumstances that contextualize the processes. In doing so, a speaker not only signals to conversation partners what she thinks of constellations of entities in the world (e.g., 41, 'she's your grandma'), but also offers food for their thoughts, and thus sets parameters for the shared cognitive space.

In this conversation, Ms Beatrice offers 37 opening moves (or 21.14% of her total moves). Of these, 19 are statements, as compared to 14 questions, 2 offers, and 2 attending moves. She thus shows a preference for using a declarative mood configuration (though often, as illustrated in Example 1, accompanied by rising intonation) to introduce new content for negotiation. Mood choices signal interactional stances, for instance, of a speaker presenting herself as someone who has information to share, as opposed to eliciting information. However, they also guide conversation partners' thinking along a path chosen by the speaker: 'well y'all must know her then' (45) offers the mental process of 'knowing' as highly probable (note the presence of modality, 'must'), rather than as an equally probable or improbable possibility ('do you know her?'). Ms Beatrice's opening moves are in essence hypotheses that she forms on the basis of the available evidence and that she tests against her conversation partners' responses.

Negotiating People and Places: Dividing Cognitive Space, and More Hypothesis Testing

During the course of Ms Beatrice's participation, we see repeated attempts to learn more about Mary and Rose. Ms Beatrice brings the conversation back to the students in turn 78 (between turns 48 and 77, talk was about her friendship with Ms Frances, and her husband), by appraising first Rose and then Mary as 'a beautiful lady'. As well as offering an evaluation for negotiation, this refocuses attention on the visitors. Ms Beatrice's attempt to confirm her working out of the visitors' relationship with Ms Frances is however thwarted in this instance by Ms Frances, who pursues her own agenda of getting to know the students.

Example 2

| 78 | Beatrice: | you're a beautiful lady. |
| 79 | Rose: | {LV thank you, ((laughs))} |

80	Beatrice:	you too.
81	Mary:	*{LV thanks. ((laughs))}*
82	Frances:	yeah they both (.) beautiful women.
83	Beatrice:	uhuh.
84	Frances:	ya'll both married, =
85	Beatrice:	=ya'll are kin to her?
86	Mary:	no I'm not married.
87	Beatrice:	[ya'll are kin to her?*
88	Frances:	[you're not married?*
89	Rose:	[m: mhm,* (.) no.
90	Mary:	no. *((2 sec. unintelligible; several voices overlap))*
91		*{louder* just friends,*}*
		(2.0)

The compliment used as an opening move (78) involves Rose as the topical theme of the clause, in the role of the carrier of an attribute ('beautiful lady'), which is extended by way of an elliptical clause (80). While Rose and Mary's responses signal that they engage with and don't object to the compliment, their laughter may indicate surprise, or that they are not altogether comfortable with it. Ms Beatrice's opening gambit does however achieve that the visitors are back at the center of nego-tiation, and both Ms Frances and Ms Beatrice follow up with opening moves that, in the form of declaratives, offer attributes of social roles for discussion. Moves 84 and 85 are produced in 'latched' form, that is, so close together as to almost overlap, and are then repeated (Ms Frances rewords her opening, reversing polarity), this time overlapping. Moves 89 and 90 could potentially be responses to either opening move, while Mary's louder 'just friends' (91) extends a disagreeing response to Ms Beatrice's moves 85 and 87.

We believe it is significant that both ladies attempt to categorize the students in terms of social roles (and even status). The questions they ask are not random, but are socially appropriate, and at a minimum show that in the presence of advanced dementia, these two ladies are capable of using social knowledge to test hypotheses formed on the basis of the available evidence, that is, their sensory input, and the two young wom-en's responses to their questions: the two women are obviously young, and obviously adults, and are thus candidates for several female social roles, among them that of being married. Further, invoking social and kinship relations points to a 'contextualized' categorization, or a cultur-ally grounded sensemaking: getting married is a major milestone in the life of an adult woman (typically, in the culture against whose backdrop this conversation takes place, a young adult woman) and, arguably, much more important than, for instance, one's precise age.

Ms Beatrice's insistence on possible kinship between her friend Ms Frances and the two visitors (strangers) is also worth mentioning. Viewed in a decontextualized fashion, this could be interpreted as perseveration in consequence to dementia. Recall, though, that earlier in the conversation, her investigation of how the visitors relate to her friend was interrupted by Mary attempting to resolve where Ms Beatrice should sit. She now resumes this concern by, as it were, backtracking: while earlier on she offered a specific relationship ('grandma'), which was met with the visitors' disagreement (Example 1, moves 42, 43), and which led to her formulating the notion that (at the very least) the students 'must' be acquainted with Ms Frances, she now offers an unspecified relationship, 'kin'. Again this is met with disagreement, and Mary's extension and explanation (91) that they are 'just friends'.

Establishing and Rehearsing Information: 'You're from China?'

Over the course of Ms Beatrice's participation in the conversation, the circumstance that Rose originates from China is negotiated in five separate episodes. We loosely define an 'episode' here as a sequence of one or more exchanges that group around the same overall conversational topic. The first three of these episodes are introduced by Mary (113) and Ms Frances (128 and 169), respectively. In Example 3, Mary uses the information that Rose is from China to enhance an opening move that demands a service from Ms Frances and Ms Beatrice, to explain what 'maman' means to Rose; the enhancement, that Rose is from China, serves as a justification for the demand.

Example 3

113 M [you have to* explain to Rose what maman is. 'cause she's from China.

On the following two occasions, negotiating where Rose is from is a straightforward request for information, opening an exchange.

Example 4

128 Frances: where she's from.
129 Rose: I'm from China.
130 Frances: China,
131 Rose: yea.
132 Beatrice: China.
133 Frances: oh yeah.
134 Beatrice: that's a good ways- a little ways from here,

135	Frances:	yeah,
136	Beatrice:	it's almost at the back door.
		[((M, B, F, chuckle))]*
137.1	Frances:	[(xX)* the back door ((M chuckles))
137.2		but- yes, (3.0) 'coz I know (xX)

(Turns 138–142 negotiate that China is a beautiful country)

143	Frances:	a good way from here.
144	Rose:	uh?
145	Frances:	it's a good way from here I'd say.
146	Rose:	[a:h. *
147	Beatrice:	[yeah I* believe so. ((M chuckles))
148	Frances:	very far away.

We have discussed elsewhere that an inquiry into one's origins is one of a set of questions that Ms Frances uses to good effect to keep a conversation going (see, e.g., Müller & Mok, 2012). The repeated tracking moves (130, 132) may be occasioned by the circumstance that both ladies are somewhat hard of hearing, but also serve the purpose of rehearsing the information that Rose has just supplied. Once the fact that Rose is from China is well established, Ms Beatrice offers another opening move (134) around two contradictory propositions: China is far away, or it is not. Ms Frances's tentative agreement (affirmative, but with mid-rising intonation; 135) prompts Ms Beatrice to settle, for the moment, for the 'not far away' option, which in turn is met with a chuckle all around. Ms Frances's next two moves are unclear, in 137.1 because of an overlap, in 137.2 because her vocal intensity decreases to the point of unintelligibility. Over the next seven turns, Ms Beatrice and Rose establish that China is a beautiful country, with two overlapping unintelligible utterances from Ms Frances interspersed. Then (143) Ms Frances returns to the earlier topic initiated in move 134; her response contrasting with Ms Beatrice's elaboration in move 136. Rose's tracking rejoinder prompts a reiteration from Ms Frances, this time with the addition of a modality element hedging her certainty, 'I'd say'. Ms Beatrice signals her agreement with a mental process in move 147, and Ms Frances' elaboration in move 148 establishes the collectively accepted facts.

The discussion now (149–167) turns to what Rose is doing in this country, with Ms Beatrice eliciting further information from Rose, based on what she has learned so far.

Example 5

| 149.1 | Beatrice: | you come to stay? |
| 149.2 | | or you just come to visit. |

150	Rose:	uhm I'm here uhm I'm a student. now.
151	Beatrice:	oh you're a student. =
152	Frances:	= mhm.
		(2.0)
153	Beatrice:	you gonna stay what?
154	Rose:	I'm a student.
155.1	Mary:	*{louder, slower:* she's a student.
155.2		she goes to the university. *}*
156	Frances:	o:h ye:s:. =
157.1	Beatrice:	= (Xx) hand that over there, (10.0)
157.2		's a big (x X) to (send X) (2.0) (xxx) today's country.
157.3		*((R light laugh; quiet))* I don't know, (1.5) how true that is.
157.4		everybody think their country's the best.

Ms Beatrice's opening and continuing moves (149.1 and 149.2) seek to extend the picture she has built up thus far of Rose: a foreigner, from China, a faraway country. Even though Ms Beatrice's register move (151) appears to indicate understanding, it appears from her next tracking move (153) that she is not integrating the information represented by Rose's response, a relational experiential configuration (it presents an attribute of Rose's, she *is* a student, here and now), with her own question of whether Rose has come to stay or visit. Ms Beatrice's next turn is difficult to interpret both in terms of moves and experiential configurations, owing to the partial unintelligibility of 157.1 and 157.2. Thus it remains unclear whether Ms Beatrice intended to contribute another opening move (157.1) and expand on it in 157.2. However, it is not evident that Ms Beatrice as yet integrates the attribute of 'student' into her mental picture of Rose; in addition, the long pause times give the impression of a struggle to formulate her thoughts. The experiential meaning of Rose studying (a behavioral process) appears to become established, at least for the moment, in move 161.2, since Ms Beatrice inquires after the scope of Rose's studies. However, in her summing up of the exchange (167), she pairs 'different language' with 'different country'.

Example 6

158.1	Mary:	well she wanted to study a certain subject.
158.2		so that's why she came here.
159	Beatrice:	she what?
160	Mary:	she wanted to study a certain subject?
161.1	Beatrice:	oh yeah. (3.0)
161.2		what she kind is- what she studying (.) for. (2.0)

162	Rose:	language,
163	Beatrice:	m:?
164	Rose:	language.
165	Beatrice:	language?
166	Rose:	mhm.
		(6.0) ((M chuckles quietly)) (5.0)
167	Beatrice:	different country, different language

After another significant pause (7 seconds), which none of the other participants makes a move to fill, Ms Frances again inquires 'where you from honey' (169). Laughing, Ms Beatrice contributes an extending response (174.1) to Rose's answering response (170), at first seemingly contradicting Ms Frances's extension 'a way from here', but then in a continuing move (Example 7), Ms Beatrice affirms that China is indeed 'a good ways from here'.

Example 7

169	Frances:	where you from honey.
170	Rose:	I'm from China.
171	Frances:	o:h she's from [(x)*
172	Beatrice:	[from* China.
173	Frances:	a way [from* here.
174.1	Beatrice:	[that's* (.) at the back door.
174.2		((laughs)) that's a good ways from here maman. =
175	Frances:	= yea,
		(6.0)

We interpret Ms Beatrice's laughter as a signal that she is in fact deliberately joking when she says 'at the back door', and yet again Ms Frances and Ms Beatrice between them establish that China is far away. Note that the students do not interfere (or help, depending on one's perspective) in these negotiations.

Ms Beatrice reintroduces the topic of Rose's country of origin again in 210, after a 10-second lull in the conversation.

Example 8

210	Beatrice:	and you're from China,
211	Rose:	mhm, {quiet sure,}
		(6.0)
212	Frances:	you're [from China too,*
213	Beatrice:	[you like it in the United* States? =

214	Mary:	= no O(city).* =
215	Rose:	= [mhm*, =
216	Frances:	[oh you from* [O(city).*
217	Rose:	= [(I think it's a good* country)
		((all speak simultaneously))
218.1	Beatrice:	(xxxx ((background talk ends)) country).
218.2		well naturally. ((M laughs))
218.3		I can't say that I blame you.

After the exchange initiated in move 210 ends with Rose's minimal affirmation, there is a 6-second pause, and then both Ms Frances and Ms Beatrice take the initiative almost simultaneously, which results in two competing exchanges being negotiated over the following moves. Though this looks somewhat chaotic, it is worth noting that it is by the initiative of the two older ladies that previously introduced information is again rehearsed. Ms Beatrice uses a declarative mood configuration; she presents the opening move as a fact, rather than a request for confirmation. She brings up China once more, in turn 262, after yet another long pause (7 seconds). The lull in the conversation allows her to take the initiative once again, uncontested this time, and she links the by now established notion of Rose's Chinese origin with the possibility of her return after her studies ('when you get through'). Note though that Ms Beatrice doesn't mention the concept of 'studying', but rather keeps the purpose of Rose's stay in the country vague.

Example 9

262	Beatrice:	you're goin back to China when you get through?
263	Rose:	maybe.
264	Beatrice:	you like it (X) then?
265	Rose:	mhm.
266	Frances:	that's where she's- that's where you're from sugar.
267	Rose:	yeah.
268	Frances:	{very quiet mhm, }
		(7.0)
269	Beatrice:	I bet this country is different from yours.
270	Rose:	very different.
271	Beatrice:	eh?
272	Rose:	very different.

In turn 269, yet another long pause gives Ms Beatrice the opportunity to further follow her line of reasoning, this time by making a comparison, using a verbal projection ('I bet') to initiate an exchange that invites

Rose to agree with her stance, which Rose duly does. When Ms Beatrice is about to leave Ms Frances's room, she again invokes an attribute of Rose's, namely that she is a 'lady from a different country' (304.2), and once again uses the same verbal projection as earlier to invoke the difference between the two countries (306), and Rose duly aligns herself with Ms Beatrice's view by way of a minimal response. Ms Beatrice then moves from the specific to the general ('every country', 308), but uses modality in the form of a mental projection ('I guess'), signaling a degree of uncertainty, and again Rose affirms (309) that she shares Ms Beatrice's view.

Example 10

301	Frances:	come back and see [me now,*
302	Beatrice:	[well (x) sure* (I'll make) sure.
303	Mary:	nice to meet [you too*.
304.1	Beatrice:	[I apprec-* I appreciate that. *((M laughs:))*
304.2		met (from) a: a lady from a different country. *((end laugh))*
305.1	Rose:	yeah.
305.2		thank you *((M laughs))*
306	Beatrice:	I bet it's a lot of difference huh.
307.1	Rose:	mhm. (2.0)
307.2		yea,
		(6.0)
308	Beatrice:	I guess every country's different,
309	Rose	sure.

DISCUSSION AND OUTLOOK

At this stage, a reader may wonder whether, subsequent to this interaction, Ms Beatrice retained any of the information she went to such pains to gather from Rose. Judging from encounters with her at later dates, she did not. Therefore, what of 'cognition in the wild'? We shall argue here that what is sometimes overlooked in the discussion and assessment of cognitive skills in dementia is the 'doing' and 'getting', in favor of the 'having', that is, the more or less static and context-free retention and recall of information (and in assessment situations, typically information that has no particular immediate relevance for the person examined) is foregrounded, as opposed to the dynamic seeking out of learning and joint construction of understanding.

Over the course of her conversation with Ms Frances, Mary, and Rose, Ms Beatrice makes numerous attempts to elicit information about her visitors (we focused on Rose for the purposes of this chapter). We see a lot of repetitiveness, which is often identified as one of the hallmarks of conversations involving persons with DAT. It is thus tempting to, by default, categorize repetitiveness as a symptom of the dementia, a defect (see, e.g., Cook, Fay, & Rockwood, 2009; Cullen et al., 2005). In contrast, we suggest here that what Ms Beatrice does is in fact active learning management and conversation-based rehearsal. Note that the two ladies with dementia do the 'heavy lifting' in terms of negotiating, rehearsing, and maintaining information. They produce the largest number of opening moves (Ms Frances uses 35 and Ms Beatrice 37, while Mary produces 29 opening moves, and Rose 5), as well as by far the largest number of tracking moves (Ms Frances uses 29, and Ms Beatrice 21 tracking moves, as compared to 10 and 6 used by Mary and Rose, respectively). The two students, probably owing to their self-perceived identities as learners, students, fieldworkers, by comparison very rarely take the initiative in steering the conversation. The repetitiveness (in terms of propositions negotiated) is not random but always concerns the conversation partners present. As an aside, we may note that this characterizes all the conversations we had with Ms Frances and Ms Beatrice; repetitive opening moves, such as questions, always concerned the conversation partners. Ms Beatrice repeatedly tests her own knowledge and rehearses information she has gained about Rose.

The immediate context of functioning in this case is a conversation that has elements of the familiar and the unfamiliar: Ms Beatrice signals that she knows Ms Frances, and explains on two separate occasions how she feels about her, and why she calls her 'my little maman' (turns 53–61 and 106–111).

Example 11

106   Beatrice: I (x) that my family had abandoned me, but they were doin that- (.) (when) I was sick. (2.0) she come. (1.5) she cover my feet. o:h she said don't cry. don't cry. things gonna get better,

. . . . .

111   so I call her my little maman, ((M, F, R chuckle))

In fact, Ms Beatrice's account could not have happened quite as told: Ms Frances uses a wheelchair and is not independently mobile, and would not have been able to 'come' and 'cover my feet' (see also Müller & Mok, 2012, for further discussion of language use to construct interpersonal relationships in this conversation). What is important here is that her account, and thereby her sensemaking, of her friendship with Ms Frances is not contested by anyone; it is accepted at face value and hence becomes part of the backdrop against which the situation at hand, namely the presence of two strangers in Ms Frances's room, is negotiated.

As we discussed previously, Ms Beatrice's explorations are not random, but proceed along situationally and culturally configured pathways: she first invokes close kinship ('grandma'), then, given corrective feedback ('no we're just visiting'), she concludes that the visitors must know Ms Frances (Example 1). The use of cultural knowledge to explore a situation at hand, and to narrow down hypotheses to be tested, is thus a skill that appears to remain intact in persons with dementia in the presence of significant overall memory defects. In essence, what it points to is the ability to use old, long-established cognitive schemata to make sense of the unknown. Such schemata include knowledge about family relationships, culturally significant categories of people (married versus unmarried women, for instance), but also the ability to interpret verbal and nonverbal interactional signals (such as laughter, a good-humored voice). Ms Beatrice's culturally grounded sensemaking appears to encounter difficulties when she tries to reconcile what she knows about Rose with being a 'student' (see Example 5): Rose is obviously an adult, as well as a foreigner (that she's 'from China' has been negotiated repeatedly). Elsewhere, Mary's statement that 'I uhm I'm on my master's degree', prompts Ms Beatrice to ask 'you finish high school?' (191–192). As we saw, she does not pursue this information further.

Our experience of interacting with and of examining conversations with persons with dementia leads us to the conclusion that the *drive to know*, or the active negotiation of common ground, is a cognitive activity that is very much undervalued in the culture of dementia, and further, that if investigated systematically it could give considerable insight into a person's functioning in context, which in turn can give rise to an examination of the context of functioning and, hopefully, to a maximization of cognitive support. In the conversation discussed in this chapter, contextual support can be seen as less than optimal—if the goal is the establishment of factually accurate information, that is. The two students do not question factually inaccurate information (Ms Beatrice's account of how Ms Frances has taken care of her in the past, for instance), and they typically don't offer solutions or explanations when Ms Beatrice or Ms Frances appear to be struggling with a concept or a piece of information. They tolerate long pauses and leave the steering of the conversation to the two old ladies, as well as the resolution of ambiguity (recall the negotiation of whether China is 'a good ways' or 'a little ways' away). The students are comparatively reactive participants:

they supply information when asked, but generally do not volunteer it, and only rarely offer to explain or expand. On the other hand, their comparative passivity allows Ms Frances and Ms Beatrice ample opportunity to explore and ask the questions. Given the obvious memory deficits of both ladies, it is no surprise that the same information is elicited multiple times.

It is at this juncture that future research could fruitfully explore the cognitive task of conversing: the willingness and ability of persons with dementia to explore their environments and to actively strive to get to know them, paired with the judicious use of environmental support (verbal and nonverbal scaffolding) should not only give insight into a person's contextualized functioning, but could also contribute to quality of life. As regards insight into functioning, documenting, and tracking how an individual 'does cognition' in conversation may even lead, in due course, to a modification, or a reformulation of how we view dementia progression or severity. At present skill and deficit tends to be formulated chiefly in terms of memory impairment, with well-established patterns in the differential impairment of memory subsystems (see also Chapter 1 of this volume). What tends to get overlooked somewhat is what persons with dementia *want to know,* and how they go about finding out. What we saw in the conversation investigated here was that Ms Beatrice's explorations and negotiations showed clear signs of integrating given and new, pre-existing and contextually available multi-modal information, that is, an active, questing engagement with the environment. A communicative environment that acknowledges and gives scope to this engagement takes the person with dementia seriously as an active cognitive agent, with their own perspective and 'take' on a situation under exploration. In typical assessment encounters, the examiner is the person who asks the questions, and the person with dementia is evaluated on the basis of the answers she or he gives. We believe that listening to the questions a person with dementia asks, as a hypothesis-tester, as a meaning-maker in the moment of interaction, may provide greater insight into how they make sense of their environment and, in turn, how the environment helps or hinders sensemaking.

REFERENCES

Atkinson, J. M., & Heritage, J. (Eds.). (1984). *Structures of social action: Studies in conversation analysis.* Cambridge: CUP.

Blessing, A., Keil, A., Linden, D. E., Heim, S., & Ray, W. J. (2006). Acquisition of affective dispositions in dementia patients. *Neuropsychologia, 44*(12), 2366–2373.

Camp, C. J., Foss, J. W., O'Hanlon, A. M., & Stevens, A. B. (1996). Memory interventions for persons with dementia. *Applied Cognitive Psychology, 10,* 193–210.

Camp, C. J., & Stevens, A. B. (1990). Spaced-retrieval: A memory intervention for dementia of the Alzheimer's type (DAT). *Clinical Gerontologist, 10,* 658–661.

Cherry, K. E., Simmons, S. S., & Camp, C. J. (1999). Spaced-retrieval enhances memory in older adults with probable Alzheimer's disease. *Journal of Clinical Geropsychology, 5,* 159–175.

Clark, A. (1997). *Being there. Putting brain, body and world together again.* Cambridge, MA: MIT Press.

Clark, H. H. (1996). *Using language.* Cambridge: CUP.

Cook, C., Fay, S., & Rockwood, K. (2009). Verbal repetition in people with mild-to-moderate Alzheimer Disease. *Alzheimer Disease & Associated Disorders, 23*(2), 146–151.

Cullen, B., Coen, R. F., Lynch, C. A., Cunningham, C. J., Coakley, D., Robertson, I. H., & Lawlor, B. A. (2005). Repetitive behaviour in Alzheimer's disease: Description, correlates and functions. *International Journal of Geriatric Psychiatry, 20*(7), 686–693.

Duff, M. C., Mutlu, B., Byom, L., & Turkstra, L. S. (2012). Beyond utterances: Distributed cognition as a framework for studying discourse in adults with acquired brain injury. *Seminars in Speech and Language, 33,* 44–54.

Eggins, S. (2004). *An introduction to systemic functional linguistics.* 2nd ed. London: Continuum.

Eggins, S., & Slade, D. (2005). *Analysing casual conversation.* 2nd ed. London: Equinox.

Evans-Roberts, C. E., & Turnbull, O. H. (2010). Remembering relationships: Preserved emotion-based learning in Alzheimer's disease. *Experimental Aging Research, 37*(1), 1–16.

Ferguson, A., & Thomson, J. (2008). Systemic Functional Linguistics and communication impairment. In M. J. Ball, M. R. Perkins, N. Müller & S. Howard (Eds.), *The handbook of clinical linguistics* (pp. 130–145). Malden, MA: Blackwell.

Goffman, E. (1974). *Frame analysis: An essay on the organization of experience.* New York: Harper & Row.

Guendouzi, J. A., & Müller, N. (2006). *Approaches to discourse in dementia.* Mawah, NJ: Lawrence Erlbaum.

Halliday, M.A.K. (1975). *Learning how to mean. Explorations in the development of language.* London: Edward Arnold.

Halliday, M.A.K., & Matthiessen, C.M.I.M. (1999). *Construing experience through meaning: A language-based approach to cognition.* London: Cassell.

Halliday, M.A.K., & Matthiessen, C.M.I.M. (2004). *An introduction to functional grammar.* 3rd ed. London: Edward Arnold.

Hutchins, E. (1995). *Cognition in the wild.* Cambridge, MA: MIT Press.

Hutchins, E., & Palen, L. (1997). Constructing meaning from space, gesture, and speech. In L. B. Resneck, R. Raljo, C. Pontecorvo, & B. Burge (Eds.), *Tools and reasoning: Essays in situated cognition* (pp. 23–40). Vienna: Springer-Verlag.

Hymes, D. (1972). Toward ethnographies of communication: The analysis of communicative events. In P. P. Giglioli (Ed.). *Language and social context* (pp. 21–44). Harmondsworth, UK: Penguin.

Mok, Z. (2011). *The linguistic construction of interpersonal processes among people in dementia: An application of systemic functional linguistics.* PhD Dissertation, University of Louisiana at Lafayette.

Mok, Z., & Müller, N. (2013). Staging casual conversations for people with dementia. *Dementia.* Advance online publication, May 22, 2013. doi: 10.1177/1471301213488609

Müller, N., & Mok, Z. (2012). Applying Systemic Functional Linguistics to conversations with dementia: The linguistic construction of relationships between participants. *Seminars in Speech and Language, 33,* 5–15.

Müller, N., Mok, Z., & Keegan, L. (in press). Systemic Functional Linguistics and qualitative research in applied clinical linguistics. In M. J. Ball, N. Müller and R. Nelson (Eds.), *The handbook of qualitative research in communication disorders: In honor of Jack S. Damico* (pp. 149–170). Mahwah, NJ: Psychology Press.

Vanhalle, C., Van der Linden, M., Belleville, S., & Gilbert, B. (1998, December). Putting names on faces: Use of a spaced retrieval strategy in a patient with dementia of the Alzheimer's type. *Neurophysiology and Neurogenic Speech and Language Disorders, 2,* 17–21.

APPENDIX: TRANSCRIPTION CONVENTIONS

The Basic Layout:

Orthographic transcription of all utterances produced by the participants. Turns are numbered; where a turn includes more than one move, moves are placed on separate lines.

((coughs))	Double parentheses and italic type indicate behaviors or events other than speech that are relevant to the interaction, or comments made by the transcriber.

Prosodic Information Integrated into the Orthographic Transcription:

.	falling intonation
,	a slight rise in intonation
?	rising intonation
<u>Christ</u>mas	underlining indicates a marked added emphasis

Pauses within Utterances, and Silences between Utterances:

(.)   brief pause; shorter than 0.5 of a second (brief pauses at the end of utterances are not indicated).

(3.0)   timed pause, three seconds

Overlaps and Interruptions, and Latched Speech:

[overlap begins

*   overlap ends

=   Latching, i.e., the end of one utterance is followed immediately by the beginning of another, without overlap, but also without any pause.

Levels of Intelligibility (Transcriber's Perspective):

did you have a good Christmas	No parentheses: no transcriber doubt; fully intelligible
(did you have a good Christmas)	Transcriber's best guess at meaning; confident enough to identify intended meaning, but some doubt remains.
(did you have a xXx)	The transcriber can identify unstressed ('x') and stressed ('X') syllables.
(2.5 secs unintell.)	2.5 seconds unintelligible speech.

Voice Quality and Intensity:

{LV }	The voice quality associated with a light laugh during speech.
{quiet }	The curly brackets mark the presence of voice quality / intensity indicated by the
{slow }	descriptor in italics.

4

TALKING WITH MAUREEN

*Extenders and Formulaic Language in Small
Stories and Canonical Narratives*

Boyd Davis and Margaret Maclagan

INTRODUCTION

In this chapter we address cognitive and communicative resources available to people with dementia by analyzing a series of conversations with Maureen Littlejohn. Despite living in a Special Care community for persons with dementia, Ms Littlejohn's fluency and fast-paced, charming anecdotes cause most people who meet her to think she is unimpaired. But the fluency depends on her manipulation of formulaic and colloquial phrases, and especially extenders, and the anecdotes are beginning to be more frequently repeated within a single conversation. Her favorite stories are coalescing, behaving as if they were simply much longer formulaic units, selected to illustrate or exemplify more difficult topics.

We begin with a description of the corpus and its collection over six years (2006–2012). We then consider differences in the way listener responses signal affiliation or alignment with Littlejohn in order to highlight ways she manages floor-holding. We examine in some detail the communicative resources on which she increasingly relies for conversation management: extenders, placeholders and other formulaic and colloquial phrases. She injects rehearsed narrative and "small stories" (Georgakopoulou, 2006b) from her repertoire of topics and tales into conversations with partners who can show they align with her viewpoint or affiliate with her as a speaker. We close by exploring how Littlejohn's rehearsed stories may be considered formulaic units in themselves.

Maureen Littlejohn

"Maureen Littlejohn" was born on Halloween, 31 October 1929, in western North Carolina. She first consented to chat with university students in 2006. At that time, she lived in a retirement community in Charlotte, North Carolina. In early 2010, residence administrators moved her to a single-bedroom apartment in a secure memory care unit. In mid-2012, her family moved her to a different memory care residence in Harrisburg, NC. Long-term care residential communities in the United States, including assisted living and memory care or special care units, are not currently required to obtain specific written diagnoses of dementia, including dementia of the Alzheimer's type (DAT), and the researchers have not been given consent to administer cognitive testing to her. Her legal guardian and residence staff have told us that Littlejohn has "memory problems," particularly with finding her way outside the residence or in any place that is not part of the residence. Problems are also evident in her ability to handle details and to plan or to handle complex tasks, and with the shrinking range of topics on which she can converse. By summer 2012, her relatives noticed decreases in her conversational topics and in her conversation management, primarily linked to topic repetition. Conversations with her began when she was mildly impaired; using a three-stage model, she is currently moving into moderate impairment.

The Maureen Littlejohn Corpus

Recordings of 25 conversations with Littlejohn are available as of December 2012 and form part of the Carolina Conversations Collection (CCC), a specialized web portal housed at the Medical University of South Carolina (MUSC). The CCC is open to researchers who provide evidence of review by their institution's review board (or approved affiliative review) and agree to the conditions for publishing (http://carolina conversations.musc.edu/about/). Currently, it contains two collections of conversational interviews: one of multiethnic and multiracial men and women older than 65 with one or more chronic diseases, and one of persons with dementia, collected since 1998 (Pope & Davis, 2011).

Ten of the interactions were recorded by undergraduates enrolled in a gerontology service-learning course at UNC Charlotte (Hancock, Shenk & Davis, 2008), using Olympus 50 digital recorders. In 2010, two graduate students visited Littlejohn separately, each recording five conversations using Olympus 50 recorders (Davis, Maclagan & Shenk, in press), and two researchers began a continuing series of five conversations with her across a 2-year period. One recording used an Olympus 500 recorder, and four conversations were video recorded using a Kodak Z18 portable camcorder (Davis, Maclagan & Wright, 2012). All audio was converted to .wav files and downsampled to 22.05 kHz. Audio was stripped from the video recordings and converted to .wav files for transcription. Recordings were transcribed using Transcriber software (http://trans.sourceforge.net). Video was saved as .mp4 and .avi files in order to view and analyze in Elan video software (http://tla.mpi.nl/tools/tla-tools/elan/) and QuickTime Pro.

The total length of the corpus is 8 hours and 16 minutes or 455 minutes and 41 seconds. The total number of words is 74,750, with Ms Littlejohn contributing 52,250. Since file formats vary, we have not calculated the size of the corpus in megabytes or gigabytes.

Undergraduates and one graduate student, Lorene, were given one hour of training in conversing with older persons. They were encouraged to avoid direct questions (questions starting with WH-words, or yes/no questions) and to use go-aheads (two-syllable back-channel responses like *Uh-huh, Mmm-hmm,* or *Oh really!*) to encourage Ms Littlejohn to continue talking and to co-construct narratives with her by using quilting (Davis et al., in press). The 10 undergraduate recordings contribute a total of 158:40 minutes, with the average length of the conversational interviews being 16:28 minutes. Their interviews contained 22,959 words, with Ms Littlejohn contributing 16,338 or 71 percent of the total.

The 11 graduate student interviews contributed a total of 166:43 minutes. The average interview length differed greatly between the two graduate students. Lorene, who had received the same training as the undergraduate students, interacted well with Ms Littlejohn and averaged 23:26 minutes per interview. By contrast, Mina, who had had no training, averaged 8:15 minutes per interview. The total number of words in these interviews was 26,566, with Ms Littlejohn's contribution being 18,732 or 71 percent. The researchers had considerable experience interacting with older people with dementia. Their five interviews lasted for 139:18 minutes (average length 26:03 minutes) and consisted of 25,241 words, with Ms Littlejohn contributing 17,202 words or 68 percent.

ALIGNMENT AND AFFILIATION

In this section, we focus on the effect the listeners' responses produce on Littlejohn's interaction. We highlight listener responses that signal their alignment or affiliation with her, which allows us to clarify ways in which she manages floor-holding and how she injects rehearsed narrative into her conversations. If a conversation partner signals that he or she aligns with Littlejohn's viewpoint or affiliates with her as a speaker, Littlejohn presents a selection from her repertoire of "small stories" and canonical narratives to continue fluently with the interaction. Small stories are brief fragments of lived experience (Bamberg & Georgakopoulou, 2008); canonical narratives follow Labov's (1972) model of abstract/orientation, complication, resolution, evaluation and coda. Littlejohn tells stories to those with whom she feels some involvement and engagement, perhaps with some wish for self-representation or identity maintenance, including the identity of being a fluent conversationalist and amusing raconteur. What creates at least part of that involvement and engagement is her perception that her conversation partner is supportive of her telling a story, or supports her viewpoint and her interpretation.

Definitions of Alignment and Affiliation

Listeners signal they align with a speaker's right to talk or narrate when they acknowledge that they are hearing the information the speaker is providing and suggest that the speaker continue. They affiliate with a speaker when they endorse the speaker's perspective. Stivers (2008) finds that alignment with the telling activity is enacted by vocal continuers that we call go-aheads and Beňus, Gravano and Hirschberg (2011) call grounding responses; she adds that people use nods to signal preliminary affiliation or endorsement of the teller's position as one way to show support of the stance that the teller is conveying.

Alignment gives rise to the establishment of rapport (Buschmeier, Bergmann & Kopp, 2010), facets of which are often described in terms of language accommodation (Giles, Coupland & Coupland, 1991). Riordan, Dale, Kreuz and Olney (2011, p. 2411) draw on widely adopted findings by Clark and Brennan (1991) to say

> alignment is reached through grounding, or the establishment of mutual knowledge and beliefs, in which interlocutors provide evidence of their understanding (e.g., attentiveness, eye contact) and seek this type of evidence from their conversation partner.

Beňus et al. (2011) claim that grounding response patterns, including "turn-initial single word grounding responses such as *mmhmm, okay,* and conversational fillers *um, uh*" (p. 3001), are part of the listener's establishment of common ground and signal the dominance relationship in the conversation because of the way they manage turn-taking. Steensig and Drew (2008, p. 9) note that affiliative moves are "actions which agree with or take the same stance as co-participants." Both alignment and affiliation reflect the impact on the speaker from the actions and utterances of the listener.

The subtitle of a study of listening practices by Norrick (2012, p. 566) is "the responses responses elicit," in which he ranks verbal listener responses by their "degree of obtrusiveness." Norrick's categories of listener responses are based on what the speaker does in response to them. His initial categories indicate that

> (1) prototypical continuers like *uh-huh* signaling <u>simple recipiency</u> are the least likely to elicit a response; (2) assessments like *wow* marking <u>emotional involvement</u> in foregoing talk . . . are somewhat more likely [to elicit a response]; and (3) <u>information state tokens</u> like *oh* and *so* registering receipt of information . . . are the most likely [to elicit a response]. (p. 569; our underlining)

Alignment and Affiliation in Interactions with Littlejohn

To identify alignment and affiliation, we tabulated the kinds of responses Littlejohn returned to her listeners' responses. We selected representative interactions from the three sets of female conversation partners and coded the first half of each using Norrick's categories for recipient tokens and affective/evaluative assessments. Interestingly, the unimpaired conversationalists almost never offered information state tokens. Instead, they offered comments as responses, with some amount of information that could be affiliative or disafilliative (this is what conversation analysts might call a third turn or a third slot in a multi-turn unit; see Norrick, 2012, p. 568). We suspect their comments are a carry-over from the minimal training received by the undergraduate students in conversing with persons who have DAT: the technique we call "quilting" promotes repetition and paraphrase of utterances in accounts or stories by the person with DAT (Davis et al., in press). Table 4.1 displays what Littlejohn did in response to simple recipient responses like *mmhmm*.

In this sample, Littlejohn's conversation partners responded to her with 75 simple recipient tokens. She continued talking on the same topic for 76 percent of the time, resuming an account from earlier in the conversation for 6 percent of her responses and changing the topic in some way for the remaining 18 percent. She maintained this pattern across three years with three age groups of female interlocutors.

Table 4.2 displays Littlejohn's responses to her listeners' use of emotive or evaluative assessments. Her response is overwhelmingly to keep talking: 93 percent of her responses are either to keep talking or to keep talking and segue into resuming an earlier, related account or story. The other 7 percent of her responses change the topic.

Table 4.1
Sample by date: Littlejohn's responses to her conversation partners' simple recipient tokens (such as *mmhmm*)

Conversation partners	Response: Recipient tokens	Littlejohn's immediately subsequent response
UG: 1a (2009) taking pictures	0	0
UG: 1b (2009) viewing pictures	2	2 Keeps talking, same topic
UG: 2 (2010) each tell stories-in-conversation	22	19 Keeps talking, same topic 3 Asks question to change topic
G: Mina1 (2010) Small-talk conversation with 1 story	12	7 Keeps talking, same topic 1 Keeps talking and segues into resumption of earlier account 1 Changes topic (unrelated) 2 Asks question to change topic 1 Offers recipient token to partner
G: Lorene1 (2010) Small-talk conversation with no stories	24	16 Keeps talking, same topic 2 Questions (rhetorical or ironic) 1 Asks question to change topic 1 Changes topic (unrelated) 4 Keeps talking and segues into resumption of earlier account
R: BD (2010) each tell stories-in-conversation	7	5 Keeps talking, same topic 1 Changes topic (unrelated) 1 Asks question to change topic
UG: 3 (Feb 2012) conversation, occasional story	8	8 Keeps talking

We infer that Littlejohn may have felt that the speakers were both aligned with her telling, as with the recipient tokens, but now were also becoming affiliated with her specific stance toward her story contents, as extracts (a) and (b) show. The listeners' emotive/evaluative assessments are italicized.

(a)[1]

UG2: Oh her daughter OK.
ML: Yep.
UG2: *That's good.* – –
ML: Yeah they come by – she's a stay at home mom, her husband has to travel.

Table 4.2
Sample by date: Littlejohn's responses to her conversation partners' emotive/ evaluative assessments

Conversation partners	Response: emotive/ evaluative assessments	Littlejohn's immediately subsequent response
UG: 1a (2009) taking pictures	11	7 Keeps talking, same topic 4 Keeps talking and segues into resumption of earlier account
UG: 1b (2009) viewing pictures	6	4 Keeps talking, same topic 1 Changes topic (unrelated) 1 story (unrelated)
UG: 2 (2010) each tell stories-in-conversation	7	5 Keeps talking, same topic 2 Changes/shades topic (related)
G: Mina1 (2010) Small-talk conversation with 1 story	2	2 Keeps talking, same topic
G: Lorene1 (2010) Small-talk conversation with no stories	19	19 Keeps talking, same topic
R: BD (2010) each tell stories-in-conversation	17	17 Keeps talking, same topic
UG: 3 (Feb 2012) conversation, occasional story	16	13 Keeps talking, same topic 2 Keeps talking and segues into resumption of earlier account 1 Changes/shades topic (related)

(b)

BD: . . . *that's beautiful*
ML: well – ah – I've always liked that but I used to hang it on the door people would steal it

In the first selection, UG2 has been listening as Littlejohn explains that the daughter of her niece-caregiver will soon come to visit her. Littlejohn's "Yep" at the end of a series of turns suggests that she is finished with the topic but UG2's emotive assessment elicits additional information. In the second selection, in which BD is responding to ML's discussion of one of her homemade baskets, Littlejohn's response to the praise is a small story, the fuller version of which will surface in other conversations.

Table 4.3 displays Littlejohn's responses to the longer informational comments offered as responses by the listeners. These often provide simple information, as in the interchange in extract (c).

(c)

ML: man I'd go [shopping] anytime someone would come pick me up. (laugh)

Table 4.3
Sample by date: Littlejohn's responses to her conversation partners' informative statements: recipiency and beyond

Conversation partners	Response: longer informational utterances	Littlejohn's immediately subsequent response
UG: 1a (2009) taking pictures	8	6 Keeps talking, same topic 1 Keeps talking and segues into resumption of earlier account 1 Changes topic (unrelated)
UG: 1b (2009) viewing pictures	11	5 Keeps talking, same topic 5 Keeps talking and segues into resumption of earlier account 1 Changes topic (unrelated)
UG: 2 (2010) each tell stories-in-conversation	13	12 Keeps talking, same topic 1 Asks question to change topic
G: Mina1 (2010) Small-talk conversation with 1 story	11	5 Keeps talking, same topic 3 *Questions for clarification** 1 *Question to change topic** 1 *Emotive/affective utterance** 1 *Recipient token**
G: Lorene1 (2010) Small-talk conversation with no stories	4	4 Keeps talking
R: BD (2010) each tell stories-in-conversation	6	4 Keeps talking, same topic 2 Keeps talking and segues into resumption of earlier account
UG: 3 (Feb 2012) conversation, occasional story	2	2 Keeps talking, same topic

* In these responses, Littlejohn is actually responding to Mina, to try to get Mina to talk.

UG1:	Good thing you didn't go out on black Friday.
ML:	is that bummer?
UG1:	*yeah, it's the big shopping day.*
ML:	oh I never did for whatever the reasons, I liked sales, I liked bargains, but I never did go out on the Friday after Thanksgiving.

Not surprisingly, 80 percent of Littlejohn's responses to her listener's informative responses are to keep talking on the same topic, or to keep talking and then segue into a resumption of an earlier topic, which she either feels is connected or wishes to expand. However, longer informational comments can often be quite overt in how they signal affiliation or, on occasion, disaffiliation, as when Mina introduces herself and immediately asks a question about Littlejohn's potential knowledge in extract (d).

(d)

Mina:	I'm getting my masters in Gerontology; do you know what that is?
ML:	Uh yeah, Gerontology?
Mina:	Umm hmm.
ML:	Yeah.
Mina:	What is that?
ML:	Old people *(laughs)*. You didn't expect that huh?
Mina:	I did not! *(laughs)*
ML:	Gotcha. . . .

Littlejohn does not like what she perceives as trick questions or questions that signal an expectation of potential low performance: she had said she knew what Gerontology was with "Yeah," so that Mina's continuing to press for a definition is impolite. "You didn't expect that huh" and "Gotcha" let Mina know that she, Littlejohn, is quite aware of Mina's expectations and perhaps delighted to dash them.

Littlejohn's 80 percent of responses to informational comments where she keeps talking would doubtless be higher were it not for the imbalance of turns in this first conversation with Mina. For whatever reason, as well as asking what Littlejohn perceived as "trick" questions, Mina laid the burden of initiating and maintaining the conversation on Littlejohn, by asking yes-no questions or voicing disconnected comments. Littlejohn became the person in the conversation who offered short accounts, asked questions for clarification, and acted as the listener who gave recipient tokens, affective assessments, and finally asked questions to change the topic.

A very different situation exists when Littlejohn interacts with listeners whose responses show that the listeners are either aligned with Littlejohn's talk or affiliated with her stance or content. In extract (e), UG2 and Littlejohn are talking about driving along the Blue Ridge Parkway in the western North Carolina mountains near Littlejohn's childhood home:

(e)

UG2:　When was the last time you went to you know
ML:　oh golly it's been g~ I don't know it's been quite a while but – used to you know you just wanted to take a little drive *or something* or just get out and you know kill a little time – ah – you c~ could go up – and it's an easy drive it's not like – you're you're – the elevation is – fairly high I don't know exactly what it is – but you're constantly kind of climbing but it's such a gradual – increments that you don't really realize that you're getting up –
UG2:　yeah.
ML:　that high – but ah – it's it's a pretty area the {unclear} – it's like everything else in the mountains so it's attracting too many people. {laughing}
UG2:　so many people I meet **like you said** it's gradual like – you're basically it feels like you're driving straight but you're going all the way up.
ML:　yeah – you're kind of c~ – circling around and going on up the mountain and getting you'll – be at the top before you know it

UG2's *"like you said"* lets Littlejohn know that UG2 is not only aligned with her, in the sense of supporting her continuation of commentary, but is also affiliated with her point of view, to the extent of quoting her. While Littlejohn uses an extender, *or something,* no pauses set it off or invite another response from UG2; instead, as usual, Littlejohn keeps talking. Since the two are aligned and affiliated, there is no need for Littlejohn to mitigate or hedge any claims or commentary. Instead, the *or something* echoes the *just* and the *little* in the full phrase: here, minimizing suggests that the drive might not have a serious or work-related purpose, but could be instead to *kill a little time.*

The extracts in Tables 4.1–4.3 are arranged in chronological order. As she moves from mild to early moderate dementia, Littlejohn retains the ability to recognize and to respond to her listeners' responses. Her discourse illustrates and confirms part of the findings by Norrick (2012): in general, her response to recipient tokens such as *Mmmm* or *Mmhmm* is to keep talking. Recipient tokens suggest alignment on the part of the listener as they signal engagement with what Littlejohn is saying, and show support for her continued talking or her telling some part of a story. Emotive or evaluative assessments suggest that her listener is affiliating with her stance or content: again, she keeps talking. We have no illustrations of what Norrick calls information state tokens, such as *So*, showing a listener's recipiency of information, which he asserts will be the most likely to elicit a response. However, we do have a number of instances in which the listener signals recipiency by commentary or quotation and her response is again, to keep talking. Littlejohn is happy to talk. In these interactions, listener responses with emotive or evaluative feedback are best at enabling her to continue to converse.

If the listener does not offer a recipient token, an assessment, or an informative comment, then the listener is most likely doing the talking or asking a series of questions, which will usually shut down any effort at authentic or interactive communication with persons who have dementia. However, if the listener signals active listening with responses from any of these three categories, Littlejohn will continue with a relatively coherent conversation, maintaining topic and adding more information or evaluative commentary of her own. The greater the affiliation, the fewer the extenders she uses and the more frequent the stories and the story fragments or small stories.

While we would not be surprised at these responses to Littlejohn's listeners' responses while DAT was in its early stages, it is good to find them continuing as the disease progresses, suggesting that her ability to "read" her audience has not diminished.

COMMUNICATIVE RESOURCES

In this section, we review language features that assist people with dementia to continue to interact. We give background information on formulaic language (FL); general and idiosyncratic fixed expressions (FE), including idioms and colloquialisms; and general extenders, and we explore their use by Littlejohn.

As dementia increases, a number of language and discourse features are affected. Bayles and Tomoeda (2007, p. 63) note that in early dementia of the Alzheimer's type (DAT), speech is fluent but content may be "characterized by tangentiality and an increase in the number of 'empty' words such as 'thing' and 'it.'" They add that in mid-stage DAT, content is more greatly compromised, with fewer nouns (relative to verbs), less cohesion with decreased referentiality and greater emptiness of content (pp. 66–67). The characterization of "empty" speech is most often illustrated by the increased use of words such as "thing" or "stuff." Carlomagno,

Pandolfi, Marini, Di Iasi and Cristilli (2005) note "that difficulty in pragmatic/conceptual elaboration of discourse information content plays a substantial role in the development of reduced information content and lack of reference of DAT 'empty speech' "(p. 520). However, when discourse is examined from a pragmatics perspective, the "empty" tokens are functionally useful (Davis & Bernstein, 2005).

Formulaic Language

Formulaic language (FL), as explained by Van Lancker Sidtis (2011, p. 248; see also Wray, 2002), is non-propositional language with stereotyped form and conventionalized meaning and pragmatic usage. FL is apparently stored as unitary chunks and includes a range of types. The user can manage language interaction by choice of idiom, colloquialism, filled pause or phrasal verb. FL is often considered under the larger category of multi-word expressions (MWE), which includes nominal compounds, technical terminology, monitors such as *you know* and frequent collocational expressions such as *salt and pepper* or *bread and butter*. Because FL is stored as unitary chunks, it is presumably easier for people with dementia to access, and because formulaic items are frequent and familiar, they are presumably easier for people with dementia to understand when others use them.

Altenberg (1990, 1998) claimed that formulaicity accounts for perhaps 70 or 80 percent of adult language. Wray and Perkins (2000) found that formulaic language is defined in at least 42 different ways, with the definitions keyed to "its form, function, semantic, syntactic and lexical properties, and its relationship with novel (analytic) language" (p. 3). Others categorize FL as non-propositional speech on a continuum showing greater or less idiomaticity (Van Lancker & Kempler, 1987; cf. Wray & Perkins, 2000, p. 6). By 2002, Wray (2002, pp. 8–10) had identified 50 different terms in the literature for formulaic sequences, including chunks, fixed expressions, frozen phrases, multiword units and prefabricated routines. We follow Wray (2008) in defining formulaic language as a sequence that is prefabricated, holistically acquired and conventionalized in usage, with the conditions for its use being pragmatic.

Pragmatics and Formulaic Expressions

Much of the work in the last fifteen years, particularly across Europe, in linking different aspects of pragmatics to FL has been carried out under the umbrella of *phraseology:* see, for example, the bibliography in Cowie and Howarth (1996), publications from the 2005 Phraseology conference (Granger & Meunier, 2008), and since 2010, the publication of the *Annual Yearbook of Phraseology* (Kuiper, 2011). Researchers in speech and communication disorders focus on pragmatics in interpersonal communication, such as indirect speech acts and humor, and in thera-peutic practices, such as those directed toward autism spectrum disorders (Damico & Nelson, 2005). Politeness as evidencing social competence and hence the capacity to identify, infer or project communicative states has been a focus for a number of scholars (Temple, Sabat & Koger, 1999; Ramanathan, 1997). Hamilton's discussion of the ready-made language used by Elsie in her collection of conversations (1994, pp. 65–66, and *passim*) was a major impetus in focusing research on social interaction with speakers with DAT.

Relationship to Language Acquisition/Second-Language Learning

A relevant question when considering language in dementia is when FL is acquired: do speakers learn formulaic items as wholes, or are they ini-tially analytic and syntactic and only later become formulaic? Research-ers in child language acquisition and second-language learning have addressed this question. For second-language acquisition, Ellis (2012, p. 17) reviews his earlier (1996) claim that language acquisition is "essen-tially sequence learning" in which chunks, or lexical sequences, ground the later acquisition of "language grammar." Ellis posits a continuum that accounts for "the interplay of formulas and abstract categories in de-velopment" (Ellis, 2012, p. 35). According to Ellis, the second-language learner begins with learning "phrasal teddy bears," which are "formu-laic phrases with routine functional purposes . . . and the analysis of their components gives rise to abstract linguistic structure and creativity (p. 37). Wood (2012, p. 1) notes that speech fluency is based on master-ing a repertoire of FL "retrieved from long-term memory as if they were single words." As Wray (2002, p. 97) has discussed, this buys time for the speaker to process and organize discourse and can aid the listener's com-prehension of both the discourse and the speaker's individual and group identities. Given that formulaic language chunks are acquired early, it is likely that they will continue to be available even as dementia progresses.

Formulaic Language in Conversations with Littlejohn

As the first step in analyzing formulaic language (FL) in conversations with Littlejohn, we reviewed the occurrence of multi-word expressions (MWE) in a subset of five ordinary conversations filled with small talk between Littlejohn and the graduate student Lorene. MWEs were identi-fied using WMatrix3, an online corpus management tool interfaced with USAS and CLAWS taggers for semantic field and parts-of-speech anno-tation (Rayson, 2009). The Lorene subset contained 12,502 words, 913 of which (or 7.30 percent) were identified as MWE. Categorization was handled manually (see Figure 4.1).

The conversations with Lorene held very little in the way of canonical narrative or small stories. Through previous rehearsals, both canonical narratives and small stories could present variations in the use of colloquialisms, idioms, or extenders (*and so on; all that stuff*). In order to check the extent to which MWEs varied across conversation type, we selected student and researcher conversations from 2009 through 2012 in which narratives and small stories frequently arose (see Figure 4.2). No significant differences were found in the overall number of MWEs

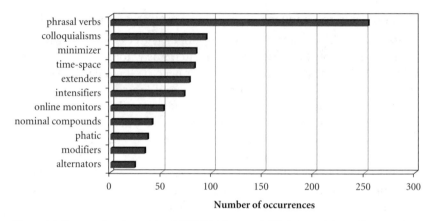

Figure 4.1 Frequent categories of MWE in Lorene-Littlejohn conversations

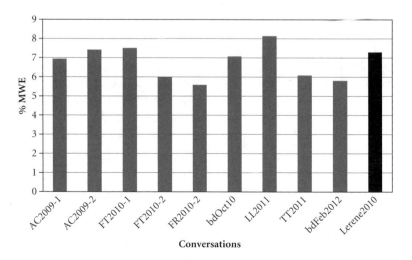

Figure 4.2 Variation in MWE across conversations with (grey) and without (black) multiple stories

between the Lorene conversations without stories and the other conversations that included stories; however, as will be discussed later, the
variation in the number of extenders is provocative.

Importance of Formulaic Language in Dementia Discourse

Examining the use of FL in dementia discourse allows us to examine
pragmatic abilities as well as linguistic structures. Ripich, Carpenter and
Ziol (2000, p. 26) observed that for persons with DAT, "As linguistic and
semantic abilities decrease, increased pragmatic efforts are utilized." For
example, in performance or rehearsed utterances, FL may index not only
the parts of rehearsed or performance narrative accessible to the speaker,
but also their efforts to adapt according to their listeners.

General and Idiosyncratic Fixed Expressions

Fixed expressions (FE) are "holistic units of two or more words" (Moon,
1998, p. 2) that are fixed in some way and are usually recalled as wholes.
FEs may have apparently standard syntax, such as *does their own thing,* or
what goes around is going to come around (to use Littlejohn's version), but
the individual words or phrases cannot be substituted, and the phrase
does not have to be created *de novo.* A phrase such as *one day at a time* is
compositional, but for a speaker like Littlejohn it has become fixed: she
can no longer think of *one week at a time* or *one month/year at a time.*

Idioms and Colloquialisms

Moon (1998, p. 19) says "there is no generally agreed set of categories [for
FEs], as well as no generally agreed set of terms. Moreover, no clear clas-
sifications are possible." They can be roughly divided into idioms such
as *kick the bucket,* where the meaning of the whole cannot be worked
out from the meanings of the individual items, and colloquialisms such
as *over and done with,* which could be more formally expressed as "finished." Both types of FEs are found in the conversations with Littlejohn.

Idioms and Colloquialisms in Conversations with Littlejohn

In the earlier interviews Littlejohn used a wide range of FEs, most of
which were idioms such as *grow like weeds, dog eat dog, monkey business*
or *chit-chat.* She also used common colloquialisms such as *another man's
junk is another man's treasure,* though here she did not quite use the standard form. In later interviews she continued to use both common idioms
and colloquialisms. In the latest interview she used *climbing the walls*
and *pushed my buttons* appropriately as well as the colloquialism *done
my share* when explaining why she was happy to no longer have to wash

the dishes. However, she also used many expressions that, although not commonly regarded as FEs, had become fixed in her speech. The most common was *as I just got through saying,* which became an introduction to a story. In addition, standard FEs were not always recalled accurately. Describing her mother's hard life, Ms Littlejohn said *she sort of fought tooth and toenail to some degree.* This combines three FEs—*sort of* which is a common modifier, *fight tooth and nail* and *to some degree,* but the second is not recalled in its usual form so that the resulting *fight tooth and toenail* sounds decidedly unusual.

Importance in Dementia Discourse

Multi-word expressions and fixed expressions provide speakers with DAT with ready-made pieces of language that they can recall as wholes. Speakers who use MWEs and FEs will sound more fluent than speakers who struggle to express ideas totally in their own words. MWEs and FEs thus allow people with dementia to continue to be part of conversations, when they find it more difficult to express novel ideas in novel sentences. For the speaker with dementia, they provide material that does not have to be created word by word. For the listener with dementia, they similarly provide sections of language that can be understood as wholes.

Extenders

Extenders are considered to play an important role in the analysis of interaction and pragmatic function (Overstreet & Yule, 2001). They may be used to invite the listener to complete a list based on presumed shared knowledge (*I ran by the store and picked up butter, eggs, and stuff like that*). Such shared knowledge may be global, local, or societal, that is, "constrained to speakers of the same culture" (Evison, McCarthy & O'Keefe, 2007, p. 154).

When they are used as evaluators (e.g., Moon, 1998, p. 252), extenders offer one way to identify places where small stories may be found in conversation (Davis & Bernstein, 2005; Maclagan, Davis & Lunsford, 2008). In Littlejohn's speech, extenders are often used in an intersubjective and even stance-marking way, as Overstreet found in her (1999) corpus-based study:

> general extenders are best viewed as multifunctional forms which do not serve a predominantly referential function, but rather have a much more interpersonally defined role. Rather than having list completion or set-marking as their primary function, these expressions are used by speakers to indicate assumptions of shared knowledge and experience, or to mark an attitude toward the message expressed, or toward the hearer. (Overstreet, 1999, p. 11)

Extenders have been studied under a variety of names: set-marking tags, generalized list completers, extension particles, vague category identifiers, imprecision bundles, vagueness tags, generalizers, vagueness markers, and vague category markers (Fernandez & Yuldashev, 2011, p. 2611), with the name indexing the particular focus of a study. Earlier work focused on the connection of extenders with vagueness (on which see Cutting, 2007). More recently, the possibility that extenders might be associated with grammaticalization has been examined (Aijmer, 2002; Pichler & Levey, 2011; Levey, 2012). Currently, their use in several varieties of English is being studied across a range of ages and populations (see, e.g., the literature review in Palacios Martínez, 2011).

The present discussion is the first detailed examination of the use of extenders in the conversations of a person with DAT. Speakers with dementia apparently retain the functions for extenders and depend on their properties, both of list making and of promoting shared social spaces in which to manage and maintain conversational discourse.

Usage by Littlejohn

Extenders may be viewed solely as issuing an invitation to complete a set or list. We note that the majority of Littlejohn's extenders ask the listener to complete a list of nouns or noun phrases. It would be clinically interesting to know if this feature helps account for the common perception that speakers with DAT are impaired for the production of nouns relative to verbs. In this discussion we focus on how extenders are used for intersubjectivity as suggested earlier by Overstreet (1999) and recently reaffirmed by Fernandez and Yuldashev (2011).

Not every person older than 60, with or without DAT, uses extenders. We checked this by examining a random sample of conversations produced by 10 men and women with dementia taken from the Carolinas Conversation Collection and 10 men and women presumably unimpaired taken from the online New South Voices collection at UNC Charlotte. We also reviewed 20 three-minute conversations by persons tested and found to be unimpaired. Many of these speakers, with and without impairment, used no extenders. However, those with dementia who do use extenders seem to use them for conversation management (Maclagan et al., 2008). The Littlejohn corpus contains 70,056 words, with 46,753, or 67 percent, by Littlejohn alone. Of those words, 251 are extenders: this total would normalize to 3,583 per million words (or 5,369 per million if they are compared to her words alone). This is a larger frequency of occurrence than in previous studies. What we term general extenders of the type *and everything*, Evison et al. (2007, p. 147) call vague category markers (VCM). They find that VCM occur at 2,940 per million words in a collection of social language, 1,873 per million words in CANCAD (Cambridge and Nottingham Corpus of Academic English) and 2,454 in *Liveline*, an Irish call-in radio program.

In general, extenders produced by Littlejohn allow her to keep her turn, keep the floor and keep conversation moving by simulating shared understanding of topic or context. Since most of her conversation partners were strangers to her, and even those who visited her frequently did so for only a few weeks, her own politeness conventions could account for her preference for disjunctive extenders. As Overstreet's study (1999, p. 104) demonstrates,

> a disjunctive general extender (e.g., *or something, or anything, or whatever*) may indicate a strategy of negative politeness. When used in certain types of utterances, these expressions seem to function as "hedges" which reduce the speaker's risk of threatening the hearer's face.

Littlejohn slightly varies her usage by her audience, as seen by her most frequent extenders for each group.

- With undergraduates: *or anything/or something* (n = 22), *and so on* (n = 16), *something like that* (n = 4), and *X like that* (n = 3)
- With graduate students: *and so on* (n = 40), *or anything/or something* (n = 40), *or what have you* (n = 10), *and stuff/and things* (n = 6)
- With researchers: *and so on* (n = 10), *or something* (n = 8), *or what have you* (n = 8), *or whatever* (n = 4), *this that and the other* (n = 4).

The conversations with the two graduate students attracted the most extenders with 140, twice as many as in the conversations with the twelve undergraduates (n = 71), even though their length (166:43 minutes) was only slightly greater than that of the undergraduates (158:40 minutes). The length of the conversations with the two researchers was shorter than either of the other sets of conversations, 129:38 minutes, and presented the fewest extenders at 42: roughly one-third of the graduate students and a little more than half of the undergraduates.

This variation could be associated with the ages of her listeners and the degree of politeness or involvement Littlejohn wanted to extend by using extenders as hedges or approximators. Undergraduates were generally in their twenties, the graduate students were in their late thirties/early forties, and one of the researchers was older than 60.

However, a compelling argument can be made for an even more interesting feature: the presence of stories. In general, the greater the number of stories, including resumed and repeated stories about earlier events in her life, the fewer the extenders. Repeating small stories in the same conversation, or across several, is not necessarily a signal of ideational perseveration or a sign of a cognitive deficit, particularly if new information is added or old information is slightly rearranged. Littlejohn usually resumed stories after an unimpaired partner made an affirmative comment. While the story might begin with a phrase from the previous rendition or the exchange, and repeat some of its details, it went on to give additional information as in extract (f).

(f)

ML: Uh, so you took your milk down there and butter *and stuff like that* and with no refrigerator it's amazing how cool you could keep it but by today's standards it probably wouldn't taste that cool. But of course at that time we didn't know any different – –
UG1b: Cool enough to keep it fresh
ML: Cool enough to keep it fresh and to not spoil and actually a lot of people would sell their extra milk and then there would be somebody that would have a milk run and would come by and pick up all your you had metal containers *or something* metal containers that you put your extra milk in. . . .

There was only one story, about her earlier work life, that was recounted to the graduate students: their interactions, which included the greatest number of extenders from Littlejohn, were almost exclusively small talk keyed to question-answer exchanges, with each exchange ranging from two to six conversational turns. However, it is clear that the undergraduate students had heard one or more stories in their earlier conversations with Littlejohn, from comments such as extracts (g) and (h).

(g)

Yeah yeah I remember you showing it, how did you make those? (UG1b 2009: line 20)

(h)

I was talking to my grandma about you living on a farm; she grew up on a farm too. (UG1b 2009: lines 105–106)

In addition to repeating a story from an earlier meeting, in 2012, Littlejohn began repeating stories in the same conversation, such as in extract (i) with BD, looking at a picture on the wall:

(i)

2 min 25 seconds into the recording

ML: These are old
   -- Labradors
   – Pollyanna was the yellow Molly's the black and Tess was the chocolate
   – and they're all, well you can see – Pollyanna when she was
   – up there swimming. The river was running high it was at flood stage and but
   – they just loved their water. . .
   [2 minutes later, ML looks up at the pictures again]

6 minutes 28 seconds into the recording

ML: Um – Bob was my husband and Pollyanna was the yellow Lab
   – Molly was the black Lab. She was the first one we got
   – Molly was black, Pollyanna was yellow – Tess – was chocolate
   -- and you can see the one up there and what the river was running at flood sh~ flood stage and she should not have been out in it
   – but she's got a stick in her mouth I had foolishly had thrown a stick out an
   -- they retrieve it

Relationship to Utterance Boundaries

The extenders *and whatever/or whatever/whatever* usually function to close a turn or a topic, or mark that the speaker is ready to produce or accept a new topic. Littlejohn usually signals she is ready for a change of topic or is willing to give up the floor by saying combinations of *and* or *but* with filled pauses such as *uh*. We chose four of Littlejohn's most frequently used extenders and tabulated whether she continued talking without a noticeable pause before or after the extender (more than 0.5 of a second), or whether she yielded the floor, or changed some aspect of the topic. Figure 4.3 demonstrates her predilection for using extenders to keep the floor while buying time to plan the next part of the utterance and sustain the interaction.

And so on may be the most interesting of her common extenders. According to Overstreet (1999, p. 8), this extender is "found primarily in

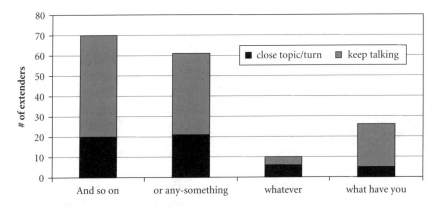

Figure 4.3 Extenders and topic maintenance

formal spoken contexts and talk among nonfamiliars." However, none of the conversations with Littlejohn occur in a formal spoken context. While three conversation partners use extenders, no other speaker in the corpus uses this particular extender, and in only 21.8 percent of its uses does it change a topic or turn, and even less often does it form part of a three-part list.

The Oxford English Dictionary says *and so on* is "used as an abbreviating phrase to avoid further description or the enumeration of further details." Littlejohn seems to use it in this sense in order to (1) remind listeners that she is "assuming" they will understand her minimal list, whether global or local, which contributes to her self-presentation as a sensitive person intent on establishing intersubjectivity and capable of using strategies of involvement and independence to indicate power distance (Scollon & Scollon, 2000, pp. 48–51; cf. Scollon, Scollon & Jones, 2012); (2) hold the floor, discouraging anything beyond tokens of response, so that she can continue with what she wants to say without looking rude, since she has just used a strategy of independence by not pausing long enough for them to speak; and (3) buy herself a fraction of time with which to plan and produce the next chunk of her utterance. In extract (j), Littlejohn demonstrates both her involvement and her independence as she asks one of the graduate students to stop visiting her. In the student's previous two interviews, Littlejohn had indicated that she did not want to converse but had not explicitly asked the student not to visit again. In this conversation, Littlejohn explicitly suggests that the student visit someone else, but she demonstrates her communicative competence by appropriately using two extenders (*this that and the other* and *and so on*) to illustrate that she actually has enough

to do and does not need visits, and by hedging and mitigating as she tries
to soften her request to the student to go talk with someone else.

(j)

> Uh look uh
> – 0.211 ya know when
> – 0.211 Pam comes she **just** takes charge and she **just**
> – 0.465 takes me out and we go do <no audible pause> *this that and*
> *the other* and **maybe** eat and **maybe**
> – 0.380 go shopping <no audible pause> *and so on* and so
> – 0.465 uh when I but the time you reach this age that I am
> – 0.423 you **just sorta** take it one day at a time and **just** rest and relax
> *and so on*
> – 0.465 and I uh appreciate appreciate your energy <no audible
> pause> *and so on*
> – 0.296 but
> – 0.296 **maybe** uh
> – 0.761 there **might** be someone
> – 0.592 that needed your care
> – 0.423 more than **maybe** I do. Do you
> – 0.338 do you how did you get in~ involved here?

Tokens such as *just, maybe, sorta* and *might* show her efforts to soften
her request; the two uses of *and so on* do not invite the conversation
partner to do much, particularly since the second one is referencing a
non-lexicalized situation. In contrast to other stretches of her discourse,
this section has very few pauses. The lack of pauses allows Littlejohn to
hold the floor; there is only one pause (0.761) between <maybe uh> and
<there might be someone> long enough for the partner to make some
kind of response without presenting herself as impolite.

Importance in Dementia Discourse

Like other types of FE, general extenders assist the speaker with DAT
who then does not have to provide an exhaustive list of the items being
referenced. More importantly, they provide a way for the speaker with
DAT to have little islands in the stream of discourse, upon which she
can perch while planning the next part of an utterance, and to create or
simulate shared understandings with the conversation partner. Extenders support the interactivity of "real conversation" and support efforts at
topic maintenance made by the speaker with dementia.

REHEARSED STORIES AND POTENTIAL FORMULAIC CHUNKS

Overview: Conversational Narrative, Repetition and Chunking

When Littlejohn tells stories or repeats story fragments, she has no need of pauses for planning to insert around her frequent formulaic apologies for retelling (*as I was just saying*), nor does she need to use extenders to keep the floor or to keep her audience involved. Her family members say she has always been a fine storyteller, a skill prized in the Carolina mountains, and she has rehearsed these stories many times over. They have become story schemas, and like icebergs, break off into chunks. According to van Dijk and Kintsch (1983, p. 336 and *passim*), chunks are stored as a textual representation in episodic memory and, we believe, can be accessed in ways similar to other formulaic expressions (see Foster, Tonkyn & Wigglesworth, 2000, on definitions for c-units and t-units as categories of spoken language units, either of which can include a number of "sentences" in the utterance; cf. Ellis, 2003, on chunking in second-language acquisition). We suggest that such story-chunks represent some of the small stories that surface in dementia discourse.

In this brief discussion of Littlejohn's repeated stories, we use "narrative" to mean talk that represents events in the past and "story" to mean "narrative with a point" (Johnstone, 2005, p. 639). For conversational narrative, we draw on Norrick (2007, p. 129). His model differs slightly from the canonical format provided by Labov (1972), and includes these components:

Orientation: background information
Narrow frame: transition into main action
Main action: only active verbs in past tense; no negatives, no continuing actions
Evaluation: interrupts main action for thoughts and feelings
Result: direct effects of main action
Resolution: what finally happened
Coda: final comment, later or present perspective

Not all of Littlejohn's repeated stories will have all of these components: several of them are coalescing into fragments and small stories, as seen later. Small stories are emergent, contingent, short narrative accounts that are conversationally embedded in everyday interactions; position the teller in relation to the hearer; and are typically unnoticed by tellers, hearers or researchers but allow the teller's experience to be "retuned" through frequent retellings and reworkings (Bamberg, 2004; Georgakopoulou, 2006a).

Ervin-Tripp and Küntay (1997) contend that repetition is one of the cultural conditions under which people lengthen and elaborate stories in conversation: it gives them "the opportunity to rehearse and reshape a story. Stories that are retold already have a basis in form, and a reteller has the knowledge of how the first occasion was evaluated by the audience" (p. 161).

Persons with dementia, however, tend to repeat stories more than twice, and this repetition has often been tied to perseveration. McCabe and Bliss (2006, p. 322) remind us of the view held by many non-impaired persons: "When narrative coherence is compromised, so is a person's perceived personality." In addition, as DAT becomes more severe, people become less able to initiate and produce full, canonical stories, producing instead story fragments that they often repeat. Their multiply-told tales may be ways in which the tellers attempt to position themselves as being worthy conversational partners.

An earlier case study (Davis, 2011) of Lucinda Greystone's rehearsed and routinized retellings of two sets of stories to 31 listeners suggested that her multiply-told tales were something more than ideational perseveration or her stepping into a rehearsed self. Greystone's stories and story fragments were her way of embodying those parts of memory she could access, those ways she could still retain of self presentation as an interesting and competent person who could still tell a good story—even though she was not always able to monitor her production sufficiently to keep from repeating it to the same person. We contend that a similar issue is at work in the rehearsed retellings by Littlejohn.

Example: Repeated Narrative and Fragments

Several stories and story-chunks surfaced repeatedly in the 25 conversations we have recorded, mostly tied to artifacts in her room. Until her most recent relocation, Littlejohn frequently recounted stories about the baskets she made, as examples of western North Carolina crafts, and "pebble people," little paperweights and decorative items made from painting local rocks by her sister, as an example of how such crafts brought money to the region and the crafter. She offered amusing anecdotes about presenting an egg basket to the Archbishop of Canterbury and about how other residents in her memory care unit often stole her baskets and hung them on their doors.

Like the childhood memories retold by Lucinda Greystone (Davis, 2011), Littlejohn has several rehearsed tales about her own childhood, particularly her love of apples and, for the last two years, about her parents' education. Littlejohn was born in 1929 and was not the old-est child; we may assume that her parents were at least 25 years older than she was. For persons living on farms in the mountains of western North Carolina to gain a college education in the period from 1915–1925 was fairly unusual: Littlejohn is proud of her parents and their ac-complishments. Interestingly, she has shared these stories only with one older student and the older researchers: both are older than 45 and are thus presumably old enough to understand the historical significance of their being educated. These stories are in response to earlier discourse in which the listeners have indicated both alignment and affiliation: for example, one researcher showed that she was familiar with Littlejohn's family name and the names of other families living in the area.

A Set of Repeated Stories

The three repetitions in the same conversation for October 2010 pres-ent a small story and its later evaluation in (k:i). In (k:ii), the backstory is presented. We learn in the orientation that it was unusual for both parents to have had some college education, and in the narrow frame, that both were schoolteachers (which presumes some college training). In the main action, she narrates the result of the main action, that the mother's college education was a fortunate accident, and then presents the main action as causal, that her brother decided not to attend and the college would not refund the pre-paid tuition. The resolution was that the mother attended instead. Just in case the listener missed the point from the orientation, that a woman's getting an education was unusual, Littlejohn expands the theme to tell the listener that women at that time were expected to marry and stay home. In (k:iii), she repeats, as evalu-ation of the whole event, the preceding orientation, that both parents were educated for that day and time.

18 October 2010

(k:i)

BD: you mentioned that – your – your dad was in South Carolina but y~
ML: my dad was from South Carolina
BD: but your momma wasn't
ML: er no she was um . they met – they m~ b~ back **it was sort of un-usual at that time my mother and father both were educated – they had been had – how much schooling they had I don't know but they both taught school** – \<mmm\> they were not teaching and my mother – ah when I was in school it would have been ah – World War Two time and *this that and the other* she did some substitute teaching but **they were both –** *educated for their time*

. . . .

(k:ii)

BD: well now your momma was she a storyteller like your daddy

ML: **oh well they were both school teachers – uh mother went to college because my grandparents had paid her brother's way to go to college as a promise said – and he decided not to go and they weren't going to refund his money so she went instead {laugh} – and she got her education**

. . . .

ML: – and ah anyway but that's that's how she got her college education because they didn't educate girls

BD: no they didn't

ML: because they were just meant to be mothers – and bear kids you know {unclear} – but ah she did become more educated so ah – but sh~ I'm very grateful for and –

. . . .

(k:iii)

ML: I don't know that I would want to go back and live that way but it wasn't as bad as a lot of people would like to make it sound {both laugh} – we in we weren't that bad **my mother and father both were –** *educated for their day and time* **they both ah w~ w~ as I say started out as school teachers**

In extract (l), ML resumes a story she had been telling about what her parents' farm produced to feed them and segues into the education story, possibly to reinforce her parents' strength and prudence.

(l)

Mid-October 2011

ML: my mother and father were just really good people – and my dad used to get a, take his corn and have it grow – We had a little grass field not too far from us – And they were both old school house teachers – **Well my mother got her education because as I probably just got through saying her brother didn't want to go to school so they weren't gonna just waste money – so she went in his place**

In extract (m), ML is telling UG4 about her mother's cooking implements and switches topic to talk about other uses for them: her mother will have used the paddle because she was a teacher, and paddling a pupil was accepted. The paddle's small story is thereby linked to a small story about her parents' education.

(m)

Late October 2011 (UG4)

ML: She had this butter paddle, – and any kid that got into any mischief – got a got a taste of the butter paddle. {laugh} – – Someone, some of the kids still have their, their paddles – And {unclear} accept it – You got – – but my mother and father **both were old one room school house teachers** – And ah – kids went – to school when they were still twenty years old

It is not uncommon for a person with dementia to self-prime: that is, to repeat what they have previously processed and produced. That may be true for rehearsed story repetition for persons with DAT. In extract (n), Littlejohn asks her audience, which now includes a young researcher, to join her amazement, moving in the backstory, from evaluation to coda with "*Can you imagine them doing that today?*" In the second clip, she repeats key components from the backstory, the result, and the resolution: they paid; he didn't go; she took his place. The evaluation is provided by the researcher and Littlejohn agrees.

3 November 2011

(n:i)

BD: Well you said your daddy taught –
ML: Yeah, and mother did too – Mother taugh~. They had paid – **Her parents had paid her way or her brother's way – tuition to go – to college – And for whatever reasons he decided he didn't want to go – So back then they let her go in his place.** – Can you imagine them doing that today? –

. . . .

(n:ii)

BD: Your mother didn't go to Limestone by /any chance?
ML: /No.
    She went, it was ah, oh god, where did she go? – It was in, in Tennessee – – And the reason she got to go to college – **as I probably just got through saying is that they had paid her brother's tuition – And he didn't want to go – and so she went in his place.**

BD: Which is lovely.
MD: It is though.

Occasionally Littlejohn simply referred to parts of the orientation, as in (o:i) and the narrowing of frame, (o:ii), which is part of a later resumption of a different story about the size of the family. Here the allusions serve as small stories that are used to emphasize family solidarity and uniqueness because of their heritage of education.

29 November 2011

(o:i)

ML: well that's true too. ah – I've done my share of hoeing corn and picking beans. {laugh}
BD: and you could do it.
ML: oh I could do it. but I did it it was not a – back then I guess it felt like pretty much like a chore, but I can look back now and it really wasn't – – my mother my parents were – ah **as I just got through saying were educated for their day and age.**

. . . .

(o:ii)

BD: so there was you and there was Louey
ML: and Mary – Lou was the my older sister, and I had one brother – actually I had two brothers one – was would have been older than I and he died in infancy it's which just so often happened ah <yeah> – back then **but mother and dad had been ah – one of the schoolhouse teachers** – and ah – we just ah we were like everybody practically there was more –

The main components of the backstory have not changed in the retelling in extract (p), which has been prompted by the researcher. Again, we find an orientation that skips to the resulting action, which is explained by the main action. This reordering is presumably for emphasis, and it is interesting that the emphasis has not changed and that once again, she repeats an evaluation that serves as coda.

26 November 2012

(p)

BD: . . . your parents – I remember – now you were telling me about your mother – – she'd gone off to school

ML: Yeah yeah she went ah sh~ ah she went to what was it? Um – – – oh I was at the time it was a well known school **but the reason she got to go is – they'd – paid for – her brother to go –**

BD: Mmm

ML: **And he didn't – changed his mind he didn't want to go – they would not refund the money – so she went in his place –**
.... {interruption}
I was very blessed at at that point in time that both mother and dad had an education – um 'cause /back then

BD: /Well that was unusual

DISCUSSION AND CONCLUSION

In this chapter we have considered some of the communicative resources that are still available to Maureen Littlejohn in spite of her progression into the moderate stage of Alzheimer's disease. Littlejohn remains willing to talk to most people and, from a single conversation, it would still be quite difficult to tell just how impaired she is. We analyzed more than eight hours of conversation to highlight the varied strategies she uses as she strives to present herself as a good storyteller and an interesting conversationalist.

One of the most important factors in enabling Littlejohn to continue to converse was her listeners' reactions to her. If listeners gave appropriate feedback so that Littlejohn felt they were aligned with her viewpoint or endorsed her perspective and so were affiliated with her as a speaker, Littlejohn was happy to carry on talking. She politely indicated her unwillingness to talk to a student who had indicated neither alignment nor affiliation with her (see extract (j)). Norrick (2012) suggested classifying listener responses as recipient tokens (*mmhmm*), emotional/evaluative assessments (*that's good*), or information state tokens (*oh*). In these conversations, emotional/evaluative responses were most efficient at allowing Littlejohn to keep talking. This is different from Norrick's suggestion that information state tokens would be most likely to encourage the speaker to continue. However, most of the student conversational partners had received some minimal training that emphasized the importance of quilting responses when conversing with someone with dementia rather than providing monosyllable responses such as *oh*. There are almost none of these simple information state responses from listeners in the conversations with Littlejohn. There are more elaborated informative statements such as *yeah, it's the big shopping day,* but these are not as effective in promoting continued conversation as the emotional/evaluative responses like *that's good* or *that's beautiful.* It makes sense that emotional responses should provoke longer responses than informative comments and continue to provoke such responses for a longer time in people with dementia.

Our analysis highlighted the importance of formulaic language and extenders in enabling Littlejohn to continue to take part in conversation. Because formulaic language is retrieved in chunks rather than having to be created afresh with each use (see Wray, 2002; Wood, 2012), it provides readymade building blocks that can be incorporated into longer utterances. It buys time for the speaker to process and organize discourse and can aid the listener's comprehension. Because formulaic items are stored and retrieved as wholes, they put less strain on a speaker's short-term memory. Formulaic language includes fixed expressions such as *by and large,* general extenders such as *and stuff like that,* placeholders such as *this, that and the other,* idioms such as *black and blue* and colloquialisms such as *over and done with.*

It is important to note that all speakers use formulaic language. Its use, therefore, is not a sign of poor language use, or lack of skill with language. On the contrary, Wood (2012, p. 1) considered that speech fluency for second-language learners is based on mastering a repertoire of appropriate formulaic language. As dementia increases, the use of formulaic language enables the speaker with dementia to continue to sound fluent.

Initially, Littlejohn was able to talk about a general subject with student visitors, taking her turn appropriately and talking about topics they brought up (e.g., post-Thanksgiving shopping as in extract (c)). However, more recent conversations with her contain more and more of her favorite stories, which are slipped into the discussion wherever she can find an appropriate hook. Her repeated stories are not simple perseveration. Littlejohn changes her stories, sometimes providing more and sometimes less detail. Sometimes different background information is provided (e.g., the butter paddles in extract (l)); sometimes a different, but still completely appropriate, evaluation is given (e.g., *can you imagine them doing that today?* in extract (n:i)); and sometimes she provides only the barest of bones. Over time, the same story has begun to be repeated more than once in a single conversation.

Littlejohn's repeated stories are a strategy to hold the conversational floor. She does not pause before or after her "apologies," such as *as I just got through saying,* or her extenders, so there is no chance for her listener to take a turn and perhaps ask a question Littlejohn cannot answer. So long as she can tell one of her repeated stories, Littlejohn's conversation is fluent, and she can control the situation.

Previously, we have investigated how people with DAT used fixed expressions and extenders (Maclagan et al., 2008) or pauses (Davis & Maclagan, 2009) as part of their on-going communication strategies.

Littlejohn's use of her preferred strategies are just as efficient at enabling her to remain part of a conversation. Nevertheless, we must emphasize that the course of dementia is different for different people: what we have found for Littlejohn may not be true for other speakers.

As other researchers have noted, the use of different categories of formulaic language is a common and pervasive feature of ordinary speech. Not all persons with cognitive impairment will make as much use of extenders as Ms Littlejohn. However, reviewing her alternation of extenders with story-chunks and her use of pauses to suggest planning and retrieval of different elements in those stories (Davis et al., in press) has prompted us to wonder whether it is time to discuss developing a retention hypotheses. Such a hypothesis would link clauses, pauses and formulaic expression of various kinds as signaling retained narrative competencies and, at the very least, a desire to continue social and linguistic interaction.

NOTE

1. In the conversational excerpts, angle brackets < > indicate a brief backchannel response from the conversation partner, / indicates overlap, non speech is in braces {laugh} and a single dash [–] represents a pause of less than half a second. Two and three dashes represent longer pauses.

REFERENCES

Aijmer, K. (2002). *English discourse particles. Evidence from a corpus.* Philadelphia: John Benjamins.

Altenberg, B. (1990). Speech as linear composition. In G. D. Caie (Ed.), *Proceedings from the fourth Nordic conference for English studies* (pp. 133–145). Copenhagen: University of Copenhagen.

Altenberg, B. (1998). On the phraseology of spoken English. In A. Cowie (Ed.), *Phraseology: Theory, analysis and applications.* Oxford: Clarendon Press.

Bamberg, M. (2004). Talk, small stories, and adolescent identities. *Human Development, 47,* 366–369.

Bamberg, M., & Georgakopoulou, A. (2008). Small stories as a new perspective in narrative and identity analysis. *Text and Talk, 28,* 377–396.

Bayles, K., & Tomoeda, C. (2007). *Cognitive-communication disorders and dementia.* San Diego, CA: Plural Publishing.

Beňuš, Š., Gravano, A., & Hirschberg, J. (2011). Pragmatic aspects of temporal accommodation in turn-taking. *Journal of Pragmatics, 43,* 3001–3027.

Buschmeier, H., Bergmann, K., & Kopp, S. (2010). Adaptive expressiveness—Virtual conversational agents that can align to their interaction partner. *Proceedings of Ninth International Conference on Autonomous Agents and Multiagent Systems (AAMAS 2010),* Toronto, Canada, May 10–14.

Carlomagno, S., Pandolfi, M., Marini, A., Di Iasi, G., & Cristilli, C. (2005). Coverbal gestures in Alzheimer's Type Dementia. *Cortex, 41,* 535–546.

Clark, H., & Brennan, S. (1991). Grounding in communication. In L. B. Resnick, J. M. Levine, & S. D. Teasley (Eds.), *Perspectives on socially shared cognition* (pp. 127–149). Washington, D.C.: APA Books.

Cowie, A. P., & Howarth, P. (1996). Phraseology—A select bibliography. *International Journal of Lexicography, 9*(1): 38–51.

Cutting, J. (Ed.). (2007). *Vague language explored.* New York: Palgrave.

Damico, J. S., & Nelson, R. L. (2005). Interpreting problematic behavior: Systematic compensatory adaptations as emergent phenomena in autism. *Clinical Linguistics and Phonetics, 19,* 405–418.

Davis, B. (2011). Intentional stance, selfhood, and Lucinda Greystone: Twice-told tales from a digital corpus of Alzheimer talk. In P. McPherron & V. Ramanathan (Eds.), *Language, body and health.* New York: Mouton de Gruyter.

Davis, B., & Bernstein, C. (2005). Talking in the here and now: Reference and narrative in Alzheimer conversation. In B. Davis (Ed.), *Alzheimer talk, text and context* (pp. 60–86). New York: Palgrave.

Davis, B. & Maclagan, M. (2009). Examining pauses in Alzheimer's discourse. *American Journal of Alzheimer's Disease and Other Dementias, 24,* 141–154.

Davis, B., Maclagan, M., & Shenk, D. (in press). Exploring questions and answers between residents and caregivers. In H. Hamilton & S. Chou (Eds.), *The Routledge handbook of language and health communication.*

Davis, B., Maclagan, M., & Wright, J. (2012). *Aw, so, how's your day going? Ways that persons with dementia keep their conversational partner involved.* Panel on Dementia Discourse, AMPRA, Charlotte, North Carolina, October.

Ellis, N. (1996). Sequencing in SLA: Phonological memory, chunking, and points of order. *Studies in Second Language Acquisition, 18,* 91–126.

Ellis, N. (2003). Constructions, chunking, and connectionism: The emergence of second language structure. In C. Doughty & M. H. Long (Eds.), *Handbook of second language acquisition* (pp. 33–68). Oxford: Blackwell.

Ellis, N. (2012). Formulaic language and second language acquisition: Zipf and the phrasal teddy bear. *Annual Review of Applied Linguistics, 32,* 17–44.

Ervin-Tripp, S., & Küntay, A. (1997). The occasioning and structure of conversational stories. In T. Givon (Ed.), *Conversation: Cognitive, communicative and social perspectives* (pp. 133–166). Amsterdam: J. Benjamins.

Evison, J., McCarthy, M., & O'Keefe, A. (2007). Looking out for love and all the rest of it: Vague category markers as shared social space. In J. Cutting (Ed.), *Vague language explored* (pp. 138–157). New York: Palgrave.

Fernandez, J., & Yuldashev, A. (2011). Variation in the use of general extenders *and stuff* in instant messaging interactions. *Journal of Pragmatics, 43,* 2610–2626.

Foster, P., Tonkyn, A., & Wigglesworth, G. (2000). Measuring spoken language: A unit for all reasons. *Applied Linguistics, 21,* 354–375.

Georgakopoulou, A. (2006a). The other side of the story: Towards a narrative analysis of narratives in interaction. *Discourse Studies, 8,* 235–257.

Georgakopoulou, A. (2006b). Thinking big with small stories in narrative and identity analysis. *Narrative Inquiry, 16,* 122–130.

Giles, H., Coupland, J., & Coupland, N. (Eds.). (1991). *Contexts of accommodation: developments in applied sociolinguistics.* New York: Cambridge University Press.

Granger, S., & Meunier, F. (Eds.). (2008). *Phraseology: An interdisciplinary perspective.* Amsterdam: John Benjamins.

Hamilton, H. (1994). *Conversations with an Alzheimer's patient: An interactional sociolinguistic study.* Cambridge, MA: Cambridge University Press.

Hancock, C., Shenk, D., & Davis, B. (2008). Integrating gerontology service-learning students as members of a research team. In P. Lan Lim (Ed.), *Service learning and gerontology education* (pp. 171–184). New York: Hampton Press.

Johnstone, B. (2005). Discourse analysis and narrative. In D. Schiffrin, D. Tannen, & H. Hamilton (Eds.), *Handbook of discourse analysis* (pp. 635–649). New York: Wiley.

Kuiper, K. (2011). *Yearbook of phraseology, 2011.* The Hague: de Gruyter Mouton.

Labov, W. (1972). *Language in the Inner City.* Philadelphia: University of Pennsylvania Press.

Levey, S. (2012). General extenders and grammaticalization; Insights from London preadolescents. *Applied Linguistics, 33,* 257–281.

Maclagan, M., Davis, B., & Lunsford, R. (2008). Fixed expressions, extenders and metonymy in the speech of people with Alzheimer's disease. In S. Granger & F. Meunier (Eds.), *Phraseology: An interdisciplinary perspective* (pp. 175–186). Amsterdam: John Benjamins.

McCabe, A., & Bliss, L. (2006). Struggling to make sense: Patterns of impairment in adult narrative discourse. *Imagination, Cognition and Personality, 25,* 321–336.

Moon, R. (1998). *Fixed expressions and idioms in English.* Oxford: Clarendon Press.

Norrick, N. (2007). Conversational storytelling. In D. Herman (Ed.), *Cambridge companion to narrative* (pp. 127–141). Cambridge: Cambridge University Press.

Norrick, N. (2012). Listening practices in English conversation: The responses responses elicit. *Journal of Pragmatics, 44,* 566–676.

Overstreet, M. (1999). *Whales, candlelight, and stuff like that: General extenders in English discourse.* New York: Oxford University Press.

Overstreet, M., & Yule, G. (2001). Formulaic disclaimers. *Journal of Pragmatics, 33,* 45–60.

Palacios Martínez, I. (2011). "I might, I might go I mean it depends on money things and stuff": A preliminary analysis of general extenders in British teenagers. *Journal of Pragmatics, 43,* 2452–2470.

Pichler, H., & Levey, S. (2011). In search of grammaticalization in synchronic dialect data: general extenders in northeast England. *English Language and Linguistics, 15,* 441–471.

Pope, C., & Davis, B. (2011). Finding a balance: The CCC corpus. *Corpus Linguistics and Linguistic Theory, 7,* 143–161.

Ramanathan, V. (1997). *Alzheimer discourse: Some sociolinguistic dimensions.* Mahwah, NJ: Lawrence Erlbaum.

Rayson, P. (2009). *Wmatrix: A web-based corpus processing environment.* Computing Department, Lancaster University. http://ucrel.lancs.ac.uk/wmatrix/

Riordan, M., Dale, R., Kreuz, R., & Olney, A. (2011). Evidence for alignment in a computer-mediated text-only environment. In L. Carlson, C. Hoelscher, & T. F. Shipley (Eds.), *Proceedings of the 33rd annual meeting of the Cognitive Science Society* (pp. 2411–2416). Austin, TX: Cognitive Science Society.

Ripich, D., Carpenter, B., & Ziol, E. (2000). Conversational cohesion patterns in men and women with Alzheimer's disease: A longitudinal study. *International Journal of Language and Communication Disorders, 35,* 49–64.

Scollon, R., & Scollon, S. (2000). *Intercultural communication: A discourse approach.* Oxford: Blackwell.

Scollon, R., Scollon, S., & Jones, R. (2012). *Intercultural communication: A discourse approach.* Oxford: Blackwell.

Steensig, J., & Drew, P. (2008). Introduction: Questioning and affiliation/disaffiliation in interaction. *Discourse Studies, 10,* 5–15.

Stivers, T. (2008). Stance, alignment, and affiliation during storytelling: When nodding is a token of affiliation. *Research on Language and Social Interaction, 41,* 31–57.

Temple, V., Sabat, S., & Koger, R. (1999). Intact use of politeness in the discourse of Alzheimer's sufferers. *Language and Communication, 19,* 163–180.

van Dijk, T., & Kintsch, W. (1983). *Strategies of discourse comprehension.* New York: Academic.

Van Lancker, D., & Kempler, D. (1987). Comprehension of familiar phrases by left- but not by right-hemisphere damaged patients. *Brain and Language, 32,* 265–277.

Van Lancker Sidtis, D. (2011). Formulaic expressions in mind and brain: Empirical studies and dual-process model of language competence. In J. Guendouzi, F. Loncke, & M. Williams (Eds.), *The Handbook of psycholinguistic and cognitive processes* (pp. 247–272). New York: Psychology Press.

Wood, D. (2012). *Formulaic language and second language speech fluency.* New York: Continuum.

Wray, A. (2002). *Formulaic language and the lexicon.* Cambridge: Cambridge University Press.

Wray, A. (2008). *Formulaic language: Pushing the boundaries.* Oxford: Oxford University Press.

Wray, A., & Perkins, M. (2000). The functions of formulaic language: An integrated model. *Language and Communication, 20,* 1–28.

5

INTERACTIONAL AND COGNITIVE
RESOURCES IN DEMENTIA
A Perspective from Politeness Theory

Jackie Guendouzi and Anna Pate

INTRODUCTION: INTERACTIONAL VERSUS
COGNITIVE RESOURCES

All communication acts involve cognition; the division between socially acquired language resources and cognitive resources that support language processing, noted in chapter one, is in some senses arbitrary. It is a necessary division that, when analyzing language, allows researchers to distinguish cognitive resources that are subconscious mechanisms (e.g., working memory) from aspects of communication that may have been socially learned and are, therefore, intentional choices a speaker makes when addressing an interlocutor. Standardized assessments of language are designed to tap into specific cognitive resources (e.g., attention, working memory, long-term memory, sentence comprehension, etc.) that support language use and often use linguistic formats (e.g., closed questions) that require specific responses. In contrast, less formal contexts such as clinical/research interviews or narrative tasks (e.g., asking a client/participant to describe their weekend or recall life-history events) can assess the language skills of an individual in a manner that overlaps (to some degree) with the structure of everyday conversations. Clinical/research interviews initially follow a question-answer format with expectations that the interviewee will produce information that is relevant and/or accurate. In this respect, clinical/research interviews may represent an interactional context that might potentially pose a threat to a person with dementia's (PWD) self-esteem if they are unable to recall the relevant information. However, it is also the case that there are elements of clinical/research interviews that offer more discursive flexibility. For example, the participants may engage in small talk and topic shift more freely. Interactions in follow-up interviews may reflect the type of conversations that take place between acquaintances or friends (Guendouzi & Müller, 2006), that is, there may be discussion of shared information that is more personal in nature (e.g., personal interests, past events or family members' well-being, etc.).

Clinical/research interviews, like standardized tests, can involve the use of questions that place stress on the PWD's long-term and short-term memory (e.g., 'what did you do yesterday'? or 'which college did you go to'?). Such questions represent a potential threat to the PWD's self-esteem in that they require a response that is relevant to the interviewer's particular request for information. Furthermore, this type of information typically consists of details that most neuro-typical people have little difficulty producing, but in the case of PWD, providing such information may prove difficult. Indeed, PWD are often acutely aware of their cognitive deficits (Guendouzi & Müller, 2006) and may manifest distress at not being able to respond to questions that most people would regard as mundane. Additionally, the semi-structured nature of clinical/research interviews may require a certain amount of cognitive agility to follow abrupt topic changes or inferred meanings. For example, the interviewer prompted by the PWD's response may introduce a secondary topic, or make a comment that is not fully explicated in his/her actual utterance. Such moments in a conversation represent a challenge to the PWD who may still be attempting to process and respond to the interviewer's prior utterance or question. In a "normal" conversation an interlocutor may simply request further information or state 'what do you mean?' For the PWD, openly admitting that you have not understood a question or comment is potentially making your cognitive deficit more salient. In the corpus of data to be discussed later, F, a woman with dementia, produced very few examples of direct requests-for-clarification in response to the researcher's questions. In order to maintain face (self-esteem) at times of potential confusion, the PWD may instead offer responses consisting of socially learned linguistic items such as politeness markers, phatic or formulaic tokens, minimal responses, or in some cases not respond at all.

This chapter explores how socially acquired communicative resources interact with declining cognitive resources in conversations between F and a researcher (the first author). In particular, we examine the use of politeness markers (Brown & Levinson, 1987), formulaic items, and phatic tokens in relation to working memory and semantic processing (Cowan, 2011; Shelley-Tremblay, 2011). We consider whether the use of such linguistic items is a compensatory strategy that PWD produce in order to fulfill the social obligation of maintaining an interaction in the face of non-comprehension of propositional information, or whether the use of these communicative items is an artifact of failing cognitive resources. In order to discuss these issues we will initially outline politeness theory and its role in the presentation of social identity (or "face") in our everyday conversations. We will then (a) briefly describe politeness markers of involvement and independence (Scollon & Wong-Scollon, 1995), (b) note some of the issues surrounding politeness theory, and (c) consider the function of politeness markers in relation to cognitive load and flexibility of use in interactions. Finally, we will illustrate how the frequent use of such socially learned conversational behaviors may be the result of diminishing cognitive resources in examples taken from conversations between F and the researcher.

POLITENESS THEORY

Politeness theory (Brown & Levinson, 1987) attempts to account for the verbal strategies interlocutors utilize to ensure all parties involved in an interaction feel affirmed. Therefore, much of the research in politeness theory has been concerned with the interpersonal function of communication. In traditional interpretations of the theory, it typically assumed that speakers use politeness markers as a discursive means of presenting "self" and expressing their relationship with other parties in the interaction. Much of the early scholarship in politeness theory drew on Goffman's examination of the concept of *face* (1967/1982). Goffman described face encounters as social situations where it was 'possible for two or more persons [. . .] to jointly ratify one another as authorized co-sustainers of a single, albeit moving, focus of visual and cognitive attention' (1982, p. 64). As Goffman suggested, talk is a system that incorporates 'ritually governed face-to-face' (1982, p. 65) actions that require interlocutors to not only monitor and process linguistic and contextual information, but also address both their own and their audience's psychosocial needs.

Brown and Levinson (1987) further developed the concept of face to suggest speakers and listeners are influenced in their linguistic choices by both *negative* and *positive* face needs. *Negative face* refers to the avoidance of imposition of both self and other(s), while *positive face* refers to an individual's need to be liked or appreciated. Thus, politeness theory proposes that individuals choose particular verbal constructions in order to attend to the psychosocial dimensions of interpersonal communication. For instance, complimenting someone (e.g., 'you look nice today') is a positive politeness strategy that attends to both the interlocutor's and the speaker's self-identity. A pragmatic paraphrase of the remark 'you look nice today' might be *and I am a nice person for saying that to you.* In the case of negative face, speakers may choose verbal constructions such as subordinate adjectival clauses (e.g., 'could you possibly'), hedges (e.g., 'mhm', 'well'), or indirect speech acts to present requests that require action on the part of the interlocutor. For example, when issuing a directive asking for assistance with a task, someone might say 'I was going to ask well mhm if it isn't too much trouble could you possibly help me with this job', or use an indirect speech act such as 'I'm a little dry' when requesting a drink.

Leech (1983), drawing on Grice's cooperative principle (1975), suggested that a politeness principle operates in conversations. He proposed speakers utilize six maxims (tact, generosity, approbation, modesty, agreement, and sympathy) in order to adhere to the politeness principle. The tact maxim suggests a speaker should minimize the expression of beliefs that imply cost to other and maximize the expression of beliefs that imply benefit to other (e.g., 'may I intrude on you for a moment?'). The generosity maxim states that a speaker should minimize the expression of beliefs that express or imply benefit to self and maximize the expression of beliefs that express or imply cost to self. Unlike the tact maxim, the maxim of generosity focuses on the speaker by suggesting that others should come before self (e.g., 'you sit back and put your feet up, I can do the laundry'). The approbation maxim states a speaker minimize the expression of beliefs that express disapproval of others and maximize the expression of beliefs that express approval of other (e.g., 'Jamie, I know you're good with words—would you help with this term paper?'). This maxim suggests it is preferable to praise others, and if this is not possible, a speaker should discursively avoid the issue, give some form of minimal response, or remain silent. The Modesty maxim states speakers minimize the expressing praise of self and maximize the expression of disparise of self (e.g., 'oh, just like me, I'm so scatterbrained, I forgot my class notes you are always so organized can I borrow yours?'). The Agreement maxim states speakers minimize expression of disagreement between self and other and maximize the expression of agreement. Leech did not suggest that people always avoid disagreement, rather they are more direct when expressing agreement than disagreement (e.g., 'yes, I agree with that' versus 'well you know I don't really think that is correct'). The sympathy maxim suggests speakers minimize ill feeling between self and other and maximize sympathy between self and other. In summary, politeness theory examines how interlocutors manage the psychosocial aspects of conversation and negotiate how to achieve their instrumental and interpersonal goals.

Some Issues in Politeness Theory

Politeness theory, particularly as put forward by Brown and Levinson (1987), is not without problems. For example, the division of politeness into the binary constructs of negative and positive face may limit the application of the theory. Although Leech (1983) noted that the expression of politeness varies from culture to culture, many recent discussions suggest that the early scholarship in politeness theory was Anglo-centric (Garcés-Conejos Blitvich, 2013) and culturally limited. A further aspect of politeness theory that has raised questions is the tendency of scholars such as Brown and Levinson (1987) and Leech (1983) to discuss politeness theory using traditional speech act categories. Constructivist theories suggest that the meaning of an utterance is created within the discourse itself and is dependent on the listener's interpretation. Thus, the function of speech acts is determined by both interlocutors, and indeed may be viewed differently by either party. An example from the author's recent experience illustrates this point. She asked one of her children (who had been to the hairstylist) 'what kind of haircut is that?' In her mind this was a genuine question attempting to elicit the name of the hairstyle, but u.ᵉ listener interpreted it as an insult (face threat) and responded with 'well I like it' (a justification).

Recent models of communication suggest that face and politeness should be studied separately (Bargiela-Chiappini & Haugh, 2009; Haugh & Bargiela-Chiappini, 2010). However, despite the need for such scholarship, it is difficult to discuss politeness without reference to face. Indeed, research in politeness theory has often concerned itself with describing the interactional strategies and resources that speakers use to address both their own and their interlocutor's face needs. Garcés-Conejos Blitvich provides a strong argument suggesting that to move forward politeness scholarship needs 'a clear understanding of the paradigms within which central, traditional concepts to the field were formulated' (2013, p. 25). As she notes, the theoretical foundations of research in politeness theory have drawn heavily on the work of Brown and Levinson (1987) and traditional Gricean frameworks (Leech, 1983). It is not the purpose of this chapter to engage in a discussion of this relevant and obviously fascinating development in politeness theory, but to remain aware of the debate. For a full discussion of these issues, we recommend Garcés-Conejos Blitvich's article (2013).

A further problem in politeness theory is the use of the terms *positive* and *negative politeness* and *positive* and *negative face*. As Scollon and Wong-Scollon (1995) noted, the choice of these particular terms has resulted in an understanding of these concepts that is sometimes confusing to readers. Indeed, the two terms may appear to imply opposing concepts, and it is the experience of the first author that students often view *negative politeness* as representing linguistic strategies that would be considered socially rude, and *negative face* in terms of the "negative" aspects of a person's character or behavior. An alternative is to consider the 'two sides of face' as the degree of 'involvement and independence' (Scollon & Wong-Scollon, 1995, p. 36) marked by a speaker's choice of linguistic construction. *Involvement* reflects the degree of intimacy or deference we accord our interlocutors. For example, active participation in a conversation reflects an interlocutor's adherence to the social obligation of involvement in an interaction with others. *Independence* on the other hand reflects a speaker's need to discursively maintain his/her own autonomy and acknowledge his/her interlocutor's independence to speak and act as a free social agent. As Goffman suggested, politeness markers act to validate the agreement of both parties to participate in a shared social event. However, whether we term this phenomenon negative or positive politeness (or degree of involvement and independence), both terms are embedded within the concept of face (Scollon & Wong-Scollon, 1995). Therefore, despite recent calls to study face and politeness separately, it is almost impossible to disentangle these constructs. Indeed, it would be difficult to attempt to explore why we use markers of politeness without noting that they appear to be an interactional resource that (typically) reduces the risk of an overt face threat to the listener. For the purposes of this chapter, we will adopt the terms of *involvement* and *independence* as used by Scollon and Wong-Scollon (1995).

POLITENESS MARKERS

Politeness markers include a wide range of interactional resources, such as greetings and partings (Laver, 1975), compliments, phatic tokens, formulaic strings, minimal responses, acknowledgements, and subordinate clauses that act as adjuncts to the main propositional message of the utterance (e.g., 'if you don't mind, do you think you could', etc.). Such items function to address issues of face in relation to both involvement and independence. In the next three sections, we will focus specifically on phatic tokens, politeness markers of involvement, and politeness markers of independence.

Politeness Markers of Involvement: Phatic Tokens

Malinowski (1923/1989) was the first researcher to focus linguistic attention on the importance of phatic communion; he described this phenomenon as 'free, aimless, social intercourse [. . .] where the meaning of the words is almost completely irrelevant' (1989, p. 313). It was perhaps the use of the terms *aimless* and *meaningless* that initially led to phatic talk being regarded as less worthy of academic study in the field of linguistics. Malinowski noted that phatic talk is a 'type of speech in which ties of union are created by a mere exchange of words' in a relationship where companionship is the goal rather than the purpose 'of communicating ideas' (Malinowski, 1989, p. 316). Thus, interlocutors, when engaging in phatic talk (e.g., greetings, inquiries about health, the weather, etc.), are addressing a social desire to connect with others and acknowledge another's presence. Much of this type of talk can be considered ritualized conversational routine (Coulmas, 1981) and is often formulaic in nature. As Malinowski suggested, the meaning of such talk resides not in the propositional content but 'in the pragmatic function' of the utterance (Bauman, 1992, p. 147). Speakers use phatic talk (i.e., small talk) to establish and maintain connections with others by acknowledging the other's presence, thus reflecting the interlocutors' degree of involvement with each other. However, as has been discussed elsewhere (Coupland & Ylänne-McEwen, 2000), small talk is also instrumental in getting the "big talk" done. Small talk thus facilitates the process of action; phatic politeness markers of involvement help initiate, extend, and complete social interactions without loss of face.

Acknowledging Speaker Involvement

Another way that interlocutors attend to face issues and maintain interactional relationships is to collaborate in maintaining a conversation over a lengthy period or sustain a particular topic thread that a speaker has introduced. These interactional tasks require acknowledgement of an interlocutor's prior turn, or a response to the current topic. It is beholden on listeners to show appropriate reciprocity and interactionally mark that they are listening to, attending to, and following the gist of what their interlocutor is saying. In addition, listeners typically offer responses that relate to, or extend the topic under discussion. In any conversational context this may be achieved through the use of a variety of communicative devices (e.g., gesture, face expression, etc.) or verbal minimal responses, such as 'mhm', 'oh yeah', or 'uh huh'. Speakers also use formulaic verbal acknowledgements (e.g., 'that's right' or 'I guess so') or idiomatic phrases that sum up previous conversational content without the necessity of actually repeating the facts or propositional content (e.g., 'at the end of the day' or 'what else could you do').

Politeness Markers of Independence

The use of politeness markers associated with the concept of independence reflect a speaker's awareness of the social obligation not to impose on others, and in that sense can be seen as an intentional use of language. That is, typically they reflect the fact the speaker is aware of the degree of imposition involved and has made the necessary adjustments in his/her choice of utterance form, thus displaying a willingness to maintain both his/her independence and respect his/her interlocutor(s) freedom of action. Politeness markers of independence include hedges, pre-requests, and formulaic carrier phrases attached to propositional clauses. Many such markers consist of routine adverbials added to a statement or request. For example, if I want to tell a family member that I am about to change the channel on the television (knowing they appear to be enjoying the program), I might say 'sorry I know you're watching this but I need to check the weather'. Such politeness markers are the elements of talk that often surround the primary propositional message and acknowledge the potential imposition of the utterance on the listener's independence. It is important to remember that although traditionally politeness markers are discussed in terms of independence (negative face) and involvement (positive face), both aspects of this two-sided coin are in operation at all times. Furthermore, any particular verbal construction can act as a marker of either involvement or independence, thus politeness markers may function to address both involvement and independence.

POLITENESS AND FACE THREATS

Any utterance that does not reflect the appropriate level of involvement or independence due particular interlocutors can be considered potential face threats. Face threats may result in discursive conflict or cause a breakdown in coherence, thus threatening the flow of conversation and/or the self-esteem of the interlocutors. For example, an utterance that shows too intimate a level of involvement might jeopardize the interlocutor's independence. Conversely, allowing too much independence may suggest the speaker has no real interest in the interaction with his/her interlocutor. Consider a scenario where a woman asks a co-worker advice about the color choice of a dress that she has indicated she really likes and the co-worker responds with, 'well with your figure I wouldn't buy either of them'. In this scenario, the co-worker's forthright remark has (a) threatened the woman's self-esteem by implying the woman is too large for the dress, and (b) misjudged the degree of involvement and social distance that is appropriate between co-workers. In addition, the co-worker's comment may affect the woman's decision to buy the item and thus imposes on the woman's independence of action. Managing face, therefore, is a complex discursive process that requires interlocutors to mark both the appropriate level of involvement and the appropriate degree of independence for the participants' perceived social roles and the particular context of the speech event.

All interactions potentially place interlocutors at risk of either producing face threatening acts or being the recipient of a face threat. Consider another workplace scenario where one employee makes a statement agreeing with a stringent new workplace policy and then questions a co-worker (who does not agree with the policy) about his/her viewpoint. For the first speaker, stating his/her opinion risks altering the listener's perception of his/her social identity and thus the status of their relationship (degree of involvement). In addition, the speaker also imposes on the listener's independence by opening up a topic that may require the listener to reveal his/her own viewpoint on the new policy. As Leech's maxim of tact suggests, a speaker should minimize the expression of beliefs that might imply cost to others, thus managing face in any context is a delicate social balancing act.

Face Threats in the Context of Dementia

In the case of PWD, the risk of being the recipient of a potential face threat is increased due to cognitive deficits. In any interaction, a listener must hold a speaker's utterance in working memory, process its meaning, then draw on long-term memory to form a relevant response. For PWD, particularly in contexts that involve the answering of questions that require specific answers (e.g., standardized assessments), the face threat is increased due to memory loss. In contrast, during informal contexts, such as everyday conversations, it is easier to avoid the "correct" response by interjecting phatic comments (e.g., a statement about the weather), responding with simple reiterations of the speaker's utterance, or changing the topic. For example, if a family member visiting a PWD asks 'what did you have for breakfast?', the PWD could potentially respond with 'it was nice' or avoid the answer by commenting on the speaker's appearance 'you look nice today'. Such interactional resources allow the PWD to acknowledge the interlocutor's question and maintain the conversation without overtly disrupting the interaction. These forms of response would not be appropriate in a more formal clinical interaction that required specific information in response to questions.

POLITENESS MARKERS: COGNITIVE PROCESSING LOAD

Certain politeness markers have a degree of structural freedom that differs in comparison to an utterance that carries specific propositional content or reflects an instrumental goal. For example, politeness markers can be used as a means to interrupt a speaker at a place in the conversation that would not normally be considered an optimal transition-relevance point (Sacks, Schegloff, & Jefferson, 1974). Interjecting a compliment, for instance, might allow a speaker to change topic without overtly appearing to dominate the conversational floor. Indeed most individuals respond well to compliments or questions about their well-being (e.g., 'you look nice' or 'how are you feeling today?'). Positive politeness markers of involvement are, therefore, interactional variables that can potentially allow speakers more structural flexibility in conversational sequences (i.e., to topic shift, interrupt, etc.).

As noted previously, politeness markers may also consist of phrases and/or clauses uttered so frequently they are often formulaic in nature. For example, greetings such as "hi how are you" are likely fixed and stored as whole gestalts in our lexicon(s) (Wray, 2002). Even phatic utterances that relate to a specific interlocutor may involve a clause level constituent that is in itself formulaic (e.g., how is the [. . .] going?), phrases that only require the speaker to insert the appropriate noun (e.g., golf, diet, thesis, job, etc.) in the paradigmatic slot. Politeness strategies may also involve the use of formulaic strings that are common expressions in everyday conversations. For example, speech acts such as comments about the weather are frequent in English-speaking cultures.

The form and usage of such politeness markers suggests the possibility that they are linguistic items that may require less cognitive processing, that is, they need less online assembly and can be inserted as whole constituents that precede (or follow) a speech act. Politeness markers that function as adverbials also have less grammatical constraint in relation to their syntactic position (i.e., before a subject, after an object, or within a verb phrase). In summary, politeness markers can serve multiple purposes in an interaction: first, as they are often constructed of fixed units they require little online assembly; second, they allow a listener to interject a comment without dominating the conversational floor; third, they allow an abrupt topic change; and, finally, they show appropriate reciprocity within a conversation. Politeness strategies of this type are therefore linguistic markers self presentation in talk that reflect (a) the speaker's desire to participate in the interaction, (b) the speaker's discursive acknowledgement of face needs (self and other), and (c) awareness of appropriate interactional social behavior.

It should be noted that politeness markers such as compliments or comments relating to a visible object may be the result of cognitive distraction rather than a purposeful attempt to address face requirements. Recent ethnographic observations by the first author have noted that many PWD are easily distracted by such objects and can at times become fixated on the object and repeatedly comment on it or touch it. In these cases, the comment appears to function, not as a politeness marker, but as the result of distraction. For example, a PWD commented on the first author's watch and then proceeded to lean over and touch the watch for several minutes in a manner that would normally be considered socially inappropriate.

Attention, Activation, and Inhibition of Semantic Information

Before proceeding to the analysis of our data, it is necessary to consider the role that working memory and attention play when interlocutors engage in conversation. Cowan (2011) suggests a model of working memory that focuses on the role of attention in processing language. He suggests that inhibition of the effect of spreading activation (Collins & Loftus, 1975) to similar or semantically related information is dependent on the individual's focus of attention. Thus, selective attention on information relevant to the context is crucial to accessing and retrieving the target. That is, working memory, in response to an interlocutor's utterance, activates a range of linguistically related information, and the focus of attention mechanism acts to inhibit the information that is not the precise target. Linguistically related information might include aspects of syntax, morphology, or semantics. Cowan suggests that related information is activated automatically but notes all information does not have the same status (or relevance). Furthermore, information activated in the working memory is only available for a limited amount of time before decaying, and Cowan suggests the focus of attention mechanism is more resistant to this decay and, therefore, plays an important role for the listener in maintaining the information that is most relevant to the interaction at hand. Cowan suggests that individuals who do well at storing and processing information efficiently are those who can best inhibit the storage or processing of irrelevant information activated by spoken or visual stimuli.

Similarly, Shelley-Tremblay (2011), in a discussion of semantic breakdown in people with aphasia and PWD, suggests a major role for attention and inhibition. He notes that PWD may have problems with word retrieval in naming tasks because of a 'failure to get a clean perceptual activation of concepts' (p. 630). Early studies (Margolin, Pate, &

Friedrich, 1996; Nicholas, Obler, Au, & Albert, 1996) found evidence of degradation across information categories within the semantic network in PWD. Margolin et al.'s work found a significant deterioration in the semantic networks of PWD even in the early stages of dementia. This suggests that the interference of semantically similar or associated information does not help support language use but may actually serve to inhibit processing in even mild cases of dementia. This is 'possibly because the eroded boundaries of the semantic network' allow multiple exemplars to become activated (Shelley-Tremblay, 2011, p. 631). Shelley-Tremblay suggests that a Central Surround Mechanism (CSM) functions to inhibit similar or related words from interfering, that is, in word priming studies, neuro-typical participants have shown increased activation for the target and decreased activation for semantically associated words. He further notes that detailed information appears to degrade first, and there may be a blurring of distinctions between categories rather than loss of semantic information. In the CSM model, the semantic deficits in dementia might result from an inability to maintain semantic mediation between or across categories for any length of time, thus the problems manifested in dementia relate to impaired organization and access rather than loss of actual items.

Thus, we could suggest that one problem for PWD in processing language is an inability to inhibit associated information or exemplars activated in their working memory by a speaker's question or utterance. The target information is not lost, but the PWD's language system may have difficulty focusing on the target when the fine-grained distinctions between categories are blurred or lost. Shelley-Tremblay (2011) suggests the possibility that abnormal action of the CSM inhibits the ability of PWD to make the decisions or comparisons across semantic categories that allow them to focus on the specific target.

This might also be the case in relation to stored cognitive frames or schemas (Minsky, 1975) of events. Frames or cognitive schemata are the organization and storage of knowledge about a particular concept. The schema contains the features or attributes that are associated with a category membership (Sims & Lorenzi, 1992). They also incorporate preconceived ideas or expectations associated with particular words, events, or objects. For example, if a speaker references a particular event (e.g., 'did you enjoy the Christmas party yesterday?') other information, general and specific that is associated with, or expected to occur at, such an event, is also activated in the working memory. General information stored within a schema for the concept "party" might include the following: items found at such events (e.g., presents, drinks, etc.), behaviors that occur (e.g., the gathering of people, the giving of gifts, the eating of food, etc.), and formulaic verbal strings commonly spoken at such events (e.g., 'it's a nice party' or 'would you like a drink?'). Other information specific to the individual might include memories of a particular experience that occurred at a party in the past (e.g., singing karaoke in public). The CSM or focus of attention must inhibit any general exemplars or personal memories not relevant to the party under discussion and focus on the information relevant to the current conversation. An inability to focus on the target information may result in the production of comments that appear to draw on the associated general information activated by the speaker's question. For example, in response to the question 'what gift did you get yesterday?' the interlocutor may say 'we always gave gifts' or 'Christmas is the time for gifts'.

The recall of personal details, particularly events that are recent, or occurred regularly throughout a person's life, is not typically a difficult task in a conversation or interview. However, for PWD, who have difficulties with both short-term and long-term memory; questions about both recent and regular life events may expose their memory loss, and therefore such questions represent potential face threats to the PWD's self-esteem. In the analyses presented in the following section, we examined whether F's responses adhered to the cooperative principle (Leech, 1983) and showed evidence of using politeness strategies of involvement. We further consider whether F's contributions were compensatory strategies motivated by a desire to show appropriate reciprocity and engage with her interlocutor. Alternatively, her contributions may have been artifacts of a compromised language processing system automatically compensating for an inability to access (or focus on) the specific information required to answer the questions the researcher asked, or (2) an inability to inhibit semantically related information primed by spreading activation.

METHOD

Participant Background

The data presented here is from a corpus of data involving conversations between the first author and F, a woman with dementia who resided in a long-term care facility. F was 80 years old and had been suffering from dementia for approximately 12 years. She had been in the long-term care facility for 7 years. F was in a wheelchair and needed assistance with acts of daily living. F suffered from hearing loss since the age of 55 and wore hearing aids. She occasionally presented with dysarthric speech production, but this appeared variable and was often dependent on her general health condition on the day of recording. The healthcare assistant introduced J to F as a volunteer visitor interested in recording the life histories of seniors in the area. F was on most occasions lively and willing to engage in conversation but on some days was unresponsive and presented with a dull affect. On these occasions, the researcher did not audio-record the interaction.

Initially, the overall goal was to collect a corpus of language samples from a PWD and an unfamiliar interlocutor in order to assess particular features of communication that appeared to be problematic for either interlocutor. The researcher chose ethnographic research interviews as a means to collect the data because, as noted previously, such interviews were semi-structured but also retained elements of everyday conversations. In addition, such interviews mirror (to some extent) the ethnographic interviews that healthcare professionals may carry out as a supplement to formal standardized tests of cognition when assessing a client or patient's functional communication skills.

Data Collection Methods

The researcher collected audio recordings of interviews with F on a monthly basis over a period of one year. The interviews were audio-recorded in F's bedroom at the long-term care facility, but on two occasions, audio-recordings were carried out in the communal lounge. The data was audio recorded on a small Marantz tape recorder using a Sony lapel microphone attached to the author's jacket. In both contexts, the first author was sitting directly opposite F approximately two feet away. The first author transcribed the data, which was then reviewed by a second researcher. For the purposes of this chapter, the first author reviewed the original audio recordings and ethnographic notes and clarified some of the utterances produced by F. Institutional Research Board (IRB) and family permissions were obtained to use the data presented in this chapter.

Transcription Conventions

As the focus of the analyses was identifying interactional acts and their semantic relevance, the transcription conventions were kept to a minimum.

- ? Signifies rising intonation associated with a question or request for clarification.
- (.) Brief pause; shorter than 0.5 of a second (brief pauses at the end of utterances are not indicated).

(3.0)	Timed pause, three seconds.
*	Overlapping sequence begins and ends.
=	Latching, i.e., the end of one utterance is immediately followed by the beginning of another, without overlap, but also without any pause.
(laughs)	Words in single parentheses in italics indicates non-verbal or contextual information.
(3 secs unintell)	Unintelligible segment.
(xXx)	Unintelligible but transcriber can identify unstressed ('x') and stressed ('X') syllables.
{T}	Tearful voice

Analytical Framework

Discourse analysis provided the framework for the initial analyses of the data, and, in particular, we drew on Interactional Sociolinguistics (see Guendouzi & Müller, 2006, for a more detailed discussion of discourse analysis). We focused on conversational acts at points in the interview where the researcher asked a question that required F to remember specific personal information or details of her life. We also drew on theories of working memory, attention, and semantic processing to consider the role cognitive processing resources played in the production of F's utterances (Cowan, 2011; Shelley-Tremblay, 2011).

Analytical Limitations

As is often the case in qualitative research, there is a risk of appearing to "cherry pick" one's examples. This is a valid concern but one that cannot be avoided when presenting extracts of conversational data, particularly given restrictions of space when reporting the data in articles. Typically, discourse analysts do tend to choose those examples that best represent the thesis or argument they are putting forward. However, the examples are either representative of patterns that appear frequently throughout a dataset or are unusual uses of language that warrant discussion. Indeed, as many of the authors in this volume would attest, PWD frequently appear to use language that includes formulaic items, phatic tokens, extenders, repetitions, and politeness markers. The framework that embedded the analyses initially drew on politeness theory because previous work (Guendouzi & Müller, 2001, 2002, 2006) noted that F used politeness markers such as routine or ritualized expressions (e.g., greetings, partings, comments about the weather, and comments on visible items such as a brightly colored blouse) in a seemingly appropriate manner. However, a recent (re)review of the corpus revealed that although F frequently used discourse markers of reciprocity (e.g., 'well' or 'oh yes') and minimal responses, there were few examples of politeness adverbials that usually accompany requests-for-action in Anglo-western cultures (e.g., 'if you don't mind' or 'could you please').

The pattern of exchanges discussed in the following section was typical of the conversations recorded within the care facility and in unrecorded conversations that occurred on occasions the researcher took F for walks in the garden. We are aware that conclusions based on a small data set of conversations involving only one PWD might be subjective and therefore should not be generalized to the larger population of all people with dementia. However, patterns that are found repeatedly in conversational data do raise important questions about how PWD process language in the context of cognitive deficits, and also suggest important avenues for future research. We are aware that the inferences drawn from the following analyses are simply the thoughts of two researchers and therefore do not hold any claim to being the "correct" interpretation; however, we hope that the potential explanations we present may help to create a future dialogue between cognitive researchers and discourse analysts.

DATA AND DISCUSSION

Prior to the recording of the following data extract, J had been informed by a healthcare assistant that F had been taken shopping by her husband the previous day to buy some clothes (see Guendouzi & Müller, 2006, pp. 212–213).

Extract 1

1 J: does your husband take you to the shop does he?
        (2.0)
2 F: does he takes me (.) shopping?
3 J: mhm
4 F: oh well (.) we get around *(nods and smiles)*
5 J: *(brief laugh)* (2.5) uhuh
6 F: when he was a (.) come (.) at first he was out shopping there and it was a nice day out (xx)and we got the essentials you know (1.5) and then we well maybe we would go and then we would go to the closest on Sunday (.) at half eleven off to- we're off to- we were going to the mass (xxx.)
7 J: mhm
8 F: and eh to them while on the road (.) I was asleep there

9 F: ehm, (.) M (xxXxxxXxx) (1.5) well
10 J: mhm,
11 F: ehm, (1.5) you want us to stay, do you?
12 J: yea. (3.5) did you use to go into town to do your shopping or did you go to (name of shop) on Williams road?
13 F: uh- uh no (.) right into town
14 J: right into town?
15 F: mhm, (2 mins) *(F does not appear to have any further information on this topic, and there is a two-minute silence)*

In the previous extract, J had asked F whether her husband takes her shopping (turn 1). As noted, J already knew that F had been on such an outing and wanted to see if this general question would prompt F to recall the event of the previous day. F's initial response is to repeat back J's question (turn 2), a move that marks reciprocity but does not supply the required information. In repeating the question, F's request-for-clarification might also "buy" her time to formulate a more specific response. F then responds to J's affirming minimal response (mhm) with the formulaic phatic comment 'we get around' (turn 4). F accompanied this comment with a smile and a nod of the head in a manner that suggested verbal play. J's responding laugh and 'uhuh' suggests J did interpret the comment as an attempt at humor. This conversational move uses both iconic non-verbal emblems and a formulaic comment that does not disrupt the conversation, nor seem overtly out of place. It appeared to enable F and J to discursively construct a shared moment of joint understanding and thus decrease the face threat associated with F's memory problems (i.e., not remembering she went shopping the previous day).

In her next turn (6), F elaborates on the topic of shopping by producing a short narrative consisting of comments that are associated to the topic but are non-specific in content. F notes that when her husband came they got 'the essentials' and then offers another formulaic comment, 'it was a nice day out'. Although F appeared unable to remember the previous day's shopping trip, the use of the word 'essentials' could refer to any items that might have been purchased on any type of shopping trip without necessarily exposing the fact that F had been unable to recall the actual event. The formulaic strings (e.g., 'we get around' and 'it was a nice day out') are utterances that could describe any event involving participants going somewhere. These two comments are commonly occurring verbal items that might be associated with a cognitive schema of "going places". F's next comment, 'well maybe we would go and then would go to the closest on Sunday', tentatively suggests the possibility that F and her husband went out on Sundays to "somewhere" nearby. These clauses have no specific object (e.g., shops), and the verb tense construction does not reference a specific time or day. However, F's care assistant informed J that, prior to her institutionalization, F and her husband made regular grocery shopping trips on Sundays to a nearby supermarket. The mention of the word 'Sunday' appears to prompt F to introduce another of her regular life activities that took place on Sundays; going to Mass. F's next turn (11) initially may appear to be off-topic, but the healthcare assistant had told J that they no longer took F to the nearby chapel as she would fall asleep during the service. J assumed that F's comment was a reference to her habit of falling asleep during mass and was thus relevant to the new topic of going to church. J then attempted to reintroduce the topic of shopping and asked F whether she shopped in town or used the stores at two nearby locations. J was aware that F actually used one of the nearby stores and formulated her question in this manner to see if F would remember the specific place where she had shopped for the past 40 years. By naming the shop, J expected her utterance would help prompt F to produce the correct response. However, F responded with the "incorrect" option ('right into town'). There were clothes shops in the center of the town in question, therefore, F's response may refer to the actual trip she made the previous day. This effect may, however, be the result of F's inability to inhibit associated information activated within a cognitive schema of "going shopping", or to inhibit the first option J stated in her prior utterance.

What then does this conversational sequence reveal in relation to both F's interactional resources and her declining cognitive resources? First, consider an interpretation drawing on politeness theory and the concept of involvement. Leech's cooperative principle (1983) suggests it is beholden on the listener to respond to a speaker's comment or question and show reciprocity by offering responses that are relevant to the topic at hand. In the prior example, F appeared to fulfill her social role of involvement by opting to contribute to the interview and attempt to supply relevant information. She used the interactional resources of recycling the speaker's initial question, producing non-specific but semantically related information, formulaic tokens (turns 4 & 6), and iconic non-verbal markers.

Next, we consider what this conversational sequence might reveal about F's cognitive processing resources. F's contributions appear to reflect the use of items that have been drawn from cognitive schemas associated with the general topics of "going out" and "going shopping" (i.e., events and places associated with shopping and going out with her husband) that were available within F's semantic network due to the process of spreading activation. That is, F's language processing system may be unable to inhibit other exemplars associated with the topic activated in her working memory and thus produces utterances that are associated with general schemas relating to the topic but not specific to J's questions. The prior sequence of talk lasts for the duration of 15 turns before breaking down, suggesting, in line with models of working memory (Cowan, 2011), that the activated information persists over a specific period of time before decaying and is then no longer available for F to access.

In the second extract, we see a similar pattern in a sequence that follows a lengthy and somewhat incoherent turn by F (see Guendouzi & Müller, 2006, p. 215).

Extract 2

1   F: we're ok she's happy *(light laugh from both)* (1.5) um (1.5) she wa- she was (Xx) except for a few days, but (1.5) to his (Xx) and so she were X, and if he doesn't wait, until then (3 secs unintell) it's his flesh. you know (1.5) so we've got to do that (.) there's only a couple of pieces left in the house you know (2.0) {T} but we tried to get (XxX) over here (xXx) = *(F then gazes directly at J)*

2   J: = mhm? (5.0) it's a nice room

3   F: mhm (3.0) it's a beautiful place

4   J: yeah it is (3.5) it's very close to your home isn't it? so (husband's name) can come =

5   F: = oh yeah yeah =

6   J: = it's just up the road

7   F: mhm

8   J: does he come every day? (1.5) does he come every day?

9   F: I think so (.) I don't know whether he (.) he's (.) he mhm he likes a pint! *(smiles, tilts head and looks towards J)*

10   J: *(light laugh from J)* where does he go?

11   F: to (XXxx) I *think* =

12   J: = a:h

13   F: = that's where he used to go (.) where I was going

14   J: what about the Catholic (.) social club?

15   F: yeah?

16   J: on West Rd?

17   F: (xXx) here takin me out some

18   J: mm:

19   F: yes, he (.) I don't know (xxx) find out (0.2) (xxxx) were children. I blamed him (.) and she left *(F appears to go off topic at this point)*

In this example of conversation, J was confused by F's incoherent turn (1) and also noted that F's tearful voice quality suggested she was becoming distressed at not being able to express herself clearly. J then made a complimentary remark about F's room. J was using a common politeness strategy to avoid expressing her confusion, address F's distress, and redirect the topic. F responded by acknowledging the room was 'beautiful' (turn 3). J then comments on the proximity of F's family home to the nursing facility. F's minimal responses (turns 5 & 7) reflected reciprocity and perhaps allowed F some time to regain her composure. At this point, the interaction reflected common small-talk routines utilized by speakers (in Anglo-western cultures) at moments where there is a potential face threat to the listener. It is an interactional move that allowed J to make an abrupt topic shift and address F's positive face needs (i.e., attempt to alleviate her distress and loss of self-esteem). J used this discursive turning point to introduce a new topic and asked whether F's husband visited on a daily basis. F's hedged response suggested uncertainty (turn 11), and she then added a comment that described her husband as liking a 'pint' (alcoholic drink). It is a formulaic expression familiar to many people in the United Kingdom, and while it does not answer the question, it does relate to her husband's daily activities. F used non-verbal emblems (a smile and head nod) when uttering this descriptor about her husband, and J's laugh suggests that she assumed F was again using humor to diffuse the potential face threat of not recalling the actual answer to J's question.

J then decided to follow up on the topic F has initiated and asked her where her husband went to drink. He had in fact visited the local Catholic social club on Friday or Saturday night for most of their married life; therefore, this is a piece of information that F should be able to recall. F's response is unintelligible, but she appeared to be attempting to name the place he frequented. F then added a qualifying remark 'I think that's where he used to go (.) where I was going' (turn 13). The first clause in this utterance signals uncertainty about the location named, but the second clause appears to suggest the place she named might be a location she herself frequented. In this sequence F, once again, offers comments that do not specifically answer J's question but may reflect a cognitive schema of information associated with either her own or her husband's activities. Although not specifically on-topic, F's contribution allowed her to sustain a participatory role in the conversation. J attempted to further prompt F's memory by suggesting the Catholic social club as a potential location, but the rising intonation in F's response indicates she isn't certain whether this is the correct information. J then provides the address of the social club as a further memory cue. F, however, responded with another non-specific reference that might be associated with a cognitive schema of "going places" by noting her husband took 'her out some'. F's next contribution is off-topic (turn 19), and the conversation temporarily breaks down.

F's interactional resources in this sequence appeared to be the use of agreement to J's compliment, minimal responses, formulaic comments, and remarks that held semantic associations to a general schema of such events. Thus, a pattern of interaction similar to that identified in extract 1 emerged in this sequence, and, as with the previous example, F could not sustain the use of such interactional resources over a lengthy period before the interaction broke down. This sequence of talk lasted over a period of 11 turns with no further elaboration on the topic by F.

CONCLUSIONS

This chapter focused on two particular aspects of politeness theory (involvement and reciprocity) in order to explore whether, in the presence of memory loss, F, a woman with dementia, would be able to use interactional resources to participate in a coherent manner to the researcher's questions. Our conclusions after completing the discourse analyses suggest that the matter is far from clear. Leech (1983) noted that most interlocutors cooperate in constructing conversations in a manner that adheres to the appropriate social expectations of the cultural milieu in which the interaction occurs, and as many of the chapters in this book demonstrate, PWD appear to retain these socially acquired communicative behaviors even in the face of dementia. However, in the context of dementia, cognitive deficits, particularly memory loss and the deterioration of the semantic network system, potentially compromise the complex process of social interaction. PWD are able to utilize a variety of interactional resources that enable them to sustain a conversational role and elaborate on topic lines, thus remaining active (and polite) conversational partners; however, is the use of these communicative strategies a deliberate compensatory strategy? Typically, researchers describe these interactional resources as compensatory strategies that aid the PWD to express self-identity and agency in their interactions. However, the use of the term compensatory *strategy* is in some ways problematic. The semantic connotations of the word strategy imply an element of volition or deliberate planning on the part of the interlocutor, but as suggested previously, the conversational behaviors manifested by F may have resulted from a degraded semantic network or deficits in the cognitive systems that support language processing (e.g., working memory and attention). In this sense, the verbal constructions used by F are "compensatory" behaviors, but they are non-volitional; that is, they are the result of cognitive deficits and are likely emergent properties of a less than efficient language processing system, that is, they are the result of an interaction between both cognitive deficits and interactional resources.

Some of the interactional resources that F used to maintain involvement, and thus present a positive self-identity, did appear to J (at the time of recording) to be volitional compensatory strategies. For example, when F produced the formulaic comment 'we get around', the accompanying non-verbal behaviors suggested to J that F "intended" to discursively create a moment of shared understanding with the researcher and thereby decrease the face threat inherent in her inability to recall a recent event in her life. However, the comment may have been one of the exemplars activated in a cognitive schema of "going places". F may not have been able to inhibit this related but non-specific formulaic comment when trying to produce the target response (i.e., confirmation that her husband took her shopping). Thus, F's comment was created by a combination of both automatic cognitive processes (degraded semantic network) and the use of habitual socially learned non-verbal accompaniers. F's contributions to the interaction were utterances that shared some semantic associations with the information in J's questions and, therefore, did not appear overtly incoherent and did act (to some extent) as cohesive ties in the conversation. They were comments that might frequently occur in such conversational contexts and therefore had structural flexibility as linguistic items. However, as was shown previously, F appeared to be unable to sustain these types of responses for a long period of time, perhaps only for the period that it took for the activated field of potential candidate exemplars to decay.

What then can we learn from considering this dataset in relation to both interactional and cognitive resources? In the extracts analyzed in this chapter, embedding the analyses in a pragmatic framework of politeness theory did appear to support the notion that F adhered to Leech's (1983) cooperative principle and attempted (on most occasions) to respond to J's questions, thus fulfilling social obligations of politeness to remain an engaged conversational partner. However, closer examination of these sequences in relation to psycholinguistic theories showed evidence that F's contributions may also reflect her inability to inhibit semantically related information, thus her responses may have resulted from deficits in her processing system. F may have had difficulty in making links across eroded category boundaries and was thus unable to integrate the target into her responses, but could produce related information or socially acceptable politeness markers. Rather than simply being examples of interactional compensatory strategies, many of F's contributions appear to be the result of an interaction between intact learned social behaviors and faulty or inaccurate cognitive systems. It is still the case, however, that in the presence of cognitive deficits, F's language system "compensated" for her processing limitations by utilizing semantically associated items to respond in a manner that appeared socially appropriate. That is, F was able to draw on activated word strings from a general field of items in the cognitive schema associated with the topic at hand. Thus, F was able to maintain her involvement in the conversations presented here and discursively insert her self-identity within the interaction.

Final Thoughts and Future Directions

Over the past decade qualitative research (e.g., Davis, 2005; Hamilton, 1994; Guendouzi & Müller, 2006; Sabat, 2001) has explored the ways in which PWD use their diminishing communicative resources to stay active social partners. The results of such studies provide valuable information that reveals (a) the communicative devices used by PWD, and (b) how PWD express self-identity by attempting discursively to remain active social partners. However, conversational data can also shed light on models of psycholinguistics and help researchers to better understand the underlying cognitive mechanisms of PWD's language system. Traditionally, there has been a division in the literature between psycholinguistic research and qualitative research. Cognition-based theories of language seek to model the automatic cognitive mechanisms that support communication. Interactional theories, on the other hand, seek to identify socially learned communicative behaviors that the speaker selects in relation to the particular interactional context. Cognitive neuroscientists, however, cannot just rely on speaker performance in experimental conditions (e.g., word naming/priming tasks, etc.) to exemplify their models; they also need to consider how both cognitive and conversational resources interact in everyday contexts, and discourse analysts need to extend their analyses beyond description within sociolinguistic frameworks.

In the data provided previously, for example, it appeared that many of F's conversational behaviors support the notion of spreading activation amongst exemplars activated within a general cognitive schema of the topic at hand. Furthermore, the data suggests the possibility that deficits in focus of attention and inhibition of competing semantic information are major factors in the PWD's inability to respond appropriately to the propositional content of questions they have been asked. If this is the case, then providing the PWD with memory prompts (visual or verbal) of similar objects, concepts, or words may not always be helpful in conversations, particularly because the data suggests that appropriate adherence to politeness requirements appears to be a social behavior that is deeply embedded in the communication system, that is, PWD often work hard to maintain a socially appropriate role in a conversation. However, the utterances produced, when the PWD cooperates and shows reciprocity, may be the result of deficits in cognition rather than interactional strategies.

It is important, therefore, when analyzing conversational data to consider the cognitive mechanisms that underpin a PWD's communicative behaviors. Caregivers often need specific answers to questions that *do* matter (e.g., questions relating to food consumption or whether the PWD has used the bathroom that morning). For example, the first author asked a PWD (who also had diabetes) if he had eaten lunch, and he replied 'oh man I only had breakfast'. As he spent the mid-morning hours alone at home it was possible he might not have eaten the food left out for his lunch. The researcher checked this information with his wife and found he did in fact have lunch that day. His remark to the researcher possibly stemmed from an inability to inhibit other exemplars activated from a schema of "meals and food". In this case, drawing on activated exemplars from a cognitive schema that included items associated with the target, resulted in producing a feasible but untrue response to the question. This could have been problematic if the researcher had assumed the man's answer was correct and had given him extra food (i.e., as a diabetic it was important to make sure he ate specific amounts of food at regular intervals).

The data presented previously suggests it is time for more dialogue between pragmatic theories of discourse and psycholinguistic accounts of language. Models of language processing should be applied to "real world" data, and, conversely, qualitative researchers should consider cognitively driven explanations when analyzing their datasets rather than relying on social theories of language behavior alone. Closer examination of the interaction between conversational and cognitive resources may ultimately allow researchers to find better interventions and suggest areas of communication theory that need further exploration.

REFERENCES

Bargiela-Chiappini, F., & Haugh, M. (2009). *Face communication and social interaction*. London: Equinox.

Bauman, R. (1992). Text and discourse in anthropological linguistics. In W. Bright (Ed.), *International encyclopedia of linguistics* (pp.145–147). Oxford: Oxford University Press.

Brown, P., & Levinson, S. (1987). *Politeness: Some universals in language usage,* Cambridge: Cambridge University Press.

Collins, A. M., & Loftus, E. F. (1975). A spreading-activation theory of semantic processing. *Psychological Review, 82*(6), 407–428.

Coulmas F. (Ed.) (1981). *Conversational routine: Explorations in standardized communication situations and prepatterned speech.* The Hague: Mouton.

Coupland, N., & Ylänne-McEwen, V. (2000). Talk about the weather: Small talk, leisure talk and the travel industry. In J. Coupland (Ed.), *Small talk* (pp. 163–182). London: Pearson Education.

Cowan, N. (2011). Working memory and language use. In J. Guendouzi, F. Loncke, & M. J. Williams (Eds.), *The handbook of psycholinguistics and cognitive processing: Perspectives in communication disorders* (pp. 75–98). New York: Psychology Press.

Davis, B. (Ed.). (2005). *Alzheimer talk, text and context.* London: Palgrave-Macmillan.

Garcés-Conejos Blitvich, P. (2013). Introduction: Face, identity and im/politeness. Looking backward, moving forward: From Goffman to practice theory. *Journal of Politeness Research, 9*(1), 1–33.

Goffman, E. (1967/1982). *Interactional ritual: Essays on face to face behavior.* New York: Pantheon.

Grice, H. P. (1975). Logic and conversation. In P. Cole & J. Morgan (Eds.), *Syntax and semantics, 3: Speech acts.* New York: Academic Press.

Guendouzi, J., & Müller, N. (2001). Intelligibility and rehearsed sequences conversations with a DAT patient. *Clinical Linguistics and Phonetics, 19*(2), 91–95.

Guendouzi, J., & Müller, N. (2002). Defining trouble sources in dementia: Repair strategies and conversational satisfaction in interactions with an Alzheimer's patient. In F. Windsor, M. L. Kelly, & N. Hewlett (Eds.), *Investigations in clinical phonetics and linguistics* (pp. 15–30). Mahwah, NJ: Lawrence Erlbaum Associates.

Guendouzi, J., & Müller, N. (2006). *Approaches to discourse in dementia.* Mahwah, NJ: Lawrence Erlbaum.

Hamilton, H. E. (1994). *Conversations with an Alzheimer's patient: An interactional sociolinguistic study.* Cambridge, UK: Cambridge University Press.

Haugh, M., & Bargiela-Chiappini, F. (2010). Face in interaction. *Journal of Pragmatics, 42*(8), 2073–2077.

Laver, J. (1975). Communicative functions of phatic communion. In A. Kendon, R. M. Harris, & M. R. Key (Eds.), *Organization of behavior in face-to-face interaction* (pp. 215–238). The Hague: Mouton.

Leech, G. (1983). *Principles of pragmatics.* London: Longman.

Malinowski, B. (1989). The problem of meaning in primitive languages. In C. K. Ogden & I. A. Richards (Eds.), *The meaning of meaning,* Supplement I (pp. 296–336). London: Routledge & Kegan Paul. Originally published 1923.

Margolin, D. I., Pate, D. S., & Friedrich, F. J. (1996). Lexical priming by pictures and words in normal aging and dementia of the Alzheimer's type. *Brain & Language, 54,* 275–301.

Minsky, M. (1975). A framework for representing knowledge. In P. H. Winston (Ed.), *The psychology of computer vision.* New York: McGraw-Hill.

Nicholas, M., Obler, L. K., Au, R., & Albert, M. L. (1996). On the nature of naming errors in aphasia and dementia: A study of semantic relatedness. *Brain & Language, 54,* 184–195.

Sabat, S. (2001). *The experience of Alzheimer's disease: Life through a tangled veil.* Oxford, UK: Blackwell.

Sacks, H., Schegloff, E. A., & Jefferson, G. (1974). A simplest systematic for the organization of turn-taking in conversation. *Language, 50,* 696–735.

Scollon, R., & Wong-Scollon, S. (1995). *Intercultural communication: A discourse approach.* Oxford, UK: Blackwell.

Shelley-Tremblay, J. (2011). The breakdown of semantics in aphasia and dementia: A role for attention. In J. Guendouzi, F. Loncke, & M. J. Williams (Eds.), *The handbook of pyscholinguistics and cognitive processing: Perspectives in communication disorders* (pp. 625–645). New York: Psychology Press.

Sims, H. P., Jr., & Lorenzi, P. (1992). *The new leadership paradigm: Social learning and cognition in organizations.* Newbury Park, CA: Sage.

Wray, A. (2002). *Formulaic language and the lexicon.* Cambridge, UK: Cambridge University Press.

6

CONFLICTING DEMONSTRATIONS OF UNDERSTANDING IN THE INTERACTIONS OF INDIVIDUALS WITH FRONTOTEMPORAL DEMENTIA

Considering Cognitive Resources and Their Implications for Care and Communication

Lisa Mikesell

INTRODUCTION

Frontotemporal dementia (FTD) is a young onset neurodegenerative dementia targeting the frontal and/or temporal lobes/(Ratnavalli, Brayne, Dawson & Hodges, 2002). Unlike many dementias, the brain degeneration associated with FTD predominantly affects social and emotional behavior, interpersonal conduct and impulse control (Grossman, 2002; Hodges & Miller, 2001; Jagust, Reed, Seab, Kramer & Budinger, 1989; Kipps, Knibb & Hodges, 2007; Miller et al., 2001) rather than basic cognitive functions such as memory and visuospatial abilities (Walker, Meares, Sachdev & Brodaty, 2005). The frontal lobes, however, are strongly implicated in a particular kind of cognitive functioning, namely executive functioning, which is defined by tasks requiring planning, complex decision making and multitasking. Traditional measures of these functional domains such as the Wisconsin Card Sorting Test have been found to be insensitive to early FTD deficits and everyday functioning (Gregory et al., 2002; Roca et al., 2013). Yet executive functioning remains a defining feature of FTD, and efforts to develop more sensitive tests to detect early impairments of these areas have been undertaken (Hodges, 2007). For instance, subjects in Torralva, Roca, Gleichgerrcht, Bekinschtein and Manes's (2009) study showed deficits in executive functioning and social cognition as reflected in performances on several tests of social and executive functioning that attempted to mirror tasks in everyday life (e.g., Multiple Errands Test, Hotel Task, complex decision making).

Preserved cognitive skills are evident in individuals' intact intellectual reasoning, that is, their capacity to demonstrate logical argumentation and rational thought. Despite such abilities to reason, individuals present with *loss of insight* (Neary et al., 1998), referring to patients' limited awareness of the behavioral and personality changes they have undergone as well as a compromised ability to accurately reflect on these changes (Kipps et al., 2007; Rankin, Baldwin, Pace-Savitsky, Kramer & Miller, 2005; cf. Avineri, 2010). Consequently, individuals with FTD often have difficulty reporting deficits or problems on which caregivers readily comment. They have also been found to conflate their abilities or positive characteristics and minimize or not report negative ones (Fernandez-Duque & Black, 2007). For instance, even if individuals are confronting significant challenges, such as losing a job or facing severe financial hardship, they may casually report to providers or loved ones that everything is fine. In this way, it appears as if individuals with FTD navigate the world without updating a sense of self and/or context despite having undergone sometimes drastic changes in character and circumstance. This, coupled with blunted emotional responses and an apparent lack of social emotions such as embarrassment and shame (Miller et al., 2001), may contribute to individuals' inaccurate reports about functional capacity and life circumstances (Fernandez-Duque & Black, 2007).

Although there is some disagreement about the reliability of such categorical descriptions (Kipps et al., 2007), two profiles of FTD have been described: an *apathetic* profile characterized by a lack of motivation and volition and a *disinhibited* profile described as unrestrained and overactive (Snowden et al., 2001). Whether characterized as apathetic or disinhibited, individuals with FTD often show intact reasoning about social expectations, but do not adhere to the social expectations of which they seem to retain knowledge. This dissociation between intact intellectual reasoning and behavior manifests in particular ways in interactions with individuals with FTD (see Mates, Mikesell & Smith, 2010). As the video data discussed later illustrate, individuals with FTD often express an intellectual reasoning that is inconsistent with their embodied practices. This situation in which individuals publicly express one understanding, which they later contradict, allows one to observe and consider the nature of understandings as they are made public in talk-in-interaction and the interactional import of such inconsistencies.

For example, in a previous work, I (2013) examined these contradictions in understandings produced by individuals with FTD to explore the "pragmatics of understanding." I noted that examining these breakdowns in interaction facilitated observations of three degrees of public understanding: claims, displays and demonstrations, which I claimed provide increasingly strong evidence about the speaker's expressed understanding. Although individuals with FTD showed little difficulty producing claims and displays, they often failed to produce demonstrations made conditionally relevant by the (claimed and displayed) understandings they expressed in the preceding turns. In this chapter, I revisit these data of FTD interactions, not to elaborate on the pragmatics or degrees of understanding in talk-in-interaction, but to consider more carefully what these inconsistencies might reveal about individuals' cognitive and communicative capacities. For instance, intact cognitive abilities are suggested by individuals' effortless productions of claims and displays in response to the immediate prior turn, but executive dysfunction seems to emerge in ordinary interactions when individuals show difficulty producing demonstrations of understanding that require longer-term planning within interactional sequences.[1] I explore the nature of these cognitive capacities and impairment in more detail later. I also discuss how these conflicting understandings produced by individuals with FTD impact interactions by examining how interlocutors respond to these inconsistencies. Exploring the interactional practices of both individuals with FTD and their interlocutors has the potential to contribute important insights about effective communicative practices.

BACKGROUND

Degrees of Understanding in Interaction: Claims, Displays and Demonstrations

My earlier (2013) discussion of the pragmatics of understanding originated in Sacks's (1992) observation that speakers can express understandings that provide varying degrees of evidence about that speaker's relationship to the just preceding turn. In the following example, Sacks discussed two kinds of understanding: claims (3a) and demonstrations (3b).

1	A:	where are you staying
2	B:	Pacific Palisades
3a	A:	oh Pacific Palisades
3b	A:	oh at the west side of town

Whereas 3a merely *claims* understanding by acknowledging the previous turn (line 2), Sacks argued that 3b *demonstrates* understanding by providing additional and less ambiguous evidence. 3b not only acknowledges the previous turn but goes further by showing how the speaker understands the town where his interlocutor is staying. That is, there is stronger evidence of understanding embedded in 3b given it provides additional information about the speaker's relationship to the previous turn that 3a does not. More specifically, 3b does more than indicate that the speaker does indeed know where Pacific Palisades is located; it also reveals what this speaker finds relevant about this place and its location, namely, that it is "at the west side of town" (and not a number of other possible characteristics).

Using videotaped data of naturally occurring interactions with individuals with FTD, this earlier work (2013) extended Sacks's observation, proposing that there are three types of understanding that speakers can provide: claims, displays and demonstrations (see Table 6.1). Following Sacks's line of reasoning, I suggested that claims, displays and demonstrations all show understanding but with varying degrees of certainty or strength because they provide different kinds of evidence or proof of understanding and possess varying properties. I further suggested that understandings such as 3b are most aptly described, not as *demonstrations,* but as *displays.* Again following Sacks, I proposed that claims, such as the one in 3a, provide minimal evidence about one's understanding or relationship to the prior turn. I described claims such as 3a as being directly parasitic on the previous turn: claims use or directly rely on resources made public by another interlocutor, frequently recycling part or all of the just prior turn. As such, claims often provide mere acknowledgement of the previous turn. The certainty of the understanding is therefore often equivocal or opaque. By re-producing the interlocutor's previous turn (or by merely acknowledging or agreeing with it), the speaker offers little evidence or proof about how the previous turn was understood or that the previous turn was understood in the way intended by its producer.

In contrast, displays such as 3b (which Sacks calls demonstrations) provide stronger evidence of one's understanding because they offer a reformulation or interpretation of the previous turn. Although displays are dependent on the previous turn because of their sequential position, they offer an independent, although partial, understanding. 3b, for instance, provides an interpretation of how the speaker understands the location provided by the interlocutor that is independently expressed and does not directly rely on the first speaker's turn; however, this understanding is partial in that it makes meaningful only one feature of the

Table 6.1

Characteristics of Claims, Displays and Demonstrations of Understanding (from Mikesell, 2013)

Claims	Displays	Demonstrations
Recycles resources made available by others in previous talk; often includes repetition; is directly dependent/ parasitic on previous talk	Reformulates another's utterance; shows independent access to prior turn (i.e., interpretation or reasoning)	Follows up sequentially; is essential for activity progress
Understanding is equivocal, evasive and opaque	Understanding appears unambiguous and semi-transparent	Understanding is definite, unambiguous and transparent
Asserts something is the case without evidence or proof	Makes a prominent exhibition of a particular type of behavior, emotion or skill; performance, for public viewing	Shows something is the case by providing evidence or proof
Limited or minimal understanding is made public	Partial understanding is made public	Complete understanding is made public
Verbal repetition or verbal alignment	Verbal interpretation	Activity-based/embodied
Can be feigned/produced without much effort	Can be feigned/produced with some effort	Genuine demonstrations are difficult to feign without assistance

location that may be relevant to the second speaker. A consequence of the varying degrees of evidence embedded in different kinds of understanding is that understandings also vary in ease of production. Given that claims merely acknowledge or align without much evidence of understanding, they can be feigned without much effort, whereas displays, because they require independent cognitive access to the turn, require some effort to produce and are therefore more difficult to feign.

I (2013) previously described demonstrations as offering relatively definitive evidence about a speaker's understanding and relationship to the previous turn and sequence. Whereas claims might be glossed as verbal acknowledgements and displays as verbal interpretations, demonstrations constitute embodied understandings. They are bound to a current activity and essential for its progressivity and, as such, tend to provide transparent understandings. That is, when the previous turn makes an action or physically visible response conditionally relevant, it is more readily apparent what understanding such a response conveys. For instance, if one is asked to measure a cup of flour and picks up a tablespoon, the embodied action provides strong evidence that the instructions were misunderstood (though there may still be room to question this demonstrated understanding for its appropriateness). In contrast to claims and displays, which can be more easily feigned, demonstrations, because they provide such strong evidence of understanding, tend to be particularly difficult to feign without some assistance or scaffolding from others.

FTD and Public Understandings

Considering these different kinds of understanding becomes especially relevant when exploring contexts in which understanding becomes topicalized or problematic. This is because in some contexts, claims or displays of understanding may be treated as adequate, while in other contexts they may be insufficient. In the previous example, Sacks provided a context in which what he referred to as a claim and demonstration (what I am referring to as a claim and display) of understanding can both be pulled off without a hitch. While response 3a in Sacks's example merely claims understanding, the context is one in which more work from the speaker may not be required or expected. One can imagine, however, situations in which a mere claim (or display) would be lacking.

Much of the time understanding is achieved, or perceived to be achieved, by participants. Schegloff (1992) makes note of this when observing that understandings are made public "en passant." Occasionally, however, misunderstandings arise and understanding is attended to explicitly: while "most of the time speakers assume that recipients will understand what they are saying and recipients respond with the assumption that they have understood," there are times when "the issue of understanding becomes topicalised" (Hindmarsh, Reynolds, & Dunne, 2011, p. 489). Hindmarsh et al. (2011) note cases in which such topicalization is more likely to occur: interactions involving novices, children, apprentices, and instances of cross-cultural communication. Interactions with individuals with FTD also provide many occasions when understanding is not simply assumed or oriented to tacitly, but rather becomes an issue for participants to deal with.

Understanding itself is not only topicalized in FTD interactions; the *ways* in which understanding is made public—whether with claims, displays or demonstrations—often become the catalyst for topicalization. In other words, understanding is often topicalized in FTD interactions not only because of *what* understanding is expressed but *how* understanding is expressed and whether the means of showing understanding is contextually appropriate. More specifically, understanding becomes topicalized because *claims* or *displays* of understanding are often followed by inconsistent or conflicting *demonstrations*. As such, individuals' demonstrations do not always fulfill the interactional goals they have agreed upon with their previous claims or displays. For instance, individuals may *claim* intermediary understandings—like that in line 3a of the previous example—thereby progressing the sequence forward, and then fail to *demonstrate* understanding when the sequence reaches a moment at which such a demonstration is required to fulfill the aims of the interactional, collaborative task.

In the following interactions, I highlight the cognitive resources that may underlie individuals' abilities to successfully produce claims and displays and the cognitive resources that seem to be impaired, resulting in difficulties producing demonstrations. In addition, I explore the interactional consequences of these available and unavailable cognitive resources. The discord between claims/displays and subsequent demonstrations often leads to interlocutor attempts at resolution. Interlocutors may attempt to resolve the resulting discord by encouraging a more appropriate demonstration by physically guiding the body of the individual to *appear* more appropriately oriented to collaborative goals or by providing direct verbal instructions for the individual to follow. The analysis that follows explores, in real time, these instances of discord as well as interlocutors' responses to them. This approach helps illuminate the cognitive and communicative resources that appear most readily available to participants and helps to consider ways to best scaffold or utilize these resources in natural interaction.

APPROACH AND SIGNIFICANCE

This chapter uses videotaped recordings of interactions involving individuals with FTD and employs conversation analysis to highlight the nature of executive impairments in early stage FTD as they emerge in everyday contexts. Exploring possible connections between executive impairment and everyday functioning is important for considering the ecological validity of standard tests of executive cognition, which has been questioned. In other words, this work allows one to understand how possible executive impairment might emerge in ways that laboratory tests might not measure, ways that may be quite subtle in comparison simply because these ways are "ordinary." Accordingly, exploring these connections in everyday interactions also allows us to answer other important questions about the nature of everyday understanding and communication: Can mutual understanding be reached when the participants' references for understanding seem to be based in a different and conflicting set of "facts"? And how is mutual understanding attempted whether it is reached or not? Moreover, what happens in those moments when participants fail to reach mutual understanding, and what might we learn about ways to engage individuals with FTD?

Participants' references for understanding were referred to by Harold Garfinkel as "shared methods of practical reasoning," which Heritage and Clayman (2010, pp. 9–10) describe in the following way:

> Garfinkel argued that all human action and human institutions, including Goffman's interaction order, rest on the primordial fact that persons are able to *make shared sense* of their circumstances and act on the shared sense they make. He further argued that co-ordinated and meaningful actions, regardless of whether they involve cooperation or conflict, are impossible without these shared understandings. Garfinkel wanted to know how this is possible, and he hit on the notion that persons use *shared methods of practical reasoning* (or "ethno-methods") to build this shared sense of their common context of action, and of the social world more generally. Thus any analysis of social action is incomplete without an analysis of how social actors use shared commonsense knowledge and shared methods of reasoning in the conduct of their joint affairs. (italics in original)

Exploring how everyday understandings unfold and are organized in real time provides insights about the shared methods of practical reasoning that individuals with FTD bring to interactions, how these individuals make their understandings public in particular contexts and how caregivers understand these understandings (and of course vice versa). Exploring how these understandings are produced (i.e., with what particular interactional practices) and how and when resulting misunderstandings are resolved, ignored or left in opposition answers the more general question of whether individuals with FTD and their interlocutors are using shared methods of practical reasoning. It also provides a unique window into the black box of interaction, which has been little explored within FTD research (see, however, Joaquin, 2010; Mates et al., 2010; Mikesell, 2009, 2010). Given that FTD has been argued to especially impact social interactions and interpersonal conduct, one goal is to explore in detail how exactly (in the moment) these interactions are disrupted (or not). Such an approach helps elucidate connections between the cognitive and the social, between the experimental and the everyday, and between the experiences of caregivers and the moments that contribute to these experiences.

Individuals with FTD have been described as inappropriate and uncaring, revealing that interlocutors perceive individuals' behaviors as motivated or as constituting agentive acts and as morally bound (see Smith, 2010). Is it enough to say that individuals with FTD are inconsiderate, self-centered or socially inappropriate? These kinds of descriptions are not unhelpful—they are expressions indexing the social nature of relationships, which are imbued with moral characterizations. That is, they are embedded with moral responsibility and accountability and are therefore not unexpected given the devastation and hurt often (especially initially) embedded in FTD caregiving experiences. But such moral accountability is not just an experience or feeling, it is itself bound up in the moment-to-moment details of social action. Each interaction is built from discriminate parts that are produced turn by turn, and it is in their unfolding that perceived inconsiderate, unthoughtful or socially inappropriate moments are constructed.

Stemming in part from the work of Garfinkel, conversation analysis (CA) enables the exploration of "the procedures participants employ to construct and make intelligible their talk, and the events that occur within it" (Goodwin & Goodwin, 2000, p. 240), and it is this approach that is used here to investigate what procedures individuals with FTD and interactants employ to (attempt to) reach mutual understanding. Goodwin and Goodwin continue, "Because participants in conversation display their analysis of prior talk, the sequential organization of conversation provides rigorous, empirical ways of understanding how participants themselves make sense of the talk they are engaged in" (2000, p. 240). What Goodwin and Goodwin are suggesting is that engaging understanding is an inevitable part of ordinary social life. Every move, every turn at talk, every embodied action is decipherable to recipients as evidence of a particular understanding. As Moerman and Sacks (1988) describe it,

> understanding matters as a natural phenomenon in that conversational sequencing is built in such a way as to require that participants must continually, there and then—without recourse to follow up tests, mutual examination or memoirs, surprise quizzes and other ways of checking out on understanding—demonstrate to one other that they understood or failed to understand the talk that they are party to. (p. 85)

CA provides a way of empirically exploring how (mis)understandings are produced in their temporal and sequential contexts, how they are monitored and the range of semiotic resources that enable their production and monitoring, including language, gestures, eye gaze and other embodied responses. It does more than characterize interactions as inappropriate or unthoughtful but helps show how they may have come to be perceived that way. By exploring how understandings are produced and monitored between individuals with FTD and their interactants, this approach provides insights into what characterizes FTD interactions; how individuals with FTD and their interlocutors claim, display and demonstrate understanding; and why these claims, displays and demonstrations may be characterized as uncaring or inappropriate.

DATA AND PARTICIPANTS

The data stem from naturalistic interactions recorded in ordinary settings for the participants, namely their homes or care facility in which they live. The data include interactions highlighting three individuals diagnosed with FTD: Steve (age 72), Romeo (age 63) and Kelly[2] (age 52), and their interactants, which include spouses, caregivers, care facility staff and the ethnographers who regularly visited them. Steve was visited for 50 hours over the course of 6 months by an ethnographer (ET), who is shown in the following data, along with Steve's hired caretaker (CT). Romeo was visited for 70 hours over 16 months and primarily interacted with his wife, Juliet, who also appears in the data extracts discussed. Finally, Kelly was, at the time of data collection, living in a care facility. Interlocutors in the following data include her husband, Bron (BR); the ethnographer (ET), who visited Kelly for 35 hours over the course of 10 months; and three staff members from the care facility: Gina (GI), Rachel (RA) and Elinor (EL).

Steve and Romeo may be characterized as apathetic (Snowden et al., 2001); they initiate few exchanges and often provide minimal responses. Kelly, on the other hand, tends to be more disinhibited, initiating conversation, telling stories and expressing preferences. Kelly also exhibits perseverative behaviors, which tend to center on checking her medication schedule and using the phone. These perseverative behaviors are often disruptive to current interactional aims (see Mikesell, 2010). The following extracts have been presented in previous forums highlighting a range of discourse and caregiver practices (Mikesell, 2008, 2009, 2010; Torrisi, 2010). The following analysis explores these interactions for a different purpose—to examine how conflicts in understanding arise and the interactional "mechanisms" that seem to underlie them. Regardless of the individuals' noted clinical behaviors and symptoms, confusion seems to arise as conflicting understandings are claimed, displayed and demonstrated within a single interaction or across temporally close sequences.

ANALYSIS

In the extracts that follow, focal understandings are marked by arrows (→). Claims of understanding—those that merely indicate a hearing of the interlocutor's turn—are marked by arrows with single letters (a →). Displays of understanding, which illustrate a "deeper" understanding by providing a cognitive interpretation of the interlocutor's turn, are marked by arrows with double letters (aa →). Demonstrations of understanding showing strong evidence embedded in an embodied response are marked by arrows with triple letters (aaa →).

Claims of Understanding and Conflicting Demonstrations

Steve

In the following extract, ET suggests to Steve (SD; age 72) that they read the comics aloud together (line 1), an activity they have engaged in before. Throughout this episode, which may be characterized as the "pre-activity," Steve produces four claims of understanding that show verbal acknowledgement of or agreement with ET's previous turns (lines 2, 7, 9 and 13).

Extract 1: Steve (SD): Claims of Understanding

```
01        ET:   Oh we should do the comics again.
02 a³→    SD:   Yes we should.((SD looking down.))
03        ET:   >Y'know where they ar:e<?
04              (16.0) ((ET shuffles through newspaper and
05              sits next to SD))
06        ET:   We can do Peanuts.
07 b→     SD:   Yes we can do Peanuts.
08        ET:   You know 'em. You know it?
09 c→     SD:   I know it.
10        ET:   Um. ( ) So you c'd be (.) this character.
11              ((pointing to newspaper))
12              And I'll be (.) this girl (.) on the phone.
13 d→     SD:   ((nods)) .okay. ((ET holds newspaper up and points
14              to mark point of initiation))
```

Steve produces a modified repeat (Stivers, 2005; see Mikesell, 2010) in response to ET's suggestion of the activity in which to engage (line 2), a modified repeat confirming the terms of ET's suggestion about which comic to read (line 7), and yet another modified repeat in response to ET's inquiry that claims knowledge or understanding of the comic (line 9). At the end of this pre-activity, Steve once again claims understanding (verbally and nonverbally) by acknowledging the terms that ET has set about who will enact which character (line 13).

Thus far Steve's claims of understanding indicate that he has not only understood the activity being proposed and the terms of its arrangement; his use of modified repeats, which have been argued to do more than mere acknowledgement or agreement but also confirmation (Schegloff, 1996), indicate a close relationship to the previous turns and therefore suggest an involved level of engagement. When participants *confirm* another's turn, they are indicating that they have full access or rights to that turn. In other words, to do confirmation, one has to have both a thorough understanding of the turn and epistemic rights to the information in the turn (Schegloff, 1996; Stivers, 2005). Steve's claims of understanding may therefore be heard as indicating an engaged stance toward ET's suggestions, one that shows that he is an equal and engaged partner in deciding on the terms of the pre-activity and not merely a passive recipient (see Mikesell, 2010). Yet, despite Steve's claims, later in the sequence he *demonstrates* an understanding that conflicts with these understandings he has just *claimed* (Extract 2, line 16).

Extract 2: Steve (SD): Inconsistent Demonstration of Understanding

```
12          ET    And I'll be (.) this girl (.) on the phone.
13 d→       SD:   ((nods)) .okay. ((ET holds newspaper up and points
14                to mark point of initiation))
15          ET:   Ready, ((ET is holding paper in front of SD.))
16 eee→           (5.7) ((ET and CT look at SD))
17          CT:   No, rea[d loud (Mr. Davies).
18          ET:         [(Ow-) out loud.
19          SD:   ((reads comic aloud))
```

In lines 13–15, ET marks the end of the pre-activity and the beginning of the activity proper by holding the newspaper up for Steve to see, by pointing to the place where Steve is to begin reading, and then by explicitly initiating the commencement of the activity by announcing *Ready*. During the pre-activity, turn-by-turn, Steve has given indications that he understands and is engaged in each step in the arrangement of the activity. Although the understandings he makes public are merely claims that show rather weak evidence of his understanding, the forms they take (i.e., modified repeats) indicate an authoritative and active stance. His interlocutor orients to these claims as unproblematic, and in the context thus far, mere claims of understanding seem to be all that are warranted. That is, the turns of the pre-activity do not require a more unequivocal understanding or evidence of understanding (Mikesell, 2013). However, following the pre-activity sequence, the start of the activity proper is initiated (line 15) and a demonstration of understanding becomes relevant (line 16). Steve's character reads first in the comic, but instead of *demonstrating* an understanding—an embodied action—consonant with the understandings previously claimed, silence ensues (line 16). The silence prompts ET and CT to look toward Steve presumably to determine the nature of the misunderstanding that has occurred.

Steve's claims of understanding presumably require some cognitive work to accomplish. Perhaps at the very least, he must attend to the design features of ET's turns—the syntax and prosodic features of the turn—to be able to produce a well-timed response (Ford & Thompson, 1996; Ford, 2004), which he does without hesitation. He must also attend to the content of ET's turns (i.e., attention) in order to remember these elements (i.e., memory) and determine which ones are appropriate to recycle or re-produce as a response. Demonstrations may require a different sort of cognitive work. Although the task of reading may contribute to and therefore complicate the cognitive work being done in this demonstration, one may speculate that producing the demonstration requires more than attention and memory. It requires Steve to determine the relevance of each individual turn to the ongoing sequence so that when the activity is to begin, Steve can appropriately demonstrate his understanding of what each turn contributed to the sequence, namely, an understanding of which comic they are enacting, which character he is responsible for reading, and when the pre-activity comes to an end and the activity proper commences. That is, he must track the cumulative meaning of each turn to determine the appropriate or desirable end result of the activity sequence. Demonstrations therefore seem to demand that one be able to project (or plan) a plausible outcome (and the likely meaning) of the larger sequence.

Claims might rely on a mechanism more aptly characterized as stimulus-response in that they do not necessarily require one to determine how a single turn or adjacency pair—which is, simply stated, a turn plus immediate response—may contribute to the overarching sequence, the crux of which may be several turns away; individual turns can be produced without the element of projection or planning that demonstrations require (although interlocutors are often likely to engage turns as contributing to a larger agenda or activity). Additionally, the work of remembering in Steve's claim is also eased. The verbal content embedded in these claims recycles much of the talk that was just immediately produced, and some of the cognitive effort is therefore offloaded to the environment. Demonstrations require one to determine the relevance of each individual turn, not only for the current adjacency pair, but for the larger activity sequence. This means that to eventually produce an appropriate demonstration one must predict each turn's possible relevance for many turns later. Projecting the relevance of each turn and how turns build cumulatively in defining the meaning of the larger sequence requires an element of planning (i.e., executive functioning) that claims do not seem to require.

Interactionally, the challenge for Steve's interlocutors is not simply a result of Steve producing turns that appear "confused." In order to progress the activity, they must also figure out what the source of the confusion might be. Retrospective consideration of how the turns have unfolded up until now may yield little help. Steve's demonstrated confusion stands in such stark contrast to his previous talk that quite seamlessly progressed—indeed, seemed designed to progress—the collaborative activity. In this way, Steve illustrates his confusion "en passant" with no indication along the way that something is amiss. In order to progress the sequence and the activity embedded within it, Steve's interlocutors now must guess the source of the trouble or abandon the activity midstream. As evidenced by the many hours of video data, this latter tactic is rarely taken.

Here, in line 17, CT addresses a possible trouble source in order to continue the activity. Steve, up until this point, has claimed understanding of each individual turn, and CT's attempt to resolve Steve's inconsistent demonstration with his previous claims capitalizes on his apparent ability to negotiate each turn as it comes. In other words, when it becomes clear that Steve's action is not forthcoming, CT provides explicit verbal direction (lines 17–18) instructing Steve on what he should do next. Her targeted source of trouble is a noticeably local one. She does not treat Steve's prior claims of understanding as somehow faulty or inappropriate by, for instance, trying to re-establish which comic Steve is supposed to read or which character he is to enact. Rather she locates the source of trouble more immediately by addressing what Steve is not doing at this moment that he was expected to do, namely, reading aloud. Her location of the trouble source and attempt at resolution therefore also respect the claims of understanding Steve has made public in the previous talk.

Whereas individuals in early stages of AD are often reflective about their cognitive decline and may acknowledge explicitly when they have difficulty with recall or when they are uncertain about how to respond, individuals with FTD publicly acknowledge troubles much less often. Even in later stages of AD when individuals have been noted to repeat themselves often and unknowingly, presumably having forgotten that they expressed the same sentiment earlier in the conversation, these repetitious turns do not tend to directly conflict with each other in the way that Steve's inconsistent understandings do. These inconsistencies result in additional responsibility for interlocutors to maintain coherent conversation because they may feel compelled to resolve the inconsistency rather than ignore it or treat it as ordinary, for instance, by responding to a question every time it is asked or by "going along with" disorientations in time or place (as can be done with many communicative troubles documented in other dementias).

Romeo

In Extract 3, Romeo (RO; age 63), his wife, Juliet (JL) and the ethnographer (ET) are working on creating a prayer box for Romeo. The box is to be decorated by taping various items to the outside. In this extract, Juliet and the ethnographer are discussing its possible color, at which point Romeo begins decorating the box using the tape. Juliet reprimands him (lines 6–7; see Joaquin, 2010), telling him that he is "jumping ahead." Although Romeo claims an understanding (line 8) by verbally acknowledging Juliet's reprimand, he continues (lines 9, 13) to apply tape to the box. Romeo's claims of understanding are mere acknowledgements ("okay") of Juliet's instructions to "hold off." Nevertheless, these claims suggest that he both understands and has no need or desire to resist her instructions. Yet, fairly immediately following each of his claims, he demonstrates an inconsistent understanding by grabbing more tape. After several rounds of this, Juliet displays her own understanding (lines 23–24), seeming to realize that Romeo's demonstrations of understanding trump his claims.

Extract 3: Romeo (RO): Inconsistent Claims and Demonstrations (from Joaquin, 2010, p. 186)

01	JL:	and that's the sort of::: hot pink. But>anyways<
02	RO:	hh
03	JL:	ugh hh
04	ET:	[well color]s kinda tricky for-
05	RO:	[now what]
06	JL:	=aw Romeo Gaw h Romeo >Romeo Romeo Romeo
07		Romeo: <your jumpin ahea:d.
08 a →	RO:	okay.
09 aaa→		(1.2) ((RO gets tape from dispenser))
10	JL:	hey lets: just hold off hold off oka:y
11		((places hands on Romeo's))
12 b →	RO:	[okay]

13 bbb →		((gets tape))
14	JL:	[hold] off [**hold off**]
15 c →	RO:	[okay] now what? What?
16	JL:	hold off (.) Do you want- Romeo.
17		Do you want Romeo's pra:yer-
18		Romeo **stop** for a second.
19		Do you want Romeo's pra:yer bo:x (.)
20		to be ha:nd printed or from the computer?
21 d →	RO:	from the computer.
22 ddd →		((places tape on box))
23	JL:	I guess I ain't gonna be able to stop him (.)
24		he's ready to finish.

Although Romeo claims an understanding with his acknowledgement in line 8 of Juliet's announcement that he is jumping ahead, he rather quickly grabs more tape from the dispenser. Juliet again (line 10) attempts to curtail the behavior, telling him twice to "hold off." She accompanies her talk with an embodied gesture: she puts her hands on Romeo's as if to convey physically the significance of her verbal instruction, and he again claims understanding with his verbal acknowledgement (line 12). This sequence repeats a second time with Romeo retrieving more tape to which Juliet requests him to "hold off" and to which he responds with a claim of understanding (line 15) followed by a request for instruction ("now what?"). The third demonstration (line 22) follows after Juliet attempts to engage him in a different course of action: she asks him if he wants the cover of the box to be hand printed or digital. Nearly simultaneous with his response indicating his preference for the cover to be digital, he places more tape on the box. At this point, Juliet announces defeat, displaying her own understanding of Romeo's participation.

The activity with Steve in Extracts 1 and 2, although briefly derailed from course, was successfully completed according to the terms agreed to in the pre-activity sequence. Steve's interlocutors were able to verbally prompt him to demonstrate an appropriate understanding, one that was consistent with his previous claims and that therefore also fulfilled the expectations of the activity in progress (i.e., reading the comics). Although Juliet attempts to prompt a response from Romeo that is consonant with his claims and with her own understanding of the progression of the activity, she seems unable to do so. One challenge for Juliet (and Romeo) in this case might relate to the fact that producing a desirable demonstration requires the inhibition or absence of behavior (which becomes relevant in the following extract as well). Juliet responds to Romeo's attempts to put tape on the box as inappropriate at this stage of the activity.

His persistence in engaging in this action means that, if Juliet desires the activity to proceed differently, she must find a way to prevent Romeo from initiating the behavior. She produces explicit directives (*hold on*) and at one point a reason for her request (*you're jumping ahead*), which only momentarily derail him. An additional challenge may also be at work here. Not only does the desired behavior (of refraining from adhering tape to the box) require the inhibition of behavior, it requires inhibition of the behavior over time. Juliet's instructions ask Romeo to inhibit this behavior, not just in response to one single turn (or directive), but throughout the course of this part of the activity in which *plans* for decorating the box seem to be taking place (as opposed to actually decorating the box).

Inhibiting a behavior across an entire interactional sequence may rely on similar executive functions as those discussed in relation to Extracts 1 and 2. Planning and complex decision-making have been found to be impaired in individuals with FTD, and although it may not be immediately obvious as to what qualifies this particular decision as "complex," it requires a demonstration and may therefore require additional cognitive resources than the claims Romeo is able to produce: The demonstration requires Romeo to not only understand what Juliet is asking of him in that moment, but to understand how this action is embedded within the larger activity sequence, which in turn requires him to determine the end goal of the activity being planned. Determining the end goal of an activity requires planning (or an understanding of someone else's planning) and presumably executive functioning. Romeo must track turns and adjacency pairs across the planning stages of this sequence and determine their relevance to a final outcome. Similar to Extracts 1 and 2, the work seems to require more than just determining the relevance of isolated, individual steps in the planning stage of this activity, but determining how each individual step helps arrive at the end goal.

Displays of Understanding and Conflicting Demonstrations

Kelly

The following extract highlights perseverative behaviors, a diagnostic criterion for FTD (see also Mikesell, 2010). In these data, Kelly repeatedly checks a medication chart that is located in her room at the facility where she is staying. This compulsive checking is often disruptive because Kelly may disengage from an activity to check the chart in her room. To render her obsessive checking less disruptive, the staff at Kelly's facility have provided her with a portable, pocket-size chart that is kept in her purse. However, Kelly still, at times, will attempt to leave her current location to go to her room to check the larger chart. In this extract, ET and Kelly are in her room discussing whether Kelly is able to teach piano[4] in the new facility. When Kelly starts to check the larger chart (line 6), ET tries to encourage her to rely on the portable chart (lines 7, 9). Similar to Steve and Romeo, Kelly produces several claims of understanding that are similarly parasitic on her interlocutor's previous turns attempting to get her to check her portable chart.

Extract 4: Kelly (KE) [2/26/07.A, 6:10–6:52]: Claims

```
01      ET:   are you able to teach anybody here? (. [  ) any
02      KE:                                      [((cough))
03      ET:   you know have any um (0.3) students (.) to teach
04            piano to?
05      KE:   so far nobody.⁵
06            (0.3)
07      ET:   che[ck your-] check your bag instead of that (.)
08      KE:      [(       )]
09      ET:   'cause I think they say the same thing.
10            (1.3)
11      KE:   's (one)?
12            (5.6)
13 a→   KE:   Oh yea, it does say the same thing.
14            (0.3)
15 b→   KE:   You're right it does.
16            (3.1)
17 c→   KE:   Yea.
18            (2.1)
19 d→   KE:   Same thing itn' it.
20      ET:   Yeah.
21            (0.3)
```

Kelly recognizes that the pocket chart contains the same information as the larger chart; that is, she claims understanding of the understanding that ET makes public earlier in the sequence (line 9). Like Steve's claims of understanding in Extracts 1–2, Kelly's claim in line 13 is also a strong verbal agreement that repeats a significant portion of ET's earlier turn in line 9 (i.e., a modified repeat). Her claim in line 13 is thus not only agreeing, but confirming ET's observation in line 9 (Stivers, 2005). Additionally, Kelly produces claims of understanding four separate times (lines 13, 15, 17 and 19) as she inspects the chart. Such a thorough inspection and comparison of the charts as well as the repetition of claims may make these "mere" claims appear adamant and genuine.

In Extract 5, Kelly "upgrades" her claims by producing a *display* of understanding (line 26). Unlike the claims of understanding, her display provides a cognitive or intellectual interpretation of ET's just prior turn; that is, Kelly produces a reformulation about why the portable chart is better that ET did not articulate. As such, Kelly's display constitutes an understanding that is independent from the understandings produced by ET. Specifically, in lines 22–23 and 25, ET reasons that the portable chart is preferable because Kelly will not "have to bother with getting up." In line 26, Kelly again agrees with ET but this time does so by reformulating ET's turn in her own words, thereby showing her independent access to ET's reasoning about why the portable chart is preferred.

Extract 5: Kelly (KE) [2/26/07.A, 6:10–6:52]: Displays

```
13 a→    KE:   Oh yea, it does say the same thing.
14             (0.3)
15 b→    KE:   You're right it does.
16             (3.1)
17 c→    KE:   Yea.
18             (2.1)
19 d→    KE:   Same thing itn' it.
20       ET:   °Yeah.
21             (0.3)
22       ET:   so that way (0.4) because it's in there (.)
23             [you don't have to bother with getting up
24       KE:   [(      )=
25       ET:   and checking it there.=
26 ee→   KE:   =keep walking o[ver.
27       ET:                  [yeah.
28             (0.4)
29       ET:   yeah.
30 f→    KE:   °'ts true.
```

As discussed in Mikesell (2013), Kelly's display shows independent agreement in ways her claims do not. Her interpretation of ET's turn therefore seems to require more cognitive work to produce. Nevertheless, such a display does not demonstrate that agreement within a larger course of action. In other words, her display of understanding, although showing independent cognitive access to ET's own reasoning, is not an embodied production of that understanding, which Kelly later fails to produce. Approximately two minutes following Kelly's claims and display of understanding about the benefits of the portable chart, Kelly is faced with an opportunity to produce such a demonstration, but she fails to do so. Instead she begins to check the larger chart in her room (line 7).

Extract 6: Kelly (KE) [2/26/07.A, 9:05–10:20]: Inconsistent Demonstrations

```
01              ET:    I have a sister.
02                     (0.4)
03              KE:    You get along with her (well)?
04                     (.)
05              ET:    yea, (.) I do. Very much so.
06                     >I saw< her this weekend.
07 aaa→                (0.3) ((KE gets up to check the large chart))
08              ET:    >check-< check your bag, not- not this one
09              KE:    Check my bag?=
10              ET:    -yeah. 'Cause remember it's in there?
11                     (3.6)
12              KE:    oh this one?
13              ET:    yeah.
14                     (1.1)
15 b→           KE:    oh yeah. It's there too.
16              ET:    yeah.
17              KE:    now I see I've g[ot (      )
18              ET:                    [ehh it's the better one.
19                     (0.6)
20 cc→          KE:    ((clears throat)) it'smaller.
21              ET:    yeah. (          ) go back once you've used that one.
22                     (1.3)
23 d(d)→        KE:    it's got exactly the same information on it.
24                     (1.4)
25              ET:    I saw you lookin' at it during, (.) church.
26              KE:    yeah.
```

Upon Kelly's inconsistent demonstration, ET reminds her to check the portable chart in her bag. Kelly inspects the chart (line 14), then claims understanding once again by agreeing with ET's turn in line 10. She further agrees with ET's assessment of the chart as "better" by displaying another understanding (line 20), that is by formulating an independent assessment of the chart that reveals why, in Kelly's opinion, the chart could be rightly assessed as "the better one" (line 18), namely because it is "smaller" (line 20). In line 23, Kelly again notes that the smaller chart is not lacking in information despite its smaller size. Although this understanding was made public by ET earlier in Extract 4, Kelly produces it here as if independently produced. These displays upgrade her previous claims, providing further insight (or independent understanding) about how Kelly perceives the portable chart.

Kelly is known to perseverate on checking about her medication, and as such it may come as little surprise that she shows difficulty demonstrating an embodied understanding that attempts to alter this behavior. Nevertheless, it is interesting that she not only claims an understanding of why the suggested alternative behavior is better, but she is also cognitively capable of formulating the logical benefits of the suggested behavior, which reflect Kelly's intact intellectual reasoning. Such intact intellectual capacities may render her conflicting demonstrations more surprising to an unfamiliar interlocutor, although a familiar interlocutor may learn to realize the limits of the understandings she makes public. Indeed, as Mikesell (2010) discusses, whereas ET (a somewhat unfamiliar interlocutor) might continue to reason with Kelly for quite some time, accepting at face value her negotiation of individual turns that indicate agreement about the use of the portable chart and willingness to comply with the alternative behavior, her husband, rather than continuing to reason with her, often deflects the sequence fairly quickly to new topics.

Such topic shifts may ease caregiver burden because if carers can maintain Kelly's focus on a conversational activity, they are less likely to be required to monitor her demonstrations and resolve discrepancies. Additionally, these conversational topic shifts seem to enable Kelly to participate in ways that take advantage of the cognitive and communicative resources most available to her, namely her intellectual capacity. Her intellectual capacity reflects rational thought and argumentation, but perhaps little executive functioning. In Extract 3, for Romeo to inhibit his behavior and therefore produce a demonstration consonant with his claim, he would have had to track the relevance of the turns that his claims were embedded within and determine their relevance to the larger sequence. Kelly is being expected to track the relevance of these turns, not only in the immediate context, but presumably across sequences and activities. To produce displays, Kelly need not track multiple turns and anticipate how each turn contributes to a larger action sequence. Similar to claims, producing displays also does not seem to require planning or multitasking (i.e., simultaneously holding multiple turns and their significance in mind) in the way that demonstrations seem to. Providing conversational spaces that take advantage of Kelly's preserved intellectual reasoning and difficulty projecting or planning sequences allowed lengthier periods of engagement without interruption or interference from her perseverative behaviors (Mikesell, 2010).

Co-producing Demonstrations

Just as others have noted about emotional displays (Goodwin & Goodwin, 2000) and other psychological states, understanding is typically believed to originate from within an individual. Even within interactional approaches, it may be assumed that understanding—whether claimed, displayed or demonstrated—is realized and made public by a single individual. Although, in the previous extracts, the analysis highlighted the conflicting understandings produced by individuals with FTD and the different kinds of cognitive work required to produce them, it was also apparent how these understandings impact an interactional sequence and result in attempts from interlocutors to produce more consistent or desirable demonstrations. In the following extract, I continue to look at how demonstrations of understanding are co-constructed, that is, how they come to be made public through the efforts of more than one participant.

In the previous extracts, individuals with FTD produced conflicting understandings. Interlocutors often attempted to resolve these conflicts in understanding in order for the activity in progress to be achieved (Extracts 1–3) or in order for the current (and potentially future) interaction(s) to progress without interruption (Extracts 4–6). In the following extract, Kelly does not demonstrate an understanding that conflicts with a previous claim or display. Rather she demonstrates an understanding that is inconsistent with the understandings made public by the other participants. Although other participants orient to a particular activity in the following extracts, Kelly does not show a similar orientation. As a result, another interactant—her spouse—responds by physically guiding Kelly so that such a demonstration is produced.

In Extract 7 (see also Mikesell, 2010; Torrisi, 2010), Kelly and Bron are sitting around a table with ET and two facility staff members—Elinor (EL) and Rachel (RA)—eating cookies. Gina (GI), another staff member, comes in with several glasses of water on a tray. When setting them down on the table, Gina spills the water, at which point everyone tries to console her and starts helping to clean up the spill (starting at line 6). In line 39 Kelly begins to visibly disengage from the activity that the other participants are orienting to by standing up and moving away from the center of focus. Consequently, Kelly's demonstration is treated by her spouse as in need of repair, and in line 43 he works to have her embody or demonstrate a different understanding, one that aligns with the demonstrated understanding of the other participants.

Extract 7: Kelly [2/26/07.A, 9:05–10:20]: *Water Spill*

```
06   ET:   It's okay. ((begins to soak up spilled water))
07         (1.1)
08   GI:   ooo[:hh
09   EL:      [It's jus' water. ((reaches over to pick up
10         glasses))
11         (      ) ((attending to mess))
12   RA:   he he he he he heh
13   GI:      [oh
14   ET:   It's [okay. (0.5) I've done that.
15   EL:       [It's no problem.
16         (0.5) ((Gina turns around to get something))
17   ET:   I was a waiter. ((Kelly looking at her cookie))
18   GI:   Sorry. ((whispers; bumps camera))
19   RA:   Wake up.
20   GI:   he he I'm n(h)ot a w(hh)ai[(h)t(h)er.
21   KE:                             [((leans to talk to Bron))
22   BR:   What?
23         (0.5)
24   GI:   (That's alright. I'll do [it.)
25   RA:                            [That's fine. ((Kelly looks at
26         Bron, then her food))
27   GI:   ohhh
28   EL:   This is why it's good you're going into nursing.
29         ((Bron points toward the others to orient Kelly))
30   BR:   ha h[a ha:
31   ET:       [>he he he he<
32   GI:   he he (.) he he
            ((6 seconds omitted))
36   GI:   I'm fi:ne.
37         (      )
38   EL:   (Ok, it's just) water.
39 →      ((Kelly stands, looking toward table, eating cookie))
40   ET:   I've done it with lots of be:er in front of a bunch of
41         gu:[ys
42   BR:      [(sit down) sit down because it's wet (t's wet)
43 →      ((grabs Kelly's purse strap, pulls gently))
44   KE:   How long are we supposed to stay here ((to Bron))
45   ET:   'n they all like cla:pped, ((gestures clapping hands))
46         'n then I was [like he he he
47 → ET:                 [((Kelly sits down))
```

Just prior to Bron's intervention, Kelly demonstrated a very different embodied understanding toward the activity when she physically disengaged from it, one that was inconsistent with the other participants and therefore could be viewed as inappropriate or uncooperative. Indeed, Bron treats her demonstration as inappropriate and works to get her to demonstrate a different understanding. When Bron pulls on Kelly's purse strap, he prompts Kelly to demonstrate an understanding that indicates engagement with the collaborative activity of cleaning up. Although Kelly does not participate in cleaning up the spill, she is now physically positioned facing the spill and therefore oriented to the focal point of the current collaborative activity.

Kelly's demonstration possesses most of the characteristics shown in Table 6.1, but it is not her demonstration alone. Moreover, we can see how collaboratively produced demonstrations of understanding may be responsive to two levels of activity. Kelly's embodied re-orientation, which is a local response to her husband's guidance or prompting (see line 47), simultaneously embodies a response to the larger collaborative activity occupying everyone's attention in the room. Thus, the act of co-construction reveals as much about the intentions of Bron as it does about Kelly's, and these intentions may not necessarily align toward a common interactional goal. In this way, Kelly's response simultaneously addresses the more local activity of responding to her husband and (superficially) orients toward the larger overarching activity of attending to the mess on the table. Considering the cognitive work that genuine demonstrations seem to require, one may conclude that Kelly's local response to her husband's prompting does not require the same cognitive capacity. Regardless of whether Kelly does or does not want to participate in cleaning up the spill, her "demonstration," being guided and therefore local to her husband's prompting, does not require Kelly to determine the cumulative relevance of previous turns within the activity sequence, how these turns contribute to the larger activity or the relevance of her local response to the larger activity in progress.

Although Kelly's constructed demonstration may visibly show an embodied understanding more consistent with those around her, one may question how Kelly herself perceives this demonstration given that it is initiated by someone else. Although demonstrations may often provide definitive and transparent understandings, when such embodied demonstrations are co-constructed by multiple participants, that transparency may be reduced or become questionable. That is, Kelly's embodied actions, through the physical guidance of her husband, show on the surface a particular demonstration of understanding that Kelly herself may not intend to demonstrate but does demonstrate in her more localized response to her husband. This extract shows how understandings are at once both individual/personal and collective/public and that it can be difficult to tease these worlds apart.

While this may pose analytic difficulties, there are perhaps some insights that can be drawn. In the previous extracts, demonstrations of understanding seemed particularly challenging for carers to inhibit or prevent. This difficulty seems to be exacerbated when behaviors deemed inappropriate by carers are undesirable throughout the course of a sequence or activity or even beyond the bounds of that single sequence/ activity (i.e., when a carer might also intend to prevent a later inappropriate behavior as in Extracts 3 and 4–6). Individuals with FTD seem to be particularly adept at responding locally to individual turns with claims or displays of understanding. Challenges arise more frequently when one must track these local turns across sequences or activities, resulting in more permanent or ongoing changes in demonstrated understandings. This kind of tracking may pose considerable (cognitive) burden. These undesirable demonstrated understandings are not just undesirable at that one moment and therefore require planning; they require one to extrapolate the meaning of the current prompted demonstration to later in the sequence or across sequences. Producing more desirable demonstrations of understanding, such as in Extracts 1 and 2 with Steve and in Extract 7 with Kelly, may appear more successful because Steve and Kelly produce demonstrations that are locally prompted (Extract 1 and 2) or co-produced (Extract 7). These prompts and co-productions may require less executive functioning to produce. By lessening the executive cognitive work for those in their care to produce appropriate demonstrations, carers are acting as external frontal lobes (Joaquin, 2010). While demonstrations may be particularly difficult to feign and also appear more challenging for individuals with FTD to independently produce, they are more easily co-produced given that they are visible understandings produced by bodily practices (as opposed to verbal and cognitive displays). Individuals can be locally prompted to produce (or co-produce) them even if one's cognitive understanding does not change.

DISCUSSION
Cognitive and Communicative Resources

Individuals with dementia are often characterized as confused. The previous analysis examines the nature of such confusion by exploring claims, displays and demonstrations of understandings in ordinary interactions involving individuals with FTD. From this examination, it seems that this confusion does not, in most cases, stem from a simple lack of or poor access to informational or procedural knowledge, nor does confusion seem to stem from deficits in linguistic or perceptual impairment that might be more commonly assessed on standard measures of (neuro)cognition. Confusion was embedded in how individuals made ordinary understandings public. Specifically, individuals with FTD often produced verbal claims and even displays of understanding that aligned with the activity being introduced and negotiated. These understandings indicate that certain cognitive capacities, particularly those that enable individuals to respond to individual turns and illustrate intellectual reasoning, are unproblematic. However, these claims and displays appear to be excessively local in scope (Mikesell, 2008)—they respond immediately to the previous turns and indicate an intention to follow through when a demonstration might be required. But when that demonstration of understanding becomes relevant, individuals often express a conflicting understanding by producing an embodied action that is incongruent with their previous claims and displays. Such mixed messages, which become apparent with the (absent) production of the demonstrations, often stalled the activity-in-progress and elicited "intervention" by other participants.

Interestingly, both loss of insight (suggesting cognitive decline) and intact reasoning (suggesting cognitive stability) may contribute to these conflicting demonstrations. First, loss of insight may result in individuals holding an inaccurate perception of what they are capable of accomplishing, which may in turn lead them to assert more authority or stronger forms of understanding than they possess. In other words, these inflated perceptions about one's capacity may contribute to individuals' acknowledgements and confirmations of interlocutors' individual turns, which often indicate a more authoritative stance or involved level of engagement in the activity in progress. However, the work required to maintain this indicated or perceived level of engagement throughout a sequence may pose additional burdens, which individuals may also inaccurately perceive, and the result is a conflicting demonstration of understanding.

Second, intact intellectual reasoning, memory and perceptual abilities may also contribute to individuals' ability to produce claims and displays of understanding, which may, perhaps surprisingly, verbalize logical analysis of another's turn and rational argumentation (Extracts 5 and 6). This ability to intellectually reason and interpret another's turn, however, does not seem sufficient for an individual to appropriately anticipate or project the relevance of the reasoning or translate that reasoning into action. This dissociation between reasoning and action has been most commonly characterized as a capacity to know the rules but an inability to follow them. For instance, when asked why shoplifting is inappropriate, an individual with FTD might be able to explain the negative consequences that may result and yet still not behave in accordance with this articulated reasoning. This dissociation seems to manifest as well in ordinary talk and interaction. Although the consequences or repercussions of the dissociation may seem less significant or severe in these contexts, interlocutors face them regularly.

Although tests of executive functioning, as it has been traditionally measured in neuropsychology, have produced an inconsistent profile of the cognitive abilities of FTD (see Roca et al., 2013; Shallice & Burgess, 1991), more recent tests of executive functioning attempt to capture executive skills in real-life tasks and contexts (e.g., Burgess, 2002; Manly, Hawkins, Evans, Woldt & Robertson, 2002). Planning, multitasking and more complex decision-making have been shown to be impaired (Torralva et al., 2009), and this chapter revealed how these deficits to plan and multitask might emerge in everyday interactions. In order to produce an appropriate demonstration, one must not only *remember* and *attend to* the previous turns or intellectually reason an immediate or local response (which may require unaffected cognitive skills such as memory, attention and intellectual reasoning), one must also be able to track and project their significance to a larger context and overarching agenda of the entire sequence and sometimes beyond a single sequence. Such projection requires an element of planning and may even be considered multitasking in the most everyday sense since the interactional significance of the previous turns and adjacency pairs have to be considered simultaneously.

Traditional tests of executive functioning have been criticized for lacking ecological validity, and the case of FTD has brought this concern to the fore. Torralva et al. (2009), for instance, remark that regarding FTD, "traditional testing environments may fail to induce executive deficits, making assessment of this cognitive domain particularly challenging" (p. 1307). They also note that if one's "environment poses little demand on certain skills, executive deficits may have no impact on real-life settings" and that "minor executive deficits can become especially impairing in highly demanding environments" (p. 1307). The tests of these skills, for example, the Multiple Errands Test (Burgess, 2002) and Hotel Task (Manly et al., 2002), may certainly be considered everyday tasks that any typical individual would be expected to be able to perform and that may be absent from the environments of individuals with FTD. However, the videotaped data I explore in this chapter suggest that the skills implicated in executive tasks such as multitasking and complex planning do indeed emerge in ordinary interactions—in environments that are presumably not "highly demanding"—but may do so in unexpected ways or in ways not immediately recognizable as "executive." These more ordinary interactional and conversational tasks are more difficult for carers to scaffold or remove from individuals' natural environments, and as suggested from the previous data, the task of demonstrating understanding seems to be one of these more ordinary tasks in which these executive impairments emerge.

Exploring real-world interactions between individuals with FTD and their carers is crucial for accomplishing two complementary aims. This work helps characterize the cognitive abilities and impairments of individuals with FTD in everyday contexts in order to establish connections between traditional laboratory tests of executive functioning and the real world. Additionally, characterizing these abilities and impairments in ordinary contexts may also provide caregivers with insights about how they might engage individuals they care for. Much research on caregivers of individuals with FTD aims to better understand carers' perceptions of their caregiving experiences and related burden and anxiety (Mioshi, Bristow, Cook & Hodges, 2009; Piguet, Hornberger, Mioshi & Hodges, 2011). However, little work has been done to examine problems of communication and misunderstanding with individuals with FTD as they unfold in real time. Such an investigation contributes to a better understanding of the nature of communication breakdowns—where do breakdowns occur and why do carers of FTD report such high levels of frustration—and to more careful consideration of potential strategies carers may use to reduce misunderstanding and caregiver burden and anxiety (see next section).

Caring for and Communicating with Individuals with FTD

An interactional approach to everyday understandings in dementia discourse may enhance caregivers' awareness of what kinds of interactional challenges are common and where problems are likely to occur. This awareness may help foster more productive interactions and less frustration because caregivers have clearer expectations about the kinds of problems that may arise and may be more prepared to handle and understand them. Although I have suggested connections between executive impairments as discussed in the neuropsychological literature and challenges in producing demonstrations of understanding, these data cannot definitely point to the precise mechanisms responsible. Regardless, examining the interactional challenges (of whatever cognitive impairments are responsible) may be most beneficial for caregivers since they are likely to experience difficulties as interactional challenges and not as cognitive dysfunction. Interactionally, claims and displays of understanding produced by individuals with FTD often do not seem to be in the service of an overarching activity, but rather they seem to be activities in their own right. That is, they don't appear to be a means to an end, but ends in themselves. In this way, individuals are oriented locally to turns when their interlocutors are often oriented to larger activities. In a sense, participants with FTD can maintain conversations in a turn-by-turn fashion, but there is often little "follow-through."

One consequence is that in interactions that are brief, structured and require primarily local responses to turns, participants might perceive the individual with FTD as being cooperative and caring because the interactional context only requires a claim or display of understanding and no awareness of a larger, overarching activity. However, in collaborative activities in which a demonstration becomes appropriate or relevant, participants may experience the individual with FTD as being uncooperative or uncaring. In short, individuals with FTD can engage in ways that are experienced as cooperative and caring and can engage in ways that are experienced as quite the opposite. Understandably, caregivers may find this inconsistent and perhaps motivated.

Additionally, and as the interactional data discussed previously may suggest, the "motivation" underlying these conflicts of understanding is likely to be difficult to perceive since sometimes these conflicts are produced over a brief interval of time and sometimes they are produced over a longer time interval. That is, because the resulting conflict seems dependent on the nature of the activity in progress and because activities vary considerably, it may be challenging for caregivers to experience these inconsistencies as patterned or as resulting from an individual's incapacity (which may in turn contribute to perceptions of the individuals' actions as uncaring and uncooperative). Indeed in my own discussions with caregivers, they were themselves often confused by the confusion of their loved ones. On the surface, confusion may appear random and inconsistent and caregivers seemed to at times experience it this way. One caregiver, for instance, noted that "yes might mean no and no might mean yes" but seemed unable to articulate when this might be the case.

An understanding of the nature of the breakdowns that occur in interactions may be important in increasing awareness and reducing frustration since caregivers may be able to predict when conflicts in understanding may arise or be less surprised when they do. Beyond awareness, this work highlighting the available cognitive and communicative resources also provides insights about ways caregivers might engage individuals that allow more balanced and effective participation. For instance, when misunderstanding became apparent in Extracts 1 and 2, Steve's caregiver located the trouble source locally in the very prior turn or demonstration, and her response resulted in a quick fix that prompted Steve to address the immediate source of trouble. Had she tried to locate the trouble source elsewhere in the sequence, for instance, by re-establishing the terms of the pre-activity, this might have created more confusion and perhaps frustration as well.

Although Juliet eventually surrenders to Romeo's persistence with the tape, we learn something about the nature of his engagement in collaborative activities that may also help caregivers consider best practices. Indeed her surrender may not be considered a defeat. Many caregivers in the larger study from which these data were drawn felt it important that individuals in their care participate in activities but often felt conflicted about the goal: the successful completion of the activity or mere participation in the activity. Nevertheless, most caregivers felt it important that their loved ones remain engaged and involved and made significant efforts to organize activities in which those in their care could participate. The examined interactions, because they indicate that collaborative activity may be challenging for individuals to accomplish without being prompted more locally at each step, may help caregivers organize activities for which the finished product is not required to be precise, in which caregivers also wish to be highly involved and/or which require few steps to accomplish (and therefore do not require attending across many turns and sequences to an overarching aim).

Given lack of insight and waning social emotional responses, FTD has been described as disrupting the quality of life and satisfaction of the family members more than of the individuals themselves, in part because disruptions in everyday life appear more severe than those described for individuals with Alzheimer's (Piguet et al., 2011). FTD caregivers report considerably high needs, burden and amounts of emotional distress, more so than those reported by caregivers of individuals with Alzheimer's disease (Nicolaou, Egan, Gasson & Kane, 2010; Mioshi et al., 2009; Piguet et al., 2011; Riedijk et al., 2006). FTD caregivers also report less relationship satisfaction (Ascher et al., 2010). Pronounced caregiver burden has been linked to behavioral changes of patients as well as patients' (in)ability to manage daily functioning (Piguet et al., 2011). In interviews with caregivers from the larger project, caregivers also expressed concerns about how much agency to attribute to the patient. While caregivers did not typically voice this dilemma as an issue of "agency," they expressed uneasy feelings about trust, believability and knowing limits.

At the same time, they often, to varying degrees, discussed individuals' behaviors as meaningful in particular ways even when behaviors were not immediately interpretable. Thus, on the one hand, caregivers questioned individuals' agency and lamented that their words could not always be trusted, their reflections and reports were not always accurate, even opinions and preferences did not always appear to be genuine. On the other hand, caregivers responded to questionable or ambiguous behaviors as motivated for particular purposes. The kind of work that caregivers underwent to come to terms with these apparently conflicting beliefs about individuals' agency seemed particularly challenging. These are fundamentally concerns about how individuals with FTD make understandings public and how interactants in turn come to perceive these understandings. The discussion presented here was intended to help caregivers make some sense of these understandings—to help caregivers more easily recognize the cognitive and communicative resources available to individuals with FTD, provide them a framework for engaging communicative misunderstandings and inconsistencies, and hopefully inspire insights about how to better communicate with those they care for.

NOTES

1. Turns and sequences are described rather extensively in Schegloff (2007), but what is most relevant for this chapter is an awareness that turns at talk build larger sequences. The following passage from Schegloff (2007) becomes particularly relevant for the analyses that follow: Each turn "can be inspected by co-participants to see what action(s) may be done through it. And all *series* of turns can be inspected or tracked (the parties and by us) to see what course(s) of action may be being progressively enacted through them, what possible responses may be being made relevant, what outcomes are being pursued, what 'sequences' are being constructed or enacted or projected. That is, sequences of turns are not haphazard but have a shape or structure, and can be tracked for where they came from, what is being done through them, and where they might be going" (p. 3).
2. All names are pseudonyms. All participants (individuals with FTD and frequent interlocutors likely to be observed and recorded) were made aware of study aims and presented with Institutional Review Board–approved study consent forms. Capacity to consent was determined for individuals with FTD, and, in all cases, proxy consent was also provided by the primary family caregiver.
3. Not all claims, displays and demonstrations of understanding are highlighted in the transcripts, only those that are most relevant for the analysis being presented in the text.
4. Prior to moving into the care facility, Kelly taught piano lessons in her home.
5. This turn also constitutes a display of understanding, but is not highlighted here because it is not relevant for the current discussion (see note 3).

REFERENCES

Ascher, E. A., Sturm, V. E., Seider, B. H., Holley, S. R., Miller, B. L., & Levenson, R. W. (2010). Relationship satisfaction and emotional language in frontotemporal dementia and Alzheimer disease patients and spousal caregivers. *Alzheimer Disease and Associative Disorders, 24*(1), 49–55.

Avineri, N. (2010). The interactive organization of 'insight': Clinical interviews with frontotemporal dementia patients. In A. W. Mates, L. Mikesell, & M. S. Smith (Eds.), *Discourse, sociality and frontotemporal dementia: Reverse engineering the social mind* (pp. 115–138). London: Equinox.

Burgess, P. (2002). Development of a simplified version of the multiple errands test for use in hospital settings. *Neuropsychological Rehabilitation, 12,* 231–255.

Fernandez-Duque, D., & Black, S. E. (2007). Metacognitive judgment and denial of deficit: Evidence from frontotemporal dementia. *Judgment and Decision Making, 2*(5), 359–370.

Ford, C. E. (2004). Contingency and units in interaction. *Discourse Studies, 6*(1), 27–52.

Ford, C. E., & Thompson, S. (1996). Interactional units in conversation: Syntactic, intonational, and pragmatic resources for the management of turns. In E. Ochs, E. A. Schegloff, & S. A. Thompson (Eds.), *Interaction and grammar* (pp. 134–184). Cambridge: Cambridge University Press.

Goodwin, M. H., & Goodwin, C. (2000). Emotion within situated activity. In A. Duranti (Ed.), *Linguistic anthropology: A reader* (pp. 239–257). Malden, MA: Blackwell.

Gregory, C. A., Lough, S., Stone, V., Erzinclioglu, S. H., Martin, L., Baron-Cohen, S., Hodges, J. R. (2002). Theory of mind in patients with frontal variant frontotemporal dementia and Alzheimer's disease: Theoretical and practical implications. *Brain, 125,* 752–764.

Grossman, M. (2002). Frontotemporal dementia: A review. *Journal of the International Neuropsychological Society, 8,* 564–583.

Heritage, J., & Clayman, S. (2010). *Talk in action: Interactions, identities, and institutions.* Malden, MA: Wiley-Blackwell.

Hindmarsh, J., Reynolds, P., & Dunne, S. (2011). Exhibiting understanding: The body in apprenticeship. *Journal of Pragmatics, 43,* 489–503.

Hodges, J. R. (2007). Overview of frontotemporal dementia. In J. R. Hodges (Ed.), *The frontotemporal dementia syndromes* (pp. 1–24). Cambridge, UK: Cambridge University Press.

Hodges, J. R., & Miller, B. (2001). Classification, genetics and neuropathology of frontotemporal dementia. Introduction to the special topics papers, part 1. *Neurocase, 7,* 31–35.

Jagust, W. J., Reed, B. R., Seab, J. P., Kramer, J. H., & Budinger, T. F. (1989). Clinical-physiologic correlates of Alzheimer's disease and frontal lobe dementia. *American Journal of Physiology Imaging, 4,* 89–96.

Joaquin, A. D. L. (2010). The prefrontal cortex: Through maturation, socialization and regression. In A. W. Mates, L. Mikesell, & M. S. Smith (Eds.), *Discourse, sociality and frontotemporal dementia: Reverse engineering the social mind* (pp. 167–198). London: Equinox.

Kipps, C., Knibb, J., & Hodges, J. R. (2007). Clinical presentations of frontotemporal dementia. In J. R. Hobbs (Ed.), *Frontotemporal dementia syndrome* (pp. 38–79). Cambridge, UK: Cambridge University Press.

Manly, T., Hawkins, K., Evans, J., Woldt, K., & Robertson, I. H. (2002). Rehabilitation of executive function: A facilitation of effective goal management on complex tasks using periodic auditory alerts. *Neuropsychologia, 40*, 2671–2681.

Mates, A. W., Mikesell, L., & Smith, M. S. (Eds.). (2010). *Discourse, sociality and frontotemporal dementia: Reverse engineering the social mind.* London: Equinox.

Mikesell, L. (2008). Common conversational practices of a frontotemporal dementia patient: Negotiating turns, getting lost in sequences. Research poster presentation. Center for Language, Interaction and Culture (CLIC), Los Angeles, CA. May 23, 2008.

Mikesell, L. (2009). Conversational practices of a frontotemporal dementia patient and his interlocutors. *Research on Language and Social Interaction, 42*(2), 135–162.

Mikesell, L. (2010). Examining perseverative behaviors of a frontotemporal dementia patient and caregiver responses: The benefits of observing ordinary interactions and reflections on caregiver stress. In A. W. Mates, L. Mikesell, & M. S. Smith (Eds.), *Discourse, sociality and frontotemporal dementia: Reverse engineering the social mind* (pp. 85–113). London: Equinox.

Mikesell, L. (2013). *The pragmatics of understanding in talk-in-interaction: Evidence from interactions with individuals with frontotemporal dementia.* Unpublished manuscript.

Miller, B. L., Seeley, W. W., Mychack, P., Rosen, H. J., Mena, I., & Boone, K. (2001). Neuroanatomy of the self: Evidence from patients with frontotemporal dementia. *Neurology, 4*, 771–780.

Mioshi, E., Bristow, M., Cook, R., & Hodges, J. R. (2009). Factors underlying caregiver stress in frontotemporal dementia and Alzheimer's disease. *Dementia and Geriatric Cognitive Disorders, 27*, 76–81.

Moerman, M., & Sacks, H. (1988). On understanding in the analysis of natural conversation. In M. Moerman (Ed.), *Talking culture* (pp. 180–186). Philadelphia: University of Pennsylvania Press. Originally published 1971.

Neary, D., Snowden, J. S., Gustafson, L., Passant, U., Stuff, D., Black, S., Freedman, M. . . . Benson, D. F. (1998). Frontotemporal lobar degeneration: A consensus on clinical diagnostic criteria. *Neurology, 51*, 1546–1554.

Nicolaou, P. L., Egan, S. J., Gasson, N., & Kane, R. T. (2010). Identifying needs, burden, and distress of career of people with frontotemporal dementia compared to Alzheimer's disease. *Dementia, 9*, 215–235.

Piguet, O., Hornberger, M., Mioshi, E., & Hodges, J. R. (2011). Behavioural-variant frontotemporal dementia: Diagnosis, clinical, staging, and management. *The Lancet, 10*(2), 162–172.

Rankin, K. P., Baldwin, E., Pace-Savitsky, C., Kramer, J. H., & Miller, B. L. (2005). Self awareness and personality change in dementia. *Journal of Neurology, Neurosurgery, and Psychiatry, 76*, 632–639.

Ratnavalli, E., Brayne, C., Dawson, K., & Hodges, J. R. (2002). The prevalence of frontotemporal dementia. *Neurology, 58*(11), 1615–1621.

Riedijk, S. E., De Vugt, M. E., Duivenvoorden, H. J., Niermeijer, M. F., van Swieten, J. C., Verhey, F. R. J., Tibben, A. (2006). Caregiver burden, health-related quality of life and coping in dementia caregivers: A comparison of frontotemporal dementia and Alzheimer's disease. *Dementia and Geriatric Cognitive Disorders, 22,* 405–412.

Roca, M., Manes, F., Gleichgerrcht, E., Watson, P., Ibanez, A., Thompson, R . . . Duncan, J. (2013). Intelligence and executive functioning in frontotemporal dementia. *Neuropsychologia, 51,* 725–730.

Sacks, H. (1992). *Lectures on conversation [1964–72],* 2 vols. Oxford: Basil.

Schegloff, E. A. (1992). Repair after next turn: The last structurally provided defense of intersubjectivity in conversation. *American Journal of Sociology, 97*(5), 1295–1345.

Schegloff, E. A. (1996). Confirming allusions: Toward an empirical account of action. *The American Journal of Sociology, 102*(1), 161–216.

Schegloff, E. A. (2007). *Sequence organization in interaction: A primer in conversation analysis, Vol. 1.* Cambridge: Cambridge University Press.

Shallice, T., & Burgess, P. W. (1991). Deficits in strategy application following frontal lobe damage in man. *Brain, 114,* 727–741.

Smith, M. S. (2010). Exploring the moral bases of frontotemporal dementia through social action. In A. W. Mates, L. Mikesell, & M. S. Smith (Eds.), *Discourse, sociality and frontotemporal dementia: Reverse engineering the social mind* (pp. 49–84). London: Equinox.

Snowden, J. S., Bathgate, D., Varma, A., Blackshaw, A., Gibbons, Z. C., & Neary, D. (2001). Distinct behavioural profiles in frontotemporal dementia and semantic dementia. *Journal of Neurology, Neurosurgery, and Psychiatry, 70,* 323–332.

Stivers, T. (2005). Modified repeats: One method for asserting primary rights from second position. *Research on Language and Social Interaction, 38*(2), 131–158.

Torralva, T., Roca, M., Gleichgerrcht, E., Bekinschtein, T., & Manes, F. (2009). A neuropsychological battery to detect specific executive and social cognitive impairments in early frontotemporal dementia. *Brain, 132,* 1299–1309.

Torrisi, S. (2010). Social regulation in frontotemporal dementia: A case study. In A. W. Mates, L. Mikesell, & M. S. Smith (Eds.), *Discourse, sociality and frontotemporal dementia: Reverse engineering the social mind* (pp. 23–48). London: Equinox.

Walker, A. J., Meares, S., Sachdev, P. S., & Brodaty, H. (2005). The differentiation of mild frontotemporal dementia from Alzheimer's disease and health aging by neuropsychological tests. *International Psychogeriatrics, 17,* 57–68.

Part Three

EXPRESSIVE APPROACHES TO ENRICHING ENGAGEMENT

7

"IN MY OWN WORDS"
Writing Down Life Stories to Promote Conversation in Dementia

**Ellen Bouchard Ryan, Debra Crispin,
and Michelle Daigneault**

Writing is a form of memory.

(Alan Dienstag)

INTRODUCTION

Communication is central to sustaining personhood for individuals with dementia, as demonstrated by the conversation analyses presented earlier in this volume. Our applied dementia focus concerns the collaborative elicitation of life story fragments in conversation and the use of written recordings of these stories as triggers for future conversation in longterm care settings. In this chapter, we briefly overview one-on-one work with conversational remembering boxes and life story binders. Then, we present two case studies for a program of group storytelling and life story binders implemented on two hospital units: a complex care unit where patients may stay for months or years and a unit for patients with dementia awaiting, often for months, placement in longterm care. The objective is to record the individuals' own words to optimize their chances of retrieving stories from their lives for sharing, elaboration, and personal connections with staff, peers, and family.[1]

As seen in all the chapters of this book, eliciting language from persons with dementia can be challenging. Here, we have highlighted successes to raise expectations of what is possible (Thompson, 2011). Many portions of conversational or group sessions were very difficult, with residents passive and responding minimally. Often it took multiple sessions before individuals accessed more language and extended cognition, usually because of a topic of interest or greater comfort over time or just a good day.

We begin with an overview of the literature concerning the impoverished communication environment of longterm care and the use of reminiscence and storytelling to enrich opportunities for individuals with dementia to interact meaningfully.

COMMUNICATION ENVIRONMENT FOR INDIVIDUALS WITH DEMENTIA IN LONGTERM CARE

Overcoming Communication Predicaments of People with Dementia in Institutional Care

Research over the past 30 years has established many aspects of the Communication Predicament of Aging (Ryan et al., 1986) whereby conversational partners often make it difficult for older adults to communicate effectively because of stereotype-driven communication (Harwood, 2007). This negative feedback cycle contributes to excess disability, especially for elders with cognitive, sensory, or physical impairments and for those in institutional environments (Ryan, 2010). For example, the use of elder speak (characterized by high pitch, exaggerated intonation, simplified vocabulary and grammar, nicknames, and repetitions) has been associated with decreases in self care and resistance to care in longterm institutions (Williams, 2011). Figure 7.1 displays the Communication Predicament of Aging Model, including the opportunity for elders to be supported in using selective assertiveness to resist patronizing, dismissive, and overly nurturing behaviors (Ryan, 2010).

Over this same period, researchers have introduced models for counteracting the overly controlling, overly nurturing, or efficiency-oriented approaches typical in nursing homes. Lubinski (2011) emphasizes the importance of creating a positive communication environment to optimize communication. To reduce excess disability and limit behavioral problems associated with boredom and loneliness, Montessori methods focus on modifying the task and preparing a supportive task environment to optimize the chance for performance success and gradual improvements (Orsulic-Jeras & Camp, 2000). The Communication

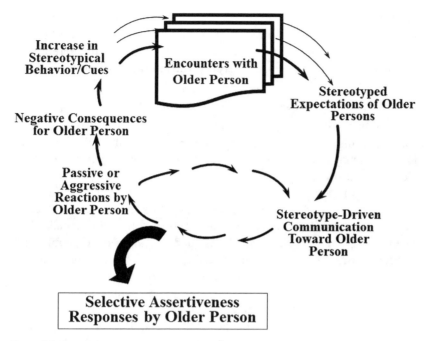

Figure 7.1 The Communication Predicament of Aging: Interrupting the Cycle with Selective Assertiveness (Reprinted with permission from Ryan, 2010, p. 78.)

Enhancement Model with its health promotion emphasis can be applied for work in dementia to improve conversation through individualized assessment of remaining abilities and sensory impairments, high expectations, mutual support, and optimized settings (Orange, Ryan, Meredith, & MacLean, 1995). As the individual is empowered, interactions become more reciprocal and fulfilling for them as well as staff (Davis, 2005; Hagens, Beaman, & Ryan, 2003; Ryan, 2010).

In line with all these models, Kitwood (1997) demonstrated the role of personhood-oriented approaches in reducing excess disability among longterm care residents with dementia. With the support of others, individuals with dementia can maintain communication, connection, and well-being. Family and caregiving staff serve the person by holding on to the memories and using them to support conversation (see Backhaus, 2011; Basting, 2009; Davis, 2005; McFadden & McFadden, 2011).

Such relationship-sustaining approaches foster resilience among persons with dementia. That is, sharing life story memories can enhance the capacity for well-being despite declining abilities (Purves, Savundranayagam, Kelson, Astell, & Phinney, 2011). Given the time and listening attention, individuals with moderate dementia can access longterm memories. As the person connects with their life story, language fluency improves and related memories come forth. Orientation to current person, place, and time can even emerge as the interaction continues.

Reminiscence for Personal Conversation

Reminiscence (also called personal storytelling and life story work) has gained prominence for promoting conversations with individuals with dementia since longterm memories are retained longest (Killick & Allan, 2001; Thompson, 2011).

Support for personal narratives to add meaning to lives within dementia is increasing. Those with dementia can tell stories that retain the conventional storytelling structure, and they find this social activity engaging and enjoyable (Fels & Astell, 2011). Moreover, people with dementia exhibit higher discourse quality within a reminiscence group than in a formal assessment (Moss, Polignano, White, Minichiello, & Sunderland, 2002). For a small sample of people with dementia, reminiscence sessions led to higher verbal fluency in post-test than regular everyday conversational approaches (Okumura, Tanimukai, & Asada, 2008). Nonverbal interchanges among peers also improved over the five group sessions.

Through a meta-analysis of reminiscence studies, Bohlmeijer, Roemer, Cuijpers, and Smit (2007) have shown a significant influence on life satisfaction and emotional well-being, somewhat stronger for community dwellers than longterm care residents. Bohlmeijer et al. (2007) imply that benefits in dementia are constrained by the reluctance to engage in therapeutic life review reminiscence as opposed to an overprotective focus on positive reminiscence alone.

Moos and Bjorn (2006) did a systemic review of evaluations of interventions using storytelling specifically with individuals with dementia. Benefits identified include communication, social integration, and positive affect (see also Moss et al., 2002). Storytelling in dementia stimulates creative expression, which is associated with increased well-being for older adults of all levels of functioning (Sierpina & Cole, 2004). However, Moos and Bjorn (2006) do argue that the focus on intervention studies for dementia may be premature and that more qualitative research on how to support creative expression in dementia is needed.

Writing Down the Words to Promote Conversation

In writing story fragments, we want to take the benefits of a personhood-oriented conversation or a reminiscence group beyond the moment, as a trigger for future satisfying conversations.

The StoryCorps Dementia project offered the public in many locations across the United States the chance to record a conversation between a person living with dementia and a family member (Basting, 2009; Purves et al., 2011). Each family member was prepared with prompts emphasizing emotion-based or experience-based questions, rather than facts and specific details. The audio recording of the co-constructed story afforded a positive experience in the present, future moments with the storyteller, and a family legacy. TimeSlips programs for dementia group storytelling (Basting, 2009) highlight the value of collaborative story creating (without stressing recall) that stimulates growth, humor, and emotional connection—creating a script and performing at a high standard for audiences. In both of these approaches, a record of the story takes the benefits beyond the initial storytelling.

Our main goal in the chapter is to explore the impact of writing down life story fragments of individuals with dementia. A few individuals in early stage dementia began in the 1990s to publish narratives of their dementia experiences (see Ryan, Bannister, & Anas, 2009), and then to create the Dementia Advocacy and Support Network International (DASNI) for mutual support primarily through writing on the Internet. A successful first goal of these original authors/leaders was establishment of support groups within Alzheimer's Societies for themselves—those with dementia, not just for caregivers. Access to the writings of dementia peers has confirmed to many newly diagnosed individuals that living with dementia is a possibility; it's not just a terminal illness. By putting individual faces on the illness, these stories of living with dementia decrease societal stereotypes and may reduce the communication predicaments endured by peers. The writings vividly demonstrate that dementia is experienced in highly varied ways and that remaining abilities, purpose, and a supportive environment can help individuals maintain satisfying lives well beyond what experts anticipated (Ryan et al., 2009). For readers with dementia as well as authors, published dementia stories can renew a positive sense of identity, including feelings of accomplishment and belonging (Ryan et al., 2009).

Dienstag (2003) reports on Lifelines Writing Group, created for community-dwelling people with early stage dementia. Members of the writing group, recruited from a larger support group, were already acquainted with each other. For three years, even while abilities declined, participants wrote briefly with topic prompts and read their work to each other. Story selections and participant quotations highlight how similar the creative process and outcomes were to writing groups everywhere. Working with non-dementia groups in longterm care, Schuster (1998) observed that sharing their written stories enabled residents to explore past and current identities.

But what about those people with more advanced dementia, those in institutional care? How can writing assist them? One should first probe alternate ways for the individual to read and write (Ryan, Spykerman, & Anas, 2005). Although handwriting typically deteriorates, use of a marker pen and wide-lined paper or even a computer with enlarged font can support writing in some residents—especially highly educated people and those admitted to longterm care for medical reasons with an earlier stage of dementia. Oral reading is a long-retained skill—probably with enlarged print in a simple font. Reading one's own dictated words is a skill lasting even longer (Hagens et al., 2003; Moore & Davis, 2002).

Various dementia programs have incorporated written memory aids in longterm care to manage everyday life and to support memory for important current information (Bourgeois, 1993; Elliot, 2011; Orsulic-Jeras & Camp, 2000). The use of prosthetic memory aids builds upon the longer-retained skill of oral reading. Moreover, personalized life story memory books with visual images accompanied by short sentences have nurtured conversations with family caregivers and nursing home staff—increasing factual statements; decreasing ambiguous, incorrect, and un-intelligible utterances; and enhancing topic maintenance (Egan, Berube, Racine, & Leonard, 2010; Hoerster, Hickey, & Bourgeois, 2001; Maclagan & Grant, 2011).

Most often in longterm care, individuals with dementia need to have their stories written down for them—or audio or video recorded. Their stories can be shared in future conversations based on the written record, audio or visual recordings, or transcripts (see Davis, 2005; see also Davis & Maclagan, chapter 4, this volume). A communication partner can make use of recorded stories to support retelling and elaboration within future conversations, in particular by prompting with the exact words and phrases previously used by the person with dementia (Hagens et al., 2003; Moore & Davis, 2002).

John Killick began visiting nursing homes in the 1990s to write down the words of residents—to honor persons with dementia by attending to their words so specifically (Killick & Allan, 2001; Killick, 2003). He has urged us to preserve the communicative moment in writing so as to re-spect personhood, as well as to individualize care (Killick, 2003). Killick (2003) arranged the words from individual interviews into poems for the speakers to share with staff and families. Sharing their writings, the person can be repeatedly 'seen' in an environment typically inducing invisibility.

After years studying communication predicaments in nursing homes (Ryan, 2010), the first author used storytelling and then storywriting to shift focus to enhancing communication with older adults with dementia

(Ryan & Schindel Martin, 2011). We began with a reminiscence group for five people with dementia (Hagens et al., 2003). From the beginning, we sought ways to write down life story fragments for sharing beyond the group. Collaborative poems were created from the reminiscence sessions—taking advantage of the unique role of metaphor, ambiguity, and discontinuities in poetry, as opposed to prose—to use the language of dementia and to combine memories across individuals. Participants' words were written large in front of the group and re-read for elaboration during pauses. In between sessions, the facilitator arranged the words into a poem, which was then reviewed by the group. Group poems were posted in the residents' rooms to encourage reading aloud with staff and visitors. To stimulate future conversations, individual interviews were used to write down elaborations on recollections originating in the group and also to create an individual poem based on the participant's own words. Objects, photographs, and favorite audio/visual tapes were collected with the help of family into a Conversational Remembering Box together with the written stories and poems. Anecdotal evidence indicated positive response to subsequent uses of the boxes for conversations with facilitators, staff, and family. Residents could often identify their own words without remembering storytelling groups or the memory box. Continuing work in longterm care underlined the value of dementia group poems for reminiscence by other peers and for reading aloud the poems with one's own words later on during palliative care (Hagens, Cosentino & Ryan, 2006).

Although life story work, especially writing down life stories for future conversations, offers a great deal of promise, only exploratory research has been conducted. As Moos and Bjorn (2006) and Thompson (2011) both argue, additional qualitative research is needed to enrich our sense of the process of writing stories down and using them later on as well as to identify the range of possible communication and psychological benefits and the conditions most conducive for those benefits.

To provide this type of qualitative data, we have conducted a number of case studies. In the two sections that follow, we explore one-on-one and then group activities for prompting, producing, recording, and sharing reminiscence or life stories.

ONE-ON-ONE WORK: CONVERSATIONAL REMEMBERING BOXES AND LIFE STORY BINDERS

In this section we highlight six case studies selected from recent student projects to paint a broad picture of the process and impact of written conversational memory aids. The undergraduate students of gerontology or health studies were in their early 20s, native-like speakers of English, and most had experience volunteering or working in longterm care. Each student spent at least six sessions observing in the longterm care center before their project; each student was supervised off-site by the first author as well as on-site by a field supervisor.

Across multiple longterm-care settings, each student interviewer held multiple conversations with a person with dementia, in longterm care assisted living homes or long-stay hospital units. Initial conversations focused on eliciting new stories, while the later sessions made increasing use of the written conversational aids. Staff evaluations of conversations with the memory aid are cited where available, but staff participation was difficult to recruit for unfunded student projects.

Conversational Remembering Boxes

For these four case studies, the interviewer gathered items for a Conversational Remembering Box (referred to in conversation as a memory box) during the conversation sessions, sometimes with help beforehand from family (Hagens et al., 2003). As stories were elicited, new ideas for the memory box arose. A photograph was taken of physical items that did not fit into the box. For favorite places and items no longer available, computer images approved by the participant were printed. Stories prompted by the items were written down at the time by the student as they were told. The student then typed the story and printed it out in appropriate font and size. The participant and student read the story together, and any changes suggested by the participant were made. The story was then placed in the memory box, along with a journal and pen for other conversational partners to record elaborations and new stories to enrich the memory box. Note that the stories were often only one or two sentences, sometimes a paragraph or two.

Individual Participant 1: Claire Jones

Claire Jones is a recently widowed 78-year-old female with moderate-stage dementia. Throughout the seven conversations, Claire required little prompting. However, she was prone to repeating and going off on tangents.

The process of finding items for the memory box and gathering stories were two threads braided together. Claire's family (both deceased and living members), her role as a twin, and leisure activities with her husband were important to her. Claire actively brainstormed with the interviewer about how to represent her music and gardening in her memory box. The interviewer strived to ensure that the stories were recorded in Claire's exact words. Claire supported the idea of the memory box: "I forget a lot and I think the Memory Box would help."

The staff member using Claire's remembering box to converse with her reported the conversation to have been "very educational, in ten minutes I learned a lot about Claire, her children, twin sister, husband and what she enjoyed in her life." The memory aid was especially beneficial because she had only recently begun working at the facility. She recommended placing signs outside or in the resident's room inviting staff or visitors to make use of the resident's memory box.

Individual Participant 2: Gary Dufresne

Gary Dufresne, 82 years old and exhibiting mild dementia, participated in eight sessions. At first in the conversations Gary was apathetic, making only passive responses. The turning point for him was becoming engaged in gathering items that he believed would best represent him for the memory box, especially reflecting his passion for the farming life. Gary was especially proud of a detailed family history book that dated back to his grandfather and could tell stories as he went through the pictures. A photograph of the book's cover was included in the memory box in order to encourage others to make use of this resource.

A staff member engaged Gary in a conversation with the memory box, whose contents he was happy to show her. Through her short conversation with him, she was able to tell that this memory box was an important way for him to keep his name alive. She believed it was beneficial to have the box in his room not only for staff and visitors but also so "he can look through the box when he is feeling blue and see everything he has done."

Individual Participant 3: Julia McDow

Julia McDow, in her 80s, has moderate dementia accompanied by visual and hearing problems. Even so, she was able to relate to her personal photos in the memory box, and sometimes she could read her stories from the box. In addition to photographs, the memory box included a journal of stories that Julia had written two decades earlier for her grandson, a crocheted blanket, and a needlepoint seat cover. She began to relate to the interviewer and the project in the fourth (of seven) session when together they read excerpts from her old journal. She began to show reciprocity by asking about the interviewer and to converse with her (e.g., "I'm happy to see you again"). Repetitive questioning disappeared in later sessions.

Story

I have a lot of grandchildren. My granddaughter Anna and grandson Frank live in Alberta. I don't think I have ever been there. I have been up north to Yellowknife and the United States. I don't see my great grandchildren that often but I do see my grandchildren from time to time. I got to watch my grandkids sometimes. That was fun. I don't see them too much now. Cooper is an actor in New York. Cooper, Patrick and Lisa are Mandy's children.

Conversation about family photos after reading the story aloud:

Julia: I like this part about my grandchildren. It makes me miss them.
Interviewer: Does looking at their pictures make you feel better?
Julia: Sometimes. I look at those pictures sometimes. (Referring to conversational box)
Interviewer: That's nice to hear. When your grandchildren visit, you should show them. They would love it.
Julia: Yeah. (laughing)

Individual Participant 4: Larry Morrison

Larry Morrison, in his 80s, had been diagnosed with dementia and Parkinson's disease. He did not move much, used little eye contact, and had few comprehensible words throughout the nine sessions. He was almost exclusively interested in watching television, especially sports. For him, the memory aid became his story! His wife was keen and helped him select items for his Conversational Remembering Box—golf, bicycle and carpentry gear, and, interestingly, his old wallet containing IDs.

Since he was so attentive to the television and experienced so much motor difficulty with speech, Larry was seen as a good candidate for a computerized Conversational Remembering Box (see Purves et al., 2011, for discussion of computerized memory aids and the use of generic memory cues). A PowerPoint slide presentation (available in his memory box in both CD-Rom and DVD formats) was created with photos and generic images of his sports interests, including audio and video clips. The interviewer was only able to elicit two- to three-word phrases, but Larry consistently engaged very directly nonverbally with the slide show and showed his comprehension and appreciation. Here's a brief exchange that served as a 'graduation' conversation. After spending time looking at a collage of pictures during the final session, the interviewer asked Mr. Morrison which picture was his favorite.

Larry:	Up at the top
Interviewer:	This one?
Larry:	No, above that picture (pointing to the only picture above)

Life Story Binders

In other student projects, we focused more on the written stories by placing them in life story binders. The students wrote down the story fragments as they occurred in conversation, entered each one in the computer, and printed it out for the participant, who suggested elaborations and changes as they wished. Sometimes this process was repeated a few times for elaborations. Then the revised printed story was placed in their binder. Most of the time these stories would be at least a paragraph long—not as brief as the ones in the Conversational Remembering Box. These stories served to spark conversations in interchanges for eliciting and editing them together and in subsequent use of the story binder.

Individual Participant 5: Max Alden

Max Alden, in his mid 70s—our sole participant with Korsakoff's dementia—had been in medical isolation for several months. Although he agreed to participate, he began the sessions verbally and nonverbally expressing reluctance. Content to be on his own, he repeated "don't need anybody." By the third session, he was speaking more readily, especially about his family and how he had always taken care of his children. In the latter sessions, he expressed his sense of humor and enthusiasm to talk. For instance, in the fourth visit, he greeted the investigators with "I'm in a very good mood today. Ask me anything you want!" and later "Do you guys know about it? I must tell you then!" His change in attitude may well have been due to the fact that student interviewers became more comfortable in the intimidating medical setting and more skilled in talking with him about his experiences rather than facts.

His stories were rich in detail, but he told the same ones over and over. For example, pointing to a youth pictured in a graduation gown, he said,

He's not my biological son. Took care of him since he was a baby. He was the son of a family friend down the street. They had some problems, so I took him in. He graduated, became RCMP. Now studying to become an officer. His name is S. He listens to me. You know why? Because he respects me. No matter how rough things were, I always looked after my kids. So when he brought his girlfriend here, I noticed she was a smoker and I told him to dump her, and he did. Then he brought B. As soon as I saw, I said he hit the jackpot. I said, "Marry her" and he did.

This story was part of an ongoing process of life review, searching for meaning and connection. He found himself with severe health issues and strained relationships with his children. He was trying to reframe his life by talking about a positive relationship. He saw himself as an expert with wisdom to share—telling stories and talking about the written stories promoted his sense of connection to himself and others.

Individual Participant 6: John Yorks

John Yorks, age 93 and exhibiting disorientation to time, place, and person, participated in nine sessions. Although he was socially isolated, not connecting with others in the home, he showed enjoyment and active engagement from the start. He stands out because of his pride in the physical binder.

His first response was, "How much do you want for it?" He thought the binder was very good and it deserved to be paid for. As soon as he was aware that the binder was full of his own stories, he responded with, "Wow we did an excellent job, very good. I think the kids will be quite proud of this." He emphasized that "it is nice to read about yourself. It reminds me of my accomplishments and important memories."

Three staff members used the story binder with John. One reported, "I saw him visibly go back in years in his mind and relax and enjoy the conversation, and that way I could get a better picture of the person he used to be." Another staff member indicated, "These stories allowed me to assist the resident in having a one-on-one conversation about his life experiences and the times that meant so much to him."

GROUP STORYTELLING AND LIFE STORY BINDERS

Next, we describe a group-based clinical intervention that extends our work with life story writings to support future conversation. Individual life story memory aids were created from group storytelling sessions, which themselves fostered conversation and relationship-building. This clinical life story intervention was initiated and implemented by Debra Crispin, spiritual care specialist (the second author), and Michelle Daigneault, recreation therapist (third author), on two longer-stay units of the teaching hospital where they work. The first author was involved as a consultant once writing down stories was identified as the basic approach.

The project was inspired by the necessity to find a way to get to know our patients. From our clinical experience leading reminiscence groups with cognitively impaired older adults, we sensed the potential to make better use of life story fragments elicited within the group process. Writing down these life stories could create a conversational resource to support person-centered care and the spiritual needs of the patients.

No audio recordings were made. Groups were facilitated by one or both of the leaders, who also wrote down the stories with occasional help from student volunteers. These life story fragments (our focus), after being entered into the computer and printed, were shared with the participant, who helped edit and integrate them into stories—often over multiple sessions with individuals. Especially rich fragments of conversation during the group were also written down at the time for research purposes.

The group storytelling process was based on the best of group reminiscence and life story work. Much of the literature in this area is guided by Kitwood's (1997) thesis that personhood is affirmed through connection and relationship. For instance, a study in Britain showed that older people in aged care prefer activities that include reinforcing a sense of identity and a sense of belonging (Fels & Astell, 2011). Group storytelling has been found to increase the sense of self and enhance participation for individuals in the later stages of dementia (Moos & Bjorn, 2006).

Moss et al. (2002) conducted one of the first studies examining the effects of reminiscence group activities on discourse interactions of people with Alzheimer's disease. They found that less structured environments yielded qualitatively better discourse patterns, particularly related to selecting and maintaining a topic, requesting additional information about a topic, changing a topic during conversation, and turn-taking. The same study found that some participants began with sharing, developed in mutually beneficial exchanges, resulting in a higher level of trust. The added stimulation of the group experience works to help people access memories. The group experience also promotes or improves a sense of meaning and purpose (Hagens et al., 2003; Moss et al., 2002).

Life story work yielding a resource for conversation can assist other care staff with a better understanding of their patients and insight into their values (Moss et al., 2002). For example, Hagens et al. (2003) noted that short personal stories in the memory box were used to calm sleepless or restless patients, especially helpful to unacquainted staff.

In summary, the purpose of the group storytelling and story binder program is to facilitate conversation with and between patients with dementia, get to know patients through the stories they tell in order to enhance patient-centered care, partner with families to gather stories about those who are not able to access memories independently, and use the written story as a tool to facilitate conversation between a patient and other patients, family members, and staff.

We will present our experience with two storytelling groups—the first in a complex care hospital unit with mostly cognitive and communication impaired patients, with only some participants diagnosed with dementia, and the second in a recently organized dementia unit within the same hospital. Working with the new unit allowed the opportunity to 'begin again' with a focus specifically on dementia. Group storytelling and life story binders were deemed to be especially important for these longterm patients lost in the acute hospital system—enduring stressful testing and numerous room/unit transfers without much opportunity to find a sense of belonging or even personhood.

Group Storytelling in a Complex Care Hospital Unit

The setting for this story program is a complex care unit within a large teaching hospital. Many of the medically complex patients have stayed for more than one year in this unit, which has been shifting from a long-stay unit to a 90-day slow rehabilitation focus. Initially, many patients had a diagnosis of dementia. The number is declining as the nature of the unit changes. The unit serves a highly diverse population in terms of physical, cognitive, communicative, social, and emotional impairments.

Group Storytelling Process

For 2½ years, the two facilitators have held 60-minute reminiscence-style storytelling sessions weekly with 5–15 participants. Group members range widely in cognitive and communicative abilities. The overall process will be described first, followed by elaboration through the experience of one participant with moderate but progressing dementia.

For each group session, a reminiscence theme is announced. Topics from the distant past yield the best recall: childhood best friend, the house where I grew up, my job, my first car, what I do for fun (favorite pastime), proudest moment, and greatest accomplishment. Advanced preparation includes posting topics ahead of time for patients and their families. It turned out to be especially useful to partner with families (contacted in person as opposed to mail/telephone) to obtain details for likely stories. Facilitators sometimes work one-on-one beforehand to retrieve memories and create a written story to be shared in the program. Often, it is enough to chat while guiding individuals to the session to help them remember a relevant story. Sometimes they read or tell their own story. Other times staff reads or tells it for them.

A social atmosphere is created for group sessions by sitting in a circle and beginning with introductions. Sensory prompts—photos, objects, food, smells, sounds—help to highlight the theme of the day. A flip chart can record words (one per line) as participants brainstorm words related to the topic. More spontaneously, articles from the daily newspaper, often with photos of local people and places, can create an environment for discussion. Concrete questions elicit more talk, but the facilitator works to broaden or deepen the discussion to access other experiences or feelings.

Some prompts work especially well, such as "Tell us about music—what music do you like?" One person responded by singing a complex song that he had sung for his mother in his teens. Misunderstood questions need a follow-up to clarify, such as, "Tell us where you came from" (looking for country of origin)—misunderstood: "from my room," "from home," "from Hamilton"—switch to "Where were you born?"

As the goal is to involve everyone, it is important for participants to take turns for conversation and questions. "Clapping" to show appreciation is a good way to finish each person's contribution/story. This activity builds individual confidence and group social identity. Importantly, clapping as a signal to stop also reinforces turn-taking. For some with physical limitations, "clapping" is a symbolic movement of foot or finger acknowledging appreciation of the story. However, reinforcing turn-taking by clapping may also inhibit spontaneous conversation. Facilitators need to watch and listen for responses from other group participants before clapping is initiated. A small group session may lend itself to more back and forth conversation, so clapping might be out of place.

Group management problems do, of course, arise. Participants who interrupt can be reoriented to topic and activity or reminded of turn-taking. It helps to position a facilitator or helper directly beside individuals who may require extra support due to cognition, hearing, vision, or anxiety.

Apart from the specifics of starters and continuers, the approach and "presence" of the facilitators play a significant role in the success of the encounter. Open posture and gestures, engaged eye contact, and appropriate touch to help direct and maintain attention create a safe space for conversation and sharing. Facilitators need to be prepared for emotional reaction to topics, questions, or someone else's story. Often, given time, members of the group support a tearful or anxious member. After seeing and hearing a co-patient crying and talking about missing his wife, a patient whose speech was rarely oriented to the situation looked compassionately at his co-patient and said, "Your lunch is waiting," pointing to staff delivering lunch nearby. Members are even quicker to support happy or proud comments with congratulations or cheers. The level of caring and encouragement among group members has been impressive. The sense of community and connection that is created within the group even rolls out to interactions between members of the group outside the group setting. One patient encouraged another during physiotherapy with personal knowledge gained from the story group.

Indicators of group-ness observed in these sessions include nonverbal signals such as sympathetic facial expressions, gestures, or even hand signals, hugs, and hand holding. One participant gave the facilitator a hug and said, "You can come again," meaning she enjoyed the experience and would like to do it again. She has severe word-finding difficulty and is not able to join in conversation easily.

Throughout the group sessions, a key goal is to write down life story fragments for the individuals. Stories (brief episodes of a few sentences or more complex stories of a few paragraphs) are transcribed and printed for the participants. The stories are placed into binders for each patient, which are kept in their room to be read by families, staff, and volunteers. New stories are posted on the wall in the patient's room. These are used as prompts to help the participant access elaborations or new memories— which are then recorded. The goal is for staff and family to use these stories as conversation starters.

We continue to look for ways to facilitate staff involvement. Time for in-service training is a continuing problem. New stories are now posted in each patient's room before being put in the binder to ease staff access. We have created a Best Practice poster for display on the unit for staff, patients, and others. Perhaps most important for encouraging staff, we now refer in the unit to the story fragments as *conversation starters* instead of 'stories.'

A section has been created on the individual patient rounds sheet where information is shared that may promote greater person-centered care. This might be from the story project, or knowledge staff have gained through conversation during personal care or from family. With the support of the unit manager, each week we post a new story/conversation starter about a patient in the nursing station.

An especially positive response occurred after the facilitators read a conversation starter at nursing rounds about a patient who can't speak much but can write. Many people don't take time to wait for her to write, so they were amazed when we told her detailed story. It had practical clues for how to be with her. Some reactions from the nursing staff are, "I can't believe that you got that story from that patient," and "Now we will know what to do with her to make her happy like sing her a song or play music for her."

Complex Care Group Participant: Ray Harrison

Resident on the unit for more than 10 years, Ray Harrison is in his late 70s with moderate dementia. Over the 2½ years, we noticed significant progression of the disease. He more frequently did not know where he was or identify any staff. We elaborate on the impact of the storytelling activity by describing Ray's experiences.

Ray attended storytelling group weekly approximately 40 times (30 with stories). Initially, he was a passive participant. He enjoyed sitting in the group, attended all sessions, and was well known to group regulars. He initially did not contribute due to difficulty accessing memories and social anxiety. Pre-group preparation with Ray proved the key to enabling him to participate more actively. The facilitator worked with Ray individually just prior to group time to help put his story together based on the topic, and then read Ray's story aloud for him in the group. Ray was able to elaborate on the story and answer questions from other participants.

As staff accumulated knowledge of Ray's life and experiences through recorded stories, they could help elicit more conversation during the group, occasionally eliminating the need for advanced preparation. Ray would tell detailed stories of his experiences once he was reminded of his accomplishments, as illustrated in this discussion of Thanksgiving in the group.

Asked about his memories of Thanksgiving, he said, "No, nothing to add." The facilitator then reminded him and the group of his years volunteering as a cook at the Mission. Asked if he participated in preparing a special meal for the people, he spoke easily. The story unfolded of the day put on for the people who came to the mission. He spoke of the food they would prepare, the choir, the real feeling of home and community he tried to create. He spoke compassionately about families and individuals.

Telling this story to the group reconnected him to his contributions. It reconnected him to his faith and his genuine caring personality. The group clapped, affirming social identity and acceptance. The group congratulated Ray for his years of volunteering in the community. Feeling validated and affirmed, Ray smiled.

Ray's life story binder served as a tool for staff from time to time. When Ray was anxious and confused, the Recreation Therapist brought his book to him. The book helped settle Ray, reminding him of how he shared many stories with the group, contributing to the 'community' on the unit. He would reflect on his stories, memories of events and family, his contributions and work, his qualities and strengths. Ray relives the events as the stories are read back to him, and this helps to reconnect Ray to his community and to himself. Sometimes when Ray would be just sitting, staff and patients would engage him in conversation based on the stories shared. When Ray only had a few stories collected, he showed the book to staff with the comment, "My whole life is in this book."

The story binder served as a transition tool when Ray was recently transferred to a longterm care facility. The binder serves as a concrete reminder to Ray of his time at the hospital. Group facilitators suggested to staff at the new facility ways they could use the binder and followed up with a visit after two months. Although supportive comments were received initially from a nurse about the binder, on follow up, she admitted she did not work closely with the patient and did not know any details from the binder. We have learned to speak with direct care providers. We also learned it would have been helpful to have some stories in the book about the people he knew at the hospital, where he had spent 10 years.

Group Storytelling in a Transition Dementia Hospital Unit

With two years' experience on the first unit, the storytelling program was introduced on a recently created Alternate Level of Care (ALC) unit within the same hospital. This is for patients who no longer have acute medical issues. Most have dementia and are awaiting longterm care. They might spend months on this unit. Some with difficult-to-manage problems such as exit-seeking, aggression, and sexually inappropriate behavior will wait even longer. Ages range from 50s to 90s.

Storytelling groups are held twice a week: one morning group and another more deliberately social afternoon affair ("Coffee, Tea and Me"). Groups have from 4–12 participants, often the same in both groups. Approximately 40 percent of the participants speak English as a second language. Whoever is up and interested is welcome, depending on the level of staff support available. Individual stories are transcribed and the printed pages hung in the patient's room. Staff are informed of ways these could be used as 'conversation starters.' After the first few months, based on our experience in complex care, 'conversation starters' for specific patients were shared at weekly clinical rounds.

Group sessions proceed in a manner similar to those for the first unit. The two weekly sessions highlight the relative strengths of small and larger groups. Small groups allow easier accommodation for hearing, vision, and attention as well as more opportunity for individual engagement. An all-inclusive group conversation is more feasible. Yet, larger groups with those of mixed cognitive/communicative ability can make it possible for those with very limited ability to experience the benefits of socialization, to participate in the group nonverbally, and sometimes to contribute, with support, after hearing the stories of others. Early on in the sessions, a series of autumn/Thanksgiving topics were presented, with leaves, chestnuts, wild flowers, and pumpkin pie as prompts. Newspaper articles were useful, especially one about the 175th anniversary of the local Farmers' Market, which included old photos of farmers bringing their goods to market and townspeople making purchases. Related to this theme, we present a small group conversation and the case of one participant to illustrate how the program has elicited conversation and connections.

Dementia Group Conversation Excerpt

Participants in a small group of six responded to a photo prompt showing a woman surrounded by shelves of preserves. Dave, unable to initiate memories, had named her "Woolie." He has a great sense of humor, and everyone laughed at the name. He could not explain why he chose it but appreciated the laughter.

Facilitator:	Dave, what do you think this woman's name is?
Dave:	Woolie.
F:	Woolie?
Dave:	Yes, Woolie.
F:	Why did you choose that? Does that mean something to you?
Dave:	No. (He laughs and everyone else joins in.)
F:	OK, This woman's name is Woolie. What else can we tell about her?
Lucy:	She is a farmer's wife and she does the preserving every year.
Charlie:	There is a lot of food. She must live on a big farm in the country.
Anna:	It could be in Saskatchewan.
F:	What else can we tell about her from the picture?
Robert:	She looks happy and is enjoying what she has done. She must have a lot of people to feed or perhaps she sells things at the market.
Alice:	I can remember my mother sitting on the back porch peeling baby onions all day with a piece of bread in her mouth.
Anna:	Why did she have bread in her mouth?
Alice:	She said it kept her eyes from watering.
Anna:	I didn't know how to peel anything. When we moved to our house in Davidson, I had a wood and coal stove. The women had to teach me how to use it. They were very patient and very kind.
Alice:	I don't know how to preserve anything. My mother did it all. You learn it from your mother or you don't do it.
Elizabeth:	I enjoy the fall weather. People cook nice things.

This group conversation is a combination of jointly creating a story about the picture and telling stories from individuals' own lives. While our focus is usually on life stories, responding creatively to this prompt yielded engagement among the patients. As Basting (2009) has demonstrated through her TimeSlips program, inviting a group to create a story takes the pressure off remembering while at the same time building upon participants' own stories. Each comment follows appropriately from previous ones. The final comment—a great summary of the experience of fall—showed that Elizabeth, otherwise a passive participant, had been engaged throughout. Anna's setting of the story in Saskatchewan reinforces the idea that even without specific recall, what they do creatively may tell their story anyway. Dave's use of humor supports his lifelong self-identity and gives him an important role in the group even after memory and initiation skills are gone.

Dementia Group Participant: Charlie Strand

Charlie Strand, 82 years of age, has moderate dementia. He awaited transfer to geriatric psychiatry due to aggression and sexually inappropriate behavior. He was teary about not being with his wife. He attended group sessions regularly but rarely initiated. During this series of four consecutive story groups, he progressed from contributing very little to not being able to stop. The written versions of the stories told across sessions are presented here. In the first session, Charlie only interacted with the story facilitator and offered lists of food and family at the dinner. In the second session, he recounted concrete details of the typical walk in the woods after Thanksgiving dinner.

> **Thanksgiving When I Was a Child:** For Thanksgiving when I was a child we would have the whole family around the table: brothers Phil, George, Reg, and my sister May and my Mom and Dad. We would have a chicken or turkey, pumpkin pie, squash, turnip, tomatoes, parsnips, carrots, cranberries, stuffing and gravy.
> **The Woods at Thanksgiving:** Sometimes at Thanksgiving we would take a walk back in the bush. We would look at the beautiful leaves on both sides of the path. We saw blackberry canes and sometimes we saw mushrooms. We picked them and ate them.

In the third session, in response to photographs of horses and wagons at a farmer's market, Charlie continued his story throughout the entire story time, even though we thanked him and clapped at the end of his time. He thought each question that was asked was asked of him. He stopped when the facilitator changed places at the table so she was not directly across from him.

Our Animals: We had 8 or 9 pigs. In the fall we would sell them out. I would hitch up the horses to the wagon and we would take them to the market. We had 7, 8, or 9 ducks. We used to have 8, 9 or 10 chickens and a rooster "cock a doodle doo"! (Big smile on his face.) We had a special rooster that got a prize at the fair.

The next day Charlie was singing a barnyard animal song at lunch time. In the fourth story session with the picture of a woman surrounded by preserves, he gave many details of caring for the apple trees and making cider. Although he was not oriented to others in the group, they were interested and told their own stories about apple cider.

Making Cider: The windfall apples were good for cider. We used to get a gallon or gallon and a half of juice from them. First of all you have to squeeze the juice out. The cider mill was over in Lynden. We put it in a milk can. Then you heat it up and put it in jars and can it. We used to have apple crates that we stored the apples in. We put them in a clean, cool place.

Conversation between Charlie, His Family,
and a Group Facilitator

The facilitator read Charlie's stories to him and his niece and sister-in-law. After the others had asked him about many things he did not remember, Charlie related this story about playing baseball:

C: Sometimes we would ride our bikes into Lynden and play baseball. All the bases were fixed up good. We had two good bats and a real good ball.
Facilitator: Did you have a glove?
C: No, not many had gloves.
Niece: I bet you were a good hitter!
C: I hit the ball pretty good.
Niece: I bet you hit home runs!
C: No, but I was a good hitter. (C explained that once someone was out they went out to play in the field and everyone moved forward. It was a rotation type of game.) After the game we would take off home from Lynden.

When Charlie was transferred on a Friday, the team gathered his stories and sent the binder along with him. Very grateful to have the binder, the nurse on the new unit reported on Monday, "We read it from cover to cover and used it every day over the weekend. It was very *helpful in this time of transition, in getting to know his family and work history.*

I think Charlie is finding it easier to trust us because we know about him. It is helpful to have a source of concrete and familiar stories to help distract and bring pleasant memories."

Charlie recognized the words and stories as his own when they read it to him. The binder is kept by his bedside, and more information is added as they go. It is encouraging to have staff recognize the value of the stories to support communication and as a tool to avoid triggers of reactive behavior. After 2½ years of working with this program, we continue to look for ways to engage direct-care staff in incorporating the stories into care, both in our own setting and in receiving facilities.

Lessons Learned from the Dementia Group

Some practical lessons include the following: to provide one-to-one preparation when necessary to make group participation possible; position facilitators, any helpers, and participants strategically; and limit noise and other distractions. At least two staff are needed, one to write as the other supports conversation. If one is required to leave for any reason, the other must try to maintain the group focus. Even so, such interruptions can instantly destroy the sense of group. Our groups have survived many uncontrollable institutional interruptions (e.g., overhead announcements, beeping IV poles, call bells, and clinical staff addressing a particular patient for medications or tests), but it would be advisable to seek out quiet spots for groups to meet. Further education of staff may help minimize interruptions. Having the group at the same time at the same place with the same facilitators is helpful to some. Looking on their activity calendar to orient themselves can help them prepare ahead of time.

Given appropriate support, everyone wants to communicate and belong: to be in relationships and connect. This program is popular—often the only activity chosen by the more reluctant or disoriented individuals. Patients not only get to tell their story, they create meaning, reclaim social and personal identity, and see beyond the presenting impairment of their fellow patient to the person (Ryan et al., 2009). One patient commented about another whose career story had just been read aloud: "I thought he was just a man in a chair. Now I know he won international awards for his work."

When conversation lags or patients are unable to access memories, it may help to direct them back to photographs or props. Writing the topic and prompts on a white board or flip chart may make it more accessible to some. Use of prior knowledge of patients may spark a memory. Sometimes patients will encourage others to share or remind them of a story they heard them tell previously. This is one advantage of having people of varying levels of cognitive ability in the same group. Debriefing helps in recognizing what has happened in the group and how the process may be improved. People with dementia are so varied and access to remaining abilities so unpredictable that the facilitators learned to prepare well and then be open to what might happen this time.

Facilitators are continually surprised by what happens in the group each week; surprised at the stories told and how previously hidden abilities can suddenly show up in conversation. This may relate to assumptions made about each patient. The group presents an opportunity to challenge ourselves, to open our minds and raise our expectations. Expectations can limit outcomes—even limit the choice of who participates in subsequent sessions. It was not clear a particular woman wanted to participate: her chair was faced away and staff were warned by others not to try to move her chair. She held her head down and closed her eyes during the session. The facilitator left her until last, not sure she would participate. It turned out she was hard of hearing. When the facilitator spoke loudly directly to her, she raised her head and gave very short responses. It felt like pulling teeth—no sign of involvement until after the session. When the facilitator touched her hand lightly and thanked her for being there, the participant clutched her hand and said, "I like you."

We are also surprised at the level of caring and community that develops amongst patients in the moment and, in some cases, over time. We are able to capture story fragments, but we are not able to capture the richness of the group process. We are particularly moved by the positive impact the group has on non-verbal patients. Often, members of the group who are able to verbalize are extremely supportive of those who cannot. It is obvious from facial expressions and gestures that they enjoy the experience of listening and benefit from being part of the group.

Sometimes difficulties in the group are due to one participant who enjoys the group but disrupts repeatedly. One very disruptive patient was eventually able to wait and take his turn after being redirected by facilitators several times. Then, a co-patient used the same strategy and language when interrupted during his turn. "We are taking turns telling stories. It is my turn right now. You can have a turn when I am finished." The other patient settled, listened, and waited. The co-patient let him know when he was finished and encouraged him to tell his story. Noticing this from outside the room, nursing staff were amazed. Once in a large group of 12 around a long table, the group was having difficulty hearing because two group members at the far end of the table were having their own conversation. Facilitators tried to get these two to stop talking while another was telling her story. It turned out that they were processing what was happening by explaining it to each other.

Even if someone is unable to access memories, they may still be able to have a meaningful conversation. One woman with advanced dementia who spoke unintelligibly almost non-stop attended a story group. This was a particularly good day for her. It was early in the morning. It was a small group, and the room was quiet. She was able to say her name when we did introductions. When it was her turn to share, she was able to say, "I don't remember." She went on to have a meaningful conversation about not remembering. At the end she said with a smile on her face, "Sometimes, it all just goes" (she shrugged her shoulders and threw hers arms up over her head). Another woman was very hesitant to be part of the group because she could not remember. With support, she was able to tell a story about herself. She then said, "Usually I don't join in conversations. I feel so embarrassed because I can't remember. I don't feel that way here." Others shared their feelings about not being able to remember.

DISCUSSION

Through individual and group case studies, we have illustrated the conversational process of eliciting life stories as well as the impact of written life stories on subsequent conversations for residents with dementia living in institutional care. In one-to-one or group conversations, paying attention to the specific words of individuals with dementia increases their conversation and their sense of connection. We have also shown how the written stories elicit continuing and elaborated conversations as well as comments of appreciation and surprise at their remaining ability. Instances of humor, mutuality, and relationship feed the conversational partner (Davis, 2005).

Through one-on-one and group collaborative storytelling we have continued to learn the importance of writing down the words of forgetful individuals whose words are often ignored. Writing down life story fragments for longterm care residents offers staff, volunteers, and family members a specific approach to overcoming communication predicaments associated with dementia and institutional living. As called for by Moos and Bjorn (2006), our qualitative research adds substance to the ground-breaking work by Killick (2003; Killick & Allan, 2001) and our own earlier efforts to use writings to support conversations (Hagens et al., 2003, 2006). In terms of models, this person-centered approach creates a prepared, enhanced communication environment enabling persons with dementia to assert their identities and connect with others on their terms (Elliot, 2011; Lubinski, 2011; Ryan, 2010).

Implications for longterm care staff and others working with individuals with dementia are many. Written life stories can be a prompt for future conversations, for chats during daily care, and for calming restless, confused, or aggressive residents. We learned to use the term *conversation starters* to entice busy staff to make use of these prompts. Information about residents' past experiences can enable staff to deliver better personalized care (Moos & Bjorn, 2006). Beyond that, using the specific words of a resident for storytelling can be a more direct way to connect to the story and the resident's sense of personhood.

In the group setting we learned how one person's story sparked conversation and connections. We also learned that priming individuals prior to the group storytelling sessions was valuable, and absolutely necessary for some. Priming could be done with reading from the life story binder or chatting about the topic on the way to the group. Groups whose participants have varying levels of ability to converse are helpful. The more able create the social experience for the less able and may act as models or provide prompts for others. As exemplified in Hagens et al. (2006), a more able resident can be recruited for three-way conversations intended to assist a less able resident to recall life story fragments or to 'write' collaborative poetry.

Written stories of persons with dementia can be used in other ways in longterm care. For example, published quotations about dementia experiences can elicit fruitful conversation in group or individual conversations—letting the authors provide the words and allowing participants to recognize those words that resonate (Ryan et al., 2009). The Hagens et al. (2006) poetry anthology is another especially good resource as it offers words from peers in a form particularly accessible in dementia—short lines, metaphor, multiple interpretations—and a form that assists conversational partners to veer away from their typical insistence on logic and reality.

One of the biggest challenges is staff education and gaining staff support. Staff feel they have no time to read stories, share the ones they hear during care, or attend information sessions. The facilitators are hard pressed to find the time to run the groups, write down the stories, type and print them, and read them with the patient before the next group. More support from management is necessary to include this work in elder-friendly and person-centered care initiatives. In Northern Ireland, the Northern Health & Social Care Trust (NHSCT) collaborated with the Reminiscence Network of Northern Ireland to establish life story work in all its residential and day care facilities serving people with dementia. In their report, the authors note the challenges of conflicting priorities, inconsistent senior management support, staff resistance or inertia, and competing demands on resources. Despite official policies, achieving an enduring change in values, ethos, and longterm care remains a huge challenge (Gibson & Carson, 2010).

Our descriptive case studies of one-on-one conversations and group storytelling point toward several directions for future research on the impact of life story writings. Before a major intervention study, it would be useful to explore the use of group storytelling in conjunction with individual conversations and the value of beginning with Conversational Remembering Boxes and aiming toward life story binders. It would seem that group storytelling and individual conversations might well support each other in terms of motivation and abilities to access memories. Memory boxes with brief conversation starters might work best for care staff, while life story binders might work best for pastoral care staff, family, and volunteers. Actually, the latter could be involved in preparing further conversation starters and locating items/images for the conversation memory box. Finally, as suggested by Bohlmeijer et al. (2007), life review in dementia might work by building up the written life story through appropriate prompts addressing both positive and negative emotions. Through all these qualitative studies, a priority should be upon developing appropriate measures for residents with dementia—for feelings of self-esteem, well-being, remembering with help, and belonging (see Purves et al., 2011).

What about personal and generic prompts to elicit life storytelling? Astell and colleagues (Astell, Ellis, Alm, Dye, & Gowans, 2010; Purves et al., 2011) have raised intriguing questions for dementia. Astell et al. (2010) present a small study in which the focus on memory with family photographs elicited lower quality speech than generic images without the press to recall specific details. Generic photos and images do elicit life storytelling as we know from Montessori materials. Astell's work creates an important distinction between personalized and individualized. Thus, generic photos and images do elicit life storytelling when choice is involved (Astell et al., 2010; Bourgeois, 1993; Elliot, 2011; Maclagan & Grant, 2011; Purves et al., 2011). Van den Brandt-van Heek (2011) uses the same generic images with a generic story or opinion/feeling questions in Theme books and a summary of the individual's own storytelling in Life Story books—thereby offering a personalized option, as needed. Thus, it seems that generic stimuli chosen for shared history can be effective in group storytelling or computer games when there are many options. Moreover, use of generic photos from participants' shared community history can be particularly effective in putting the person with dementia on a more equal footing with a healthy conversational partner and emphasizing community membership over illness (Basting, 2009; McFadden & McFadden, 2011; Purves et al., 2011).

Intervention studies can address two different aspects of the use of written life stories to foster conversations. First, short-term interventions could be evaluated in terms of improvements in specific discourse and nonverbal features of the interactions as well as psychological benefits to the individual of ongoing sessions (Maclagan & Grant, 2011; Moos & Bjorn, 2006). Second, longer term interventions, including caregiver training and emotional support for caregivers, could be evaluated. Evaluations could address group participation, care staff use of the life story memory aids, improvements in person-centered care, and psychological well-being of the residents (Davis & Smith, 2011; Egan et al., 2010; Maclagan & Grant, 2011; Thompson, 2011).

For individuals with moderate dementia, life story writings are elicited through deep listening, creativity, and openness to the moment. The writings themselves, in Conversational Remembering Boxes, life story binders, or another form, then can promote deep connections in future encounters to enrich life in a longterm care setting (see Ryan & Schindel Martin, 2011).

NOTE

1. We recognize the contributions of McMaster undergraduates who wrote down life stories as part of their honors theses: Anitaa Gregory, Cheryl Liu, Sindhura Mahendran, Justine Steckley, and Neshmi Zaman. Individuals participating in our research are identified here with pseudonyms to protect their privacy. We express our gratitude to participants and to their families.

REFERENCES

Astell, A. J., Ellis, M. P., Alm, N., Dye, R., & Gowans, G. (2010). Stimulating people with dementia to reminisce using personal and generic photographs. *International Journal of Computers in Healthcare, 1*(2), 177–198.

Backhaus, P. (Ed.). (2011). *Communication in elderly care.* London: Continuum Press.

Basting, A. D. (2009). *Forget memory: Creating better lives for people with dementia.* Baltimore, MD: Johns Hopkins University Press.

Bohlmeijer, E., Roemer, M., Cuijpers, P., & Smit, F. (2007). The effects of reminiscence on psychological well-being in older adults: A meta-analysis. *Aging and Mental Health, 11,* 291–300.

Bourgeois, M. S. (1993). Effects of memory aids on the dyadic conversations of individuals with dementia. *Journal of Applied Behavior Analysis, 26*(1), 77–87.

Davis, B. H. (Ed.). (2005). *Alzheimer talk, text and context: Enhancing communication.* New York: Palgrave Macmillan.

Davis, B. H., & Smith, M. K. (2011). Dementia care communication in residential facilities: Intersections of training and research. In P. Backhaus (Ed.),

Communication in elderly care (pp. 20–39). London: Continuum International Publishing Group.

Dienstag, A. (2003). Lessons from the Lifelines Writing Group for people in the early stages of Alzheimer's disease: Forgetting that we don't remember. In J. L. Ronch & J. A. Goldfield (Eds.), *Mental wellness in aging: Strengths-based approaches* (pp. 343–352). Baltimore, MD: Health Professions Press.

Egan, M., Berube, D., Racine, G., & Leonard, C. E. (2010). Methods to enhance verbal communication between individuals with Alzheimer's disease and formal and informal caregivers: A systematic review. *International Journal of Alzheimer's Disease.* Published online 2010 June 3, 12 pages. doi: 10.4061/2010/906818

Elliot, G. (2011). *Montessori Methods for Dementia™: Focusing on the person and the prepared environment.* Hamilton, ON: McMaster University.

Fels, D. I., & Astell, A. J. (2011). Storytelling as a model of conversation for people with dementia and caregivers. *American Journal of Alzheimer's Disease and Other Dementias, 26*(7), 535–541.

Gibson, F., & Carson, Y. (2010). Life story work in practice: Aiming for enduring change. *Journal of Dementia Care, 18,* 1351–1372.

Hagens, C., Beaman, A., & Ryan, E. B. (2003). Reminiscing, poetry writing, and remembering boxes: Personhood-centered communication with cognitively impaired older adults. *Activities, Adaptation, and Aging, 27*(3/4), 97–112.

Hagens, C., Cosentino, A., & Ryan, E. B. (2006). *You grow out of winter: Poetry in longterm care* (Writing Down Our Years Series, No. 6). Hamilton, Canada: McMaster Centre for Gerontological Studies.

Harwood, J. (2007). *Understanding communication and aging.* Newbury Park, CA: Sage.

Hoerster, L., Hickey, E., & Bourgeois, M. (2001). Effects of memory aids on conversations between nursing home residents with dementia and nursing assistants. *Neuropsychological Rehabilitation, 11*(3/4), 399–427.

Killick, J. (2003). Memorializing dementia. *Alzheimer's Care Quarterly, 4*(1), 18–25.

Killick, J., & Allan, K. (2001). *Communication and the care of people with dementia.* Buckingham, England: Open University.

Kitwood, T. (1997). *Dementia reconsidered: The person comes first.* Philadelphia: Open University Press.

Lubinski, R. (2011). Creating a positive communication environment in long-term care. In P. Backhaus (Ed.), *Communication in elderly care* (pp. 40–61). London: Continuum Press.

Maclagan, M., & Grant, A. (2011). Care of people with Alzheimer's disease in New Zealand: Supporting the telling of life stories. In P. Backhaus (Ed.), *Communication in elderly care* (pp. 62–89). London: Continuum Press.

McFadden, S., & McFadden, J. (2011). *Aging together: Dementia, friendship, and flourishing communities.* Baltimore, MD: Johns Hopkins University Press.

Moore, L., & B. Davis. (2002). Quilting narrative: Using repetition techniques to help elderly communicators. *Geriatric Nursing, 23,* 262–266.

Moos, I., & Bjorn, A. (2006). Use of the life story in the institutional care of people with dementia: A review of intervention studies. *Aging & Society, 26,* 431–454.

Moss, S., Polignano, E., White, C., Minichiello, M., & Sunderland, T. (2002). Reminiscence group activities and discourse interaction with Alzheimer's disease. *Journal of Gerontological Nursing, 28*(8), 36–44.

Okumura, Y., Tanimukai, S., & Asada, T. (2008). Effects of short-term reminiscence therapy on elderly with dementia: A comparison with everyday conversation approach. *Psychogeriatrics, 8,* 124–133.

Orange, J., Ryan, E., Meredith, S., & MacLean, M. (1995). Application of the communication enhancement model for longterm care residents with Alzheimer's disease. *Topics in Language Disorder, 15*(2), 20–35.

Orsulic-Jeras, S., & Camp C. (2000). Montessori-based activities for longterm care residents with advanced dementia. *Gerontologist, 40*(1), 107–111.

Purves, B., Savundranayagam, M., Kelson, E., Astell, A. J., & Phinney, A. (2011). Fostering resilience in dementia through narratives: Contributions of multimedia technology. In B. Resnick, L. Gwyther, & K. Roberto (Eds.), *Resilience in aging: Concepts, research, and outcomes* (pp. 231–244). New York: Springer.

Ryan, E. B. (2010). Overcoming communication predicaments in later life. In L. Hickson (Ed.), *Hearing Care for Adults 2009: Proceedings of the Second International Adult Conference* (pp. 77–86). Staefa, Switzerland: Phonak.

Ryan, E. B., Bannister, K. A., & Anas, A. P. (2009). The dementia narrative: Writing to reclaim social identity. *Journal of Aging Studies, 23*(3), 145–157.

Ryan, E. B., Giles, H., Bartolucci, G., & Henwood, K. (1986). Psycholinguistic and social psychological components of communication by and with the elderly. *Language and Communication, 6,* 1–24.

Ryan, E. B., & Schindel Martin, L. (2011). Using narrative arts to foster personhood in dementia. In P. Backhaus (Ed.), *Communication in elderly care* (pp. 193–217). London: Continuum Press.

Ryan, E. B., Spykerman, H., & Anas, A. (2005). Writers with dementia: The interplay among reading, writing, and personhood. In B. H. Davis (Ed.), *Alzheimer talk, text and context: Identifying communication enhancement* (pp. 190–198). New York: Palgrave Macmillan.

Schuster, E. (1998). A community bound by words: Reflections on a nursing home writing group. *Journal of Aging Studies, 12,* 137–147.

Sierpina, M., & Cole, T. (2004). Stimulating creativity in all elders: A continuum of interventions. *Care Management Journals, 5*(3), 175–183.

Thompson, R. (2011). Using life story work to enhance care. *Nursing Older People, 23*(8), 16–21.

Van den Brandt-van Heek, M.-E. (2011). Asking the right questions: Enabling persons with dementia to speak for themselves. In G. Kenyon, E. Bohlmeijer, & W. Randall (Eds.), *Storying later life* (pp. 338–353). New York: Oxford University Press.

Williams, K. N. (2011). Elderspeak in institutional care for older adults. In P. Backhaus (Ed.), *Communication in elderly care* (pp. 1–19). London: Continuum.

8

PREPARING FOR A THEATRICAL PERFORMANCE

Writing Scripts and Shaping Identities in an Early Memory Loss Support Group

Heidi E. Hamilton and Marta Baffy

. . . we are here to welcome you to today's performance. We are all members of the early memory loss support group that meets here at the Greenlake[1] Y. The performance today is a very personal one because the stories that you will hear came directly from our group . . . now it is with great pride that we give you To Whom I May Concern.

(Introduction to performance, May 10, 2007)

INTRODUCTION

Multidisciplinary efforts involving sociolinguists and social psychologists have highlighted the complex but clear connections between the linguistic and cognitive changes that accompany Alzheimer's disease and other dementias and an individual's social identity in everyday life; such work speaks, for example, of identity crises, loss of self, and profound changes in personality that accompany the disease (Cohen & Eisdorfer, 1986; Davis, 2005; Hamilton, 1994, 1996; Kitwood, 1997; Ramanathan, 1997; Sabat & Harre, 1992; Sabat, 2001; Shenk, 2005). In all of this work, dementia is approached as a human issue within multiple linguistic and social contexts, rather than exclusively as a slowly progressive brain disease. The motivation underlying such research comes from what Leibing (2006, p. 242ff.) calls the 'personhood movement' in dementia studies (cf. Kitwood, 1997), in which 'personhood' refers to "the person within—the reflexive, immaterial, communicable essence of a person that is located deep within the body, but that is sometimes veiled by symptoms" (Leibing, 2006, p. 243). This shift away from the more pervasive medical model of dementia is reflected in its emphasis on the "capacities of the feeling person and not only on his or her losses" (Leibing, 2006, p. 255) as well as on a redefinition of memory as "interactive and not individualized" (Leibing, 2006, p. 255). Not surprisingly, this move toward a focus on personhood has been accompanied by a heightened interest in applying the findings of basic research to help individuals with dementia and those who care for them, for example, by enhancing communication and lifting self-esteem. Most scholars working in this area are motivated by the observation that "relatively little can be done to arrest the underlying brain disease, [but] much can be done to promote health and wellbeing" (Downs et al., 2006, p. 248), resulting in a focus on the identification of active coping strategies and the enhancement of social environments for the individual with dementia.

Intersecting this line of scholarship on dementia, discourse, and identity is a robust movement in innovative programming in the arts for individuals living with the disease. Recently created scholarly societies, journals, and conferences facilitate investigations into the effectiveness of creative expression therapy in a variety of artistic domains, including music, visual arts, theater, and the writing of poetry and short stories. Proponents claim that these multi-sensory experiences are especially good at promoting the social and creative wellbeing of persons with dementia (see esp. Basting, 2009; Ryan, Bannister, & Anas, 2009). Because language is an observable representation of individuals' thoughts and emotions, fine-grained linguistic analyses of language used by participants in such therapeutic programs can arguably provide insight into their cognitive and social effects, although to our knowledge there has been no research investigating this important connection (but see Hamilton, 2011).

In this chapter, we report on our interactional sociolinguistic examination of the discourse of seven audio-recorded weekly meetings of an early memory loss support group as its members participated in several phases of an interactive theater project, *To Whom I May Concern*,[2] that was founded by Matthews (2005). The goal of this project is to open up a dialogue between people with early stage dementia and those who care for them. During the first four of these seven meetings (termed 'focus group sessions'), Matthews listened to and learned from members, eventually transforming personal experience narratives (Labov, 1972), poignant reflections, and jovial banter into a written theatrical script comprising letters addressed to family members, friends, and physicians, among others. This script was then read aloud, discussed, and edited by support group members during three subsequent meetings (termed 'script rehearsal sessions') that led up to a video-recorded live performance in front of an audience of their peers, family members, friends, care partners, and professionals.

During the three practices for their upcoming performance, the reading of these personal letters sparked a surprising number of types of communicative engagement among support group members that may provide evidence of positive cognitive and social effects of this activity. Extending far beyond the expected editing work related to this or that lexical choice or turn of phrase, members provided updates on situations represented in the letters, told 'second' stories (Sacks, 1992), recalled whose story was captured in a particular letter, evaluated a letter's content, and suggested ideas for letters that should be added to the evolving script. These preparations for performance opened up myriad opportunities for these individuals who were struggling with early memory loss. At the same time that they reported feeling increasingly powerless outside the group, these members were enacting interactional power within it (Ainsworth-Vaughn, 1998). And in performing their carefully crafted texts for an outside audience, these individuals were ultimately able to shed light on their world for those who lacked the shared experience of early dementia and to indicate to these others how they would most like to be portrayed and understood.

Within these interactions, one topic in particular—problems with a seemingly inept local paratransit service—served especially as an impetus for 'hot cognition' (Abelson, 1963; Lazarus & Smith, 1988), a lively discursive exchange of ideas that combines emotion with cognition. Members' use of epistemic, affective, and agentive stances as they co-constructed and responded to narratives of personal experience indexed the shared experience of overcoming adversity, the shared value of humor in the face of adversity (Norrick, 1997), and pointed out the irony of needing to be agentive and knowledgeable as they were having to deal with increasing dependence and memory loss. In this chapter, we argue that the enthusiasm around this shared experience empowered members to claim and hold the conversational floor in an institutional setting (Heritage & Clayman, 2011) that at other times limited their contributions to answering questions directed at them. These acts of discursive alignment then helped to shape resilient identities (Capps & Ochs, 1995; Schiffrin, 1996) for these individuals that, in turn, reinforced their membership within a group that shared these values and experiences.

In what follows, we first characterize the *To Whom I May Concern* theatrical project along with the individuals who participated in it. Next, we examine group members' discursive display of personal agency, first within the 'storytelling world' of the support group meetings and then within the 'storyworlds' (Polanyi, 1985; Schiffrin, 1990) of the personal experience narratives they recounted. We then discuss these findings in terms of the light they shed on the discursive underpinnings of the innovative project's therapeutic nature and close with implications for worlds outside of the support group environment.

THE PROJECT: *TO WHOM I MAY CONCERN*

Eager to build on the therapeutic value of their support group sessions, the two female facilitators, Abby and Nadine, of an early memory loss support group in the greater New York City metropolitan area invited the founder of *To Whom I May Concern,* Maureen Matthews, to visit their group in early March 2007. After meeting Matthews and learning about the project, the nine support group members (three males—Fritz, Jim, and Max; and six females—Alice, Amy, Jane, Jessica, Marcie, and Sophie) enthusiastically agreed to participate in the project.

Matthews joined the group for the weekly hour-long meetings in March and April. During the first four of these meetings, she asked a number of open-ended questions that encouraged highly interactive discourse that included narratives, discussion, and personal reflections from individuals regarding "the diagnostic process, impact on self perception, the reactions of friends and families, coping strategies, hopes and concerns" (http://towhomimayconcern.org). These sessions were audio recorded to facilitate the transformation of recurrent themes and salient uses of language into first drafts of letters (see Table 8.1 for a list of addressees of letters in the script) written by Matthews from the point of view of one or more group members ostensibly to a specific individual (e.g., a spouse), groups of individuals (e.g., breakfast mates), or institutions (e.g., Department of Motor Vehicles).

Once the draft of the script was written, the following three weekly meetings were turned into 'script rehearsals' in which group members read individual letters in Matthews's script aloud. In addition to practicing their parts, group members evaluated the letters, suggested editorial changes, told or retold narratives connected to the letters, and updated members on events that were captured in the letters. Matthews describes this rehearsal process as one of 'validation'; as she explains, "There is never one draft . . . Rewrites are done until the group feels a sense of ownership of the script" (http://towhomimayconcern.org). On May 10, the group performed *To Whom I May Concern* in front of a live audience that included many of the addressees of the letters in the script.

Table 8.1
Addressees of letter in *To Whom I May Concern* script

- *To Whom I May Concern*
- *Dear Museum Docent*
- *To My Dear Husband*
- *Dear Breakfast Mates*
- *Dear Doctors, Nurses, Social Workers*
- *Dear Department of Motor Vehicles*
- *Dear Chauffeu … I mean, loving wife*
- ***Dear Access-a-Ride***
- *Dear Doctor*
- *Dear Potential Group Member*

Given our interest in the discursive and social construction of identity through storytelling (Schiffrin, 1996; De Fina, Schiffrin, & Bamberg, 2006), we initially focused our attention only on the accounts arising from the first four support group meetings—in which Matthews was explicitly focused on the elicitation of personal experiences from the members. Yet upon further engagement with the three subsequent script reading and editing sessions, we discovered that group members appeared to be staking out their identities just as much, if not more, in this particular context. This is perhaps not surprising, since, in her attempts to translate members' personal experiences into scripted letters to be performed, Matthews may have selected lexical items or turns of phrase that did not mesh well with the members' thoughts and feelings.[3] It is, then, during script rehearsals that group members had clear opportunities to listen to their voices as revoiced by Matthews and to choose to accept, reject, or otherwise contest the words—and relatedly, the identities—that had been evoked within these letters. As mentioned previously, not infrequently, the reading of the letters sparked further personal experience narratives; these (re)tellings afforded group members the opportunity to reify or perhaps refine the personas that they wanted to construct and display for their group (and, although this is often unstated, for the larger audience during the final live performance).

FOCUS ON ACCESS-A-RIDE NARRATIVES

One personal experience narrative that was consistently met with enthusiastic responses throughout support group meetings (whether at focus group sessions or script rehearsals—see Table 8.2 for details) is what we have coined the 'Access-a-Ride narrative.' These tellings recounted group members' (overwhelmingly negative) experiences with Access-a-Ride, a

Table 8.2
Mentions of Access-a-Ride within support group meetings

Weekly Meetings	Focus Group Sessions	Script Rehearsal Sessions
1.	No mention of Access-a-Ride (AAR)	
2.	No mention of AAR	
3.	No mention of AAR	
4.	Max's AAR 1st telling at 32 minutes into meeting Max's AAR 2nd telling at 43 minutes into meeting Mary's personal reflection on Max's AAR tellings	
5.		Alice asks to read AAR letter Abby (facilitator) suggests adding more details to letter Alice tells own AAR narrative Jane tells own AAR narrative
6.		Alice reads AAR letter Max arrives late to meeting and tells new AAR narrative
7. Performance		Jack reads AAR letter Alice reads AAR letter Followed by comments by Jane and Alice

paratransit service operated by New York City Transit whose purpose is to provide transportation for people who, due to disability, are unable to use public bus or subway service for some or all of their trips.

In all of the narratives except one, group members lamented their Access-a-Ride experiences[4] to appreciative and knowing listeners, highlighting a variety of problems that occurred after they had reserved a trip on Access-a-Ride. Each such account involved one or more of the following (non) events: the vehicle did not arrive at all to pick up the rider; the driver left the designated pick-up area before finding the rider; the driver arrived very late; or once the rider got into the vehicle, the driver did not know the directions and/or got lost on the way to the desired destination. Importantly, the tellings also typically displayed key instances of self-advocacy and assertiveness on the part of the support group member in response to the adverse conditions he or she faced. We understand such displays to be central to the presentation of the individual's identity as a resilient human being rather than as a victim of early memory loss. In short, we argue that these Access-a-Ride narratives have a function that transcends mere 'complaining.' Indeed, we suspect that the pervasiveness of this narrative thread points to its potentially self-affirming quality for group members and, specifically, that members enjoy co-telling these stories as a way to accentuate the assertive and in-control aspects of their identities.

The final version of the Access-A-Ride portion of the *To Whom I May Concern* performance script that Matthews wrote and revised several times based on members' narratives, conversations, and reflections reads as follows:

ALICE: Actually, this letter has to be censored out of respect for every-one present. Let me just say the language is colorful, forceful, and very, very, frustrated! I'll read the cleaned up version.
Dear Access-A-Ride,
Where are you?
Why are you late?
Why do we have to go all over Queens to go two miles down the road?
WHERE ARE YOU?
I'm forced to depend on you. Why do you make it so difficult?
Signed,
Frustrated in New York

JANE: Today I came here by Access-a-Ride. I haven't done that in a long time and I must say it was very pleasant. And last week I went to a party and they picked me up at 1AM.

ALICE: Lucky you! The last time we got lost, the driver asked me if I knew the directions. And I'm the one with the memory loss!

In the upcoming analytical sections, we examine one Access-a-Ride-related conversation and three Access-a-Ride narratives, one by Alice ("I got him off that road") and two by Max ("I had words with Access-a-Ride," parts one and two), to identify the linguistic resources used by group members to 'position' (Davies & Harré, 1990) themselves and others as figures in the storyworlds as well as in the here-and-now of the storytelling situation (Goffman, 1981; Bamberg, 1997). By drawing attention to the subtle ways in which support group members use language as a tool for identity construction, we demonstrate that members portray themselves as agentive with respect to the facilitators of the in-stitutional discourse context of the support group sessions as well as to the Access-a-Ride employees.

AGENCY IN THE STORYTELLING WORLD

One of the most important sites of identity construction is the interactional situation of the script rehearsal. Indeed, it is within the realm of the storytelling world, or the here-and-now of the storytelling situation (Bamberg, 1997), that support group members built an agentive persona, particularly vis-à-vis the group facilitators. In the Access-a-Ride narratives arising out of support group meetings, we found that group members very much wanted to tell their own, and hear each others', narratives—so much, in fact, that at times they stepped on the facilitators' toes, so to speak, in order to steer the discussion toward talk about Access-a-Ride. In examining one such narrative, our aim is to determine the linguistic resources upon which group members rely to exercise interactional agency, as well as how these ultimately helped to shape the group members' identities as strong and assertive.

According to Ainsworth-Vaughn (1998), speakers use a variety of 'power-claiming discourse strategies' to wield power within an interaction. For instance, interruptions, questions, and control over discourse topic may all be employed to assert authority. These strategies are particularly salient in institutional encounters, where institutional representatives (e.g., physicians, judges, teachers) typically ask questions and direct the flow of discourse topics and events (Heritage, 1997). The support group setting is no different. Group facilitators hold the reins of the institutional and conversational agendas: they choose topics for discussion, ask questions to encourage member participation, and ensure that the group stays focused on the task(s) at hand.

Representatives' authority can nonetheless be challenged when others do not comply with the 'exchange structures' or 'participation frameworks' (Schiffrin, 1987) typically inherent in institutional encounters. A patient may, for example, stray from the distinctive question-answer pattern that characterizes the history-taking phase of a physician-patient interaction, and begin to ask questions herself, or even shift the discourse topic away from one initiated by the physician to a health concern she deems more pressing (see Ainsworth-Vaughn, 1998, for information on interactional power).

We observed several instances in which support group members exercise such agency during the script rehearsal. In the following extract, the group is in the middle of their second read-through of the *To Whom I May Concern* script. Coincidentally, as Alice begins to read the Access-a-Ride letter, Max walks in with his own Access-a-Ride story to tell.

Excerpt 1 [6. 11:40]

01	NADINE:	Oh, here's Max.
02	JANE:	"Dear Access-a-Ride."
03		Page eleven.
04	NADINE:	Here is the-
05		What-
06	ALICE:	Max you're two minutes late.
07	X:	hhh
08	MAX:	Two min-
09		I wish I was two minutes late.
10	ALICE:	Sit.
11	MAX:	I have a story boy.
12	X:	hhh
13 →	NADINE:	But [you have to wait till later.
14	?:	[About Access-a-Ride?
15 →	SOPHIE:	˅ou can write a book.
16		hhh
17	MAX:	I could.
18		I could write a whole volume of books.
19	NADINE:	Well you know what Max?
20		We just had someone else re-
21		[You know we're doing the-
22	JANE:	[Read your part.
23	ALICE:	Let him-
24		Let's go back and let him re[ad.
25	NADINE:	[Well that's what I was saying.
26		No I- I-

27 →	AMY:	No, let- let him tell us.
28	MAX:	Ehhh, it's nothing to tell.
29		'Cause if I tell you I'm only gonna get angry again.
30	X:	Aww.
31	AMY:	Well let's-
32	NADINE:	Thank y[ou-
33	MAX:	[I almost committed murder today.
34 →	JANE:	[Really.
35	?:	[Oooh.
36 →	AMY:	I think he should tell [us and then we'll ( )
37	ALICE:	[I think I can imagine
38		[the feeling.
39 →	JANE:	[That sounds very interesting.
40		hhh
41 →	AMY:	It sounds interesting and then we'll go back to page
42		eleven.
43		What the hell.

Here we see both Nadine's claim to power as the group facilitator, as well as the support group members' collective, albeit implicit, challenge to her authority. In what appears to be Max's attempt to take control of the floor, in line 11 he announces that he has a story to share with the group. This is met with immediate opposition from Nadine, who, in her role as institutional representative, rebuffs his attempt with the sharp directive, *But you have to wait till later.*

Instead of passively acquiescing to Nadine's direct attempts to assert her institutional authority, four group members engage Max with comments and even make suggestions about his future actions, almost as if they were 'in charge' themselves. Sophie comments that Max *can write a book,* while Alice contemplates the frustration he must have experienced (*I think I can imagine the feeling*). Jane nudges Max to tell his story with the continuer *really,* and then the suggestive, inviting remark, *That sounds very interesting.* Amy stands up to Nadine in a very explicit way, stating, *No, let- let him tell us* in line 27, strongly recommending that

Max be permitted to tell his Access-a-Ride story, in direct contrast to Nadine's desire to postpone the narrative telling and carry on with script reading instead. That said, in expressing her resistance and arguing for a 'say' in this matter, Amy gives a nod to the institutional order by employing the causative *let*; this indicates Amy's understanding that Nadine is indeed in charge of the conversational agenda, and further, that Amy looks to her for approval on matters related to the group discussion.

Amy, who is obviously interested in hearing Max's account, persists in her resistance to Nadine's more rigid, institutional agenda in lines 36 and 41–42, when she states, *I think he should tell us and then we'll . . .* and *It sounds interesting and then we'll go back to page eleven.* Amy's utterances are significant because they include the group members in the planning and decision-making as well. Her use of the pronoun *we*, in combination with the modal *will*, suggests that Amy considers that everyone should be involved in planning support group discussions. Thus, acting as a spokesperson of sorts, Amy positions herself and the other group members as having some control.

Excerpt 1 illustrates how group members exercise interactional agency on two levels. First, by the very act of speaking and engaging Max with comments, Sophie, Alice, and Jane disrupt the discourse activity (i.e., script reading and editing) that Nadine had planned. They ignore her directive that Max wait with his story altogether and make the implicit suggestion that he relate his unpleasant Access-a-Ride experience. Second, Amy makes use of certain lexical items (e.g., *no, we, us*) and grammatical constructions (future with *will*) that work to position the group members as at least partially 'in charge' of what counts as an appropriate discourse topic and its sequential placement within the meeting.

Although the group members' comments and suggestions contribute to their interactional agency, what is perhaps more significant is that this agency is exercised specifically with respect to an impending Access-a-Ride narrative. As we just observed, group members do not yield to the facilitator's institutional agenda, but pursue (with ultimate success) their own conversational goal of hearing Max's Access-a-Ride story. But what is it about Access-a-Ride narratives that group members find so compelling? We turn to this question in the following section.

AGENCY IN THE STORYWORLD

In addition to making agentive moves within the ongoing conversational interaction, these support group members also position themselves as agentive on the 'deeper' level of the storyworld; i.e., as characters within the stories they recount before and during script rehearsals. A great deal of identity construction occurs at this level because "in narratives, speakers typically make claims about characters and make these claims (that are said to have held for a there-and-then) relevant to the here-and-now of the speaking moment" (Bamberg, 2011, p. 103). It is this relevance of these storyworld constructions to the current, ongoing discourse that we investigate here. That is, our goal is to ascertain the following: in their narratives, what claims do support group members make about their own and other storyworld characters so as to paint an overall agentive picture of themselves? Relatedly, what linguistic resources do they use to make these claims?

Bamberg (2011) posits that identity construction in narrative, far from being haphazard, is largely accomplished along three different dimensions (constancy-change over time; sameness vs. difference; and low or high agency), the latter two[5] of which are pertinent to our current discussion. Specifically, when narrating accounts of personal experience, speakers 'navigate' their identities along the dimensions of sameness vs. difference and low vs. high agency.

Sameness versus Difference

Regarding the dimension of sameness vs. difference, Bamberg (2011) states that "it is typically through discursive choices that people define synchronically a sense of (an individual) self as different from others or they integrate a sense of who they are in terms of belonging to particular communities of others." This can be overtly done, but most often is "hinted at by way of covertly positioning self and others in the realm of being talked about" (p. 104). In the Access-a-Ride narratives that we examined, this is a vital step that narrators take in displaying agentive selves within the storyworld; i.e., support group members draw contrasts between themselves, whom they position as in-the-know and exercising clear judgment, and Access-a-Ride drivers, whom they consistently position as incompetent. It is on the backdrop of these portrayed differences that the narrators can show off their agentive moves. Alice's narrative illustrates this point:

Excerpt 2 [5A. 30:50]

01 ALICE: One day I was going home with Access-a-Ride,

02   And another person was in the car with me,

03   And we were on the Cross Island parkway,

04 →		And he doesn't get off at Utopia Parkway.
05 →		He takes us for a ride.
06		And Utopia Parkway happens to be practically the last stop
07		in [Queens
08	AMY:	[Queens,
09	ALICE:	And he's taking-
10 →		And I think to myself, "Which is the next exit?"
11 →		I said "There's another exit- the next one,"
12		The- uh-
13	AMY:	Francis Lewis.
14	ALICE:	After you get off, a little on the- the road going to the
15		Whitestone Bridge.
16 →		So luckily I got him off that road.
17	?:	Before the Whitestone Bridge.
18	ALICE:	Otherwise I would have been in the Bronx.
19	?:	(hhh)
20 →	ALICE:	They don't know where they're going.
21		I've got a better sense of direction than any
22		Access-a-Ride driver I've been with.
23	X:	(Commotion,)
24	ABBY:	That's what we're saying.
25	NADINE:	Unfortunately they don't have that, [navigator.
26	?:	[GPS
27	ALICE:	They do [have it.
28	NADINE:	[They do?
29 →	ALICE:	They do but they- they're stupid.
30	ABBY:	Well then that's really pathetic.

After providing a brief backdrop, or 'orientation' (Labov, 1972; Labov & Waletzky, 1967), to her story in lines 01–03, Alice begins to relate the events of her narrative with immediate disapproval of the driver. She specifically states, *He doesn't get off at Utopia Parkway. He takes us for a ride,* rather than driving her directly to her destination. In contrast to her depiction of her driver as rather incompetent, Alice zeroes in on her own superior problem-solving skills in lines 10–11. She begins by describing her own cognitive processes at the time (*I think to myself, "Which is the next exit?"*) and then proceeds to report her words to the driver: *I said, "There's another exit- the next one."* It becomes evident that Alice attempts to characterize herself in a far better light—in the end, it is her thoughts and actions that prevented a long 'ride' (*I got him off that road*). If he had been left to his own devices, Alice explains, the driver would have taken her all the way to the Bronx (*Otherwise I would have been in The Bronx*).

As the events of this brief narrative unfold, we get a sense of the contrast that Alice sets up between herself and the driver; however, it is within the story's 'evaluation'[6] (Labov, 1972) that Alice's negative assessment of him and her own positive self-presentation more explicitly come to light. In Alice's narrative, this can be found in lines 20–22 and 29. First, referring to Access-a-Ride drivers, she states, *They don't know where they're going.* Alice immediately follows this up with a positive self-assessment: *I've got a better sense of direction than any Access-a-Ride driver I've been with.* After minimal input from Nadine and Abby, Alice resumes her disparaging evaluation of the driver in line 29; here she goes so far as to claim that Access-a-Ride drivers are *stupid*.

Through the contrast that she creates between their two storyworld characters (see Table 8.3), Alice uses the Access-a-Ride driver as a resource for building an assertive identity for her storyworld persona. Notably, while she employs negation in relation to the driver's expected actions and knowledge (*He doesn't get off . . .; They don't know . . .*), as well as the negative adjective *stupid* regarding Access-a-Ride drivers' cognitive abilities, Alice does quite the opposite to portray herself. With simple, affirmative statements in which she alone features as the semantic agent (*I think to myself . . .; I said . . .; I got him off . . .; I've got a better . . .*), Alice positions herself as having sound cognition and problem-solving skills.

Agency Dilemma

In telling narratives of personal experience, speakers also construct their identities in relation to what Bamberg (2011) has termed the 'agency dilemma'; by this, he means that speakers either select narrative devices that

Table 8.3
Self- and other-positioning within Alice's Access-a-Ride narrative

Alice's self-positioning	Alice's positioning of the driver
	He doesn't get off at Utopia Parkway.
I think to myself, "Which is the next exit?" **I said, "There's another exit, the next one.."**	
So luckily **I got him off that road…** otherwise I would have been in the Bronx.	
	They don't know where they're going.
I've got a better sense of direction than any Access-a-Ride driver I've been with.	
	They're stupid.

lean toward a 'person-to-world' direction of fit, which indicates high personal agency, or they choose devices that construe the direction of fit from world-to-person, signaling low personal agency. In other words, some speakers depict themselves as strong, in control, and self-determined *actors;* others construct selves as less influential, less powerful, and less responsible *undergoers.* In the Access-a-Ride narratives that we examine here, group members tend to portray themselves as actors, or 'agentive self-constructers', selecting linguistic devices that underscore their active role in dealing with, or correcting, the usual Access-a-Ride blunder.

In Excerpt 2, Alice not only draws a sharp distinction between herself and the driver, but importantly, she also uses this contrast to position herself as highly agentive. As detailed earlier, Alice draws on a variety of linguistic devices to do so: she uses simple, affirmative sentences to refer to her own assertiveness and negated verbs (*doesn't get off; don't know*) to depict her driver's ineptitude. Alice also employs 'constructed dialogue' (Tannen, 1989) to represent her storyworld actions and thoughts. In doing so, she provides her character with 'speaking space' (De Fina, 2003) to spotlight the specific actions that she undertook. De Fina argues that the choice to report the speech of a storyworld character is strongly related to her agency because it foregrounds her storyworld actions. In this case, Alice's reported speech is her indirect command to the driver (i.e., *I said, "There's another exit- the next one"*); this is, without a doubt, an agentive move, especially when one considers this phenomenon within an institutional context. The professional driver *should* know directions, and a lay person, especially one with early memory loss, *should not* be expected to be able to draw on this knowledge.

In Excerpt 3, the agency dilemma plays out in a slightly different way. Max has just walked into the meeting room and begins to describe his frustrating experience getting to the support group meeting that day. He provides a partial account in lines 08–25, and then returns to his story in line 40 after getting sidetracked by the support group facilitators.

Excerpt 3 [4. 32:00]

01	ABBY:	Hi Max.
02	NADINE:	Maxwell they took you-
03	MAX:	Thank Access-a-Ride for the ( )
04	X:	(hhh)
05 →	NADINE:	I knew it, I knew it.
06 →	MARCIE:	Ac[cess-a-Ride again?
07 →	ABBY:	[They took him on a little uh-
08	MAX:	*Oh boy did I have words with them this morning.*
09	NADINE:	You're the only one that that happens to.
10		Do you think the[re's a significance?
11 →	MAX:	[I got- I got idiots who are drivers.
12		I can't help it.
13		*[Several lines omitted]*[7]
14		They sent a driver 'cause the-
15		They called him for me over there the uh, secretary.
16 →		And the driver you know what excuse he gave?
17		He was there,
18		He drove into the compound,
19		You know there's like a, backyard there where all the
20		cars are parked,
21		And he saw the, uh di- dialysis center so he knew he
22		was in the right place.

23 →		But he didn't- he didn't come to the other side and
24		say "Is Mr. Feinstein in here?"
25		(hhh)
26	ABBY:	Well you know what, come sit down, [we'll get you a nice=
27	AMY:	[(hhh)
28	ABBY:	=cup of coffee, and a cookie.
29	AMY:	He wasn't selected for his brains.
30	NADINE:	And anyway [well,
31	AMY:	[Like the first grade
32	NADINE:	Hey Maxwell, [the important thing is it's my birthday,
33	MAX:	[Yes,
34		Happy birthday.
35	X:	(hhh)
36	MAX:	((kisses Nadine)) I can't get angry,
37	MARCIE:	Have a cup of coffee
38	ABBY:	In other words, yeah.
39	NADINE:	In other words, things just happen.
40	MAX:	**So I had words with Access-a-Ride today.**
41		*[Several lines omitted]*[8]
42		It was a very exciting morning let me tell you.
43	NADINE:	You look very nice in that shirt and the green,
44		I like it.
45	MAX:	Thank you.
46	X:	(hhh)
47 →	NADINE:	For a man that was lost,
48	MAX:	Happy birthday.
49 →		I wasn't lost,
50 →		I knew what I was doing.
51 →		He didn't see me.

Interestingly, Max both begins and ends his narrative with a variant of *I had words with Access-a-Ride* (lines 08 and 40) as marked in the transcript. Indeed, it appears that these utterances function as Max's 'abstract' and 'coda' (Labov & Waletzky, 1967), that is, a brief summary of his forthcoming story and a conclusion. Max's choice to condense his experience into such statements is telling: not only does 'having words' with someone indicate the occurrence of a quarrel, but by coupling this idiomatic expression with the first person pronoun *I* (as opposed to, for example, *we had words*) Max highlights his personal, active role—and potential aggressor status—in this fight.

As suggested by Nadine and Abby's initial comments in lines 05 and 07 (*I knew it, I knew it* and *They took him on a little uh. . .*), the content of Max's subsequent narrative is somewhat predictable. Even Marcie's question, *Access-a-Ride again?*, reveals that Max has entertained the support group with Access-a-Ride narratives before; for one reason or another, he repeatedly finds himself at the mercy of incompetent drivers. While this provides good material for Max's stories, it likely takes its toll on his self-esteem. Due to his increasing memory loss and cognitive decline, Max has lost his driver's license[9]—perhaps the most emblematic symbol of independence—and is forced to rely on Access-a-Ride to get around. He makes no secret of this situation; however, it may contribute to Max's attempts to position himself as agentive specifically in these Access-a-Ride accounts.

In certain respects, Max accomplishes his storyworld positioning in a manner similar to Alice in Excerpt 2, namely, he also creates a contrast between himself and the Access-a-Ride employee (see Table 8.4). Beginning in line 11, Max uses a negative referring term regarding his drivers' cognitive abilities (*I got idiots who are drivers*) when he speaks over Nadine's question of him. Further, he employs negation in relation to his driver's expected sensible actions (*he didn't- he didn't come to the other side and say "Is Mr. Feinstein here?"*) and refers to his driver's explanation as a mere excuse (*The driver, you know what excuse he gave?*). In short, Max depicts his driver as somewhat useless, as did Alice.

When positioning himself, Max paints a generally positive picture and draws on a variety of linguistic resources to set himself apart from his 'idiot' driver. However, unlike Alice, Max does not highlight his agency by detailing the ways in which he corrected the driver's mistake. Instead, he assumes an agentive stance from the get-go, positioning himself as a disappointed 'higher up,' of sorts. For instance, with his opening abstract, *Oh boy did I have words with them this morning,* Max not only places himself in the role of semantic agent, but also suggests that he is in a position to criticize and argue with Access-a-Ride drivers. In

Table 8.4

Self- and other-positioning within Max's Access-a-Ride narrative, part 1

Max's self-positioning	Max's positioning of the driver
Damn Access-A-Ride!	
Oh boy, **did I have words with them** this morning.	
	I got **idiots who are drivers.**
	The driver, you know what **excuse he gave?**
	He was there but **he didn't come find me.**
	He didn't come to the other side **and say,** "Excuse me, is Mr. Feinstein here?"
So **I had words with Access-A-Ride** today.	
It was **a very exciting morning let me tell you.**	
(in response to Natalie who said, "For a man that was lost")	
I wasn't lost, I knew what I was doing.	

addition, when Max proclaims *I got idiots who are drivers,* he speaks as if he were somehow in charge of these employees. Finally, his remark on the driver's *excuse* intimates that Max, like a disapproving supervisor, does not accept the driver's justification as to why he was unable to pick Max up on time.

After Max seemingly concludes his narrative in line 25, Abby, Amy, and Nadine each try to appease him by offering coffee and cookies (Abby: *we'll get you a nice cup of coffee and a cookie*), disparaging the driver (Amy: *He wasn't selected for his brains*), and focusing on the more cheerful event of a birthday (Nadine: *Hey Maxwell, the important thing is it's my birthday*). It is worth noting that, unlike Amy, the facilitators attempt to shift the focus of discussion to something that is not Access-a-Ride. As noted earlier in the discussion of Excerpt 1 (Nadine: *But you have to wait till later*), the facilitators likely wish to return the support group discussion to where it had been when Max entered the room. But as discussed previously, group members resist the topical shift away from Access-a-Ride and exercise interactional agency to hear and tell these stories.

Now that he has emerged from the control he had in positioning both himself and the driver within the storyworld, Max becomes vulnerable to positioning moves by others within the storytelling world. Nadine's comment in line 47, *For a man that was lost,* is one such move. Although she appears to offer it almost as an afterthought to his narrative,

Max immediately picks up on the implication of lack of control and defends himself. After all, Max's prior narrative had centered primarily on his agentive reaction to the Access-a-Ride driver's incompetence, in that the driver had failed to find and pick up Max in the place where he usually waited. While the precise sequence of events is somewhat unclear in the brief account that Max provides, Nadine's presupposition that Max was lost essentially 'undoes' all of Max's previous positioning work. Nadine not only projects a more feeble, cognitively impaired persona onto Max (i.e., someone who gets lost even where he usually gets picked up), but simultaneously, she also arguably reveals her own perception of Max or, at minimum, her lack of attention to the point of his prior narrative. At this juncture, Max takes it upon himself to set the record straight. He immediately retorts with *I wasn't lost, I knew what I was doing. . . . He didn't see me,* putting the onus of the blame and incompetence on his driver and positioning himself as in-the-know. Nadine's comment about Max being lost is significant because it illustrates the somewhat negative other-positioning in which even support group facilitators, as individuals who are employed to assist group members, may participate. In this case, Nadine positions Max's storyworld character as the very antithesis of his preferred position: weak, confused, or 'lost.' While this portrayal is almost certainly inadvertent, Max is confronted with a face-threatening characterization of himself within the public conversation that he must decide to contest or let stand.

Approximately 10 minutes later, Max reintroduces his Access-a-Ride adventure into the discourse. He begins speaking (*So I had a very excit-*) during a lull in the conversation after Nadine has gotten up from her seat to answer the phone. He subsequently stops mid-word when Nadine drops something (as noted in line 2) and begins again with his abstract in line 6, *I had a very exciting morning yelling at Access-a-Ride.*

Excerpt 4 [4. 43:22]

01	MAX:	**So, I had a very excit-**
02		((Something drops))
03		Whoops.
04		Ya got it?
05	NADINE:	I got it.
06	MAX:	**I had a very exciting morning yelling at Access-a-Ride.**

07	AMY:	Oh.
08		That's your version of excitement huh?
09	ABBY:	It is frustrating when that happens.
10	MAX:	The guy- the driver came in,
11		But you know what?
12 →		Think.
13		It's a- the uh- where I go in the morning- the gym,
14		Excuse me.
15		It's called the cardiac rehab center.
16		*[Several lines omitted]* [10]
17		So and Access-a-Ride is my carrier.
18 →		So uh, they didn't-
19 →		They didn't show up.
20		So the hospi- the you know the facility,
21		They called Access-a-Ride and said "What happened."
22		Oh ride- the driver was there,
23		He came into the compound and he saw the place
24		where they do uh-
25	MARCIE:	Dialysis.
26	MAX:	Dialysis.
27 →		He was in the right place but he never came across
28		the you know-
29		The dri-(hhh) like-
30		We're here, and they were there.
31 →		He never came.
32	ABBY:	Yeah luckily I will say it- the- the services has- have
33		improved tremendously from-
34	MAX:	Yeah but you gotta [have-

35	ABBY:	[From a while ago.
36 →	MAX:	You gotta have somebody who can think a little bit.
37		If I'm not here look for me somewhere else.
38	ABBY:	Right.
39	MAX:	It wasn't that far,
40		It wasn't raining,
41 →		And I refuse to- on a day like today.
42		Usually I go outdoors.

His opening line, although slightly different in form from his first telling, is semantically quite similar. Here too, Max suggests that there was an unpleasant verbal exchange between him and his driver, and foregrounds his own initiating role in the argument with first person pronoun *I*, and the action verb *yell*. Notably, in his first telling, Max uses the idiomatic phrase *have words with*; however, in this second account, Max intensifies his agency with the more straightforward *yell*.

Of course, what actually transpired in the Access-a-Ride vehicle is unknown to the support group members and facilitators present at this meeting. Indeed, the only account anybody has is Max's own version of the events. The 'looking good principle' (Ochs, Smith, & Taylor, 1989) suggests that it is a common phenomenon in narratives of personal experience that narrators tend to present themselves as superior to other characters in their storyworlds. As a consequence, Max's account may well be colored by a desire to also 'look good.' He may not have actually *yelled* at the Access-a-Ride driver, but phrased it as such to appear more assertive to his audience. No matter what happened, however, Max's persistence in telling this particular narrative, and the focus on his own role in the alleged argument, strongly suggest that this story is an opportunity for Max to construct and display an agentive self.

Max's second telling is somewhat more coherent than the first; specifically, it is easier to follow than his first narrative in Excerpt 3. This is likely because he provides more background information or 'orientation' (Labov & Waletzky, 1967) in lines 13–17, as well as a more detailed account of the way in which events unfolded—that is, the 'complicating action' (Labov & Waletzky, 1967)—in lines 18–30. Max's positioning of the driver is nearly identical in this second narrative, since he depicts him as totally inept (see Table 8.5). Again, he uses negation in relation to the driver's expected actions, when he states *They didn't show up* (line

19) and *He never came* (lines 26 and 30). Unlike his previous account, Max does not explicitly assess his driver's competence (i.e., *I got idiots who are drivers*), but hints at it when he addresses an imaginary driver in line 12 and exclaims, *Think,* as well as in lines 33 and 35 when he says, *You gotta have someone who can think a little bit.* With these comments, Max positions himself as more capable than his driver, whom he depicts as unable to think on his feet.

As in his prior narrative, Max portrays himself as assertive and having some control, particularly in the beginning (with his abstract) and conclusion of his story. As he wraps up, Max remarks that it was outrageous that the driver did not think to look for him (*It wasn't far, It wasn't raining*). He then goes on to say that he *refused* to go outdoors to wait for the driver on that particular day, suggesting that he was in a position to say 'no,' or in other words, that he exercised some degree of control over what happened to him. While in this particular case Max was forced to wait for the Access-a-Ride driver (e.g., he had *no* control over the situation), by framing his storyworld action as one of refusal, he makes it clear that he did not, and will not, kowtow to the driver's interests (e.g., that he *is* in control). Through these linguistic choices, Max positions

Table 8.5

Self- and other-positioning in Max's Access-a-Ride narrative, part 2

Max's self-positioning	Max's positioning of the driver
So, I had a very **exciting** morning **yelling at Access-a-Ride**	
	The guy, the driver came in, but you know what? **Think.**
	So uh **they didn't they didn't show up.**
	The facility called Access-A-Ride and said "What happened?" Oh, the driver was there, he came into the compound, and he saw the place where they do dialysis. He was in the right place, **but he never came across the dri- we're here and he never came.**
	You gotta have **somebody who can think a little bit** I mean **if I'm not there, look for me** a little bit.
Usually I go out of doors, but **I refuse on a day like today.**	

himself as an 'agentive self-constructer,' or a "person who comes across as strong, in control, and self-determined" (Bamberg, 2011, p. 106).

As we have observed previously, in their recountings of their versions of the Access-a-Ride narrative, Alice and Max both make linguistic choices to construct not only their storyworlds but important aspects of their identities as well. Schiffrin (1996, p. 199) uses a visual analogy to highlight this phenomenon:

> Telling a story provides a self-portrait: a linguistic lens through which to discover people's own (somewhat idealized) views of themselves as situated in a social structure. The verbalization and textual structure of a story comes with its *content,* and with it *local and global contexts of production,* to provide a *view of self that can be either challenged or validated by an audience.* (emphasis not in original)

Both storytellers construct very clear differences between the service providers (the driver or Access-a-Ride as an organization) and themselves in relation to the *content* of the Access-a-Ride narrative. This identity construction is carried out within the specific *local context* of their beloved support group in the surround of friends who share their experiences of early memory loss and of institutional representatives who, while certainly amicable and supportive, are guided by institutional and professional goals and responsibilities. These friends and professionals make up the audience of which Schiffrin speaks and to which the narrators must attend as they participate in the turn-by-turn positioning dance associated with their identity work. One of the *global contexts* of production related to these specific tellings of the Access-a-Ride narratives surely must be related to a dominant master narrative of Alzheimer's disease, which, according to Basting (2009, pp. 7–11), includes the following fears: being a burden, the unknown, being out of control, and a meaningless existence. Basting elaborates:

> Alzheimer's is not only a disease of the mind but also of the environment. We live in a culture that prizes independence and the rugged individual capable of doing for him- or herself. We live in a time when the markings of age are a source of embarrassment and a sign of a lack of power. (2009, pp. 68–69)

So it is perhaps not surprising, given these local and global contexts of production, that Alice and Max construct identities for themselves as 'actors' rather than as 'undergoers' (Bamberg, 2011, p. 106), where they can be understood as "agentive self-constructers, strong, in control, self determined," rather than with "low agency, less influential, less powerful, or less responsible." It is perhaps somewhat ironic (given that problems with memory and judgment are associated with Alzheimer's disease) that the very differences that Alice and Max highlighted in their identity construction work centered on their ability to remember and reason well. But it is exactly these differences that accentuate the tellers' independence and ability to do for themselves.

CONCLUSIONS AND IMPLICATIONS

In closing, we return to the questions we posed in the introduction to this chapter—How can linguistic analysis of language used by participants in the *To Whom I May Concern* program provide insight into its cognitive and social effects as one exemplar of creative programming that seeks to be therapeutic for people with Alzheimer's disease and other dementias? What have we learned about the discursive underpinnings of the therapeutic nature of the *To Whom I May Concern* program?

Our specific focus on one particular discourse activity within these support group meetings—the recounting and evaluation of Access-a-Ride experiences—has served to highlight one of the important aspects of support group interactions: a relaxed discourse space that allows members of the group to share real-life experiences (in contrast to narrative events that might be experienced by only one individual and in contrast to experiences that are shared also by the institutional representatives). In fact, following Norrick (1997, pp. 200–203) we know that story content need not be relevant or newsworthy to grab the collective attention of a group if the possibility of co-narration holds the promise of high involvement among participants (Tannen, 1989, 2005)—and that this co-narration fosters group rapport, ratifies group membership, and portrays shared values, all clearly important activities within a support group.

This specific shared experience in the Access-a-Ride narratives is one of overcoming adversity in the form of incompetence, in which the individual with memory loss positions him- or herself as exercising better judgment and/or knowing more than the service provider does. This agency and knowing in the storyworld is important in the interaction with others, both for those who share this narrative and delight in narrative co-construction as well as for those who do not share the narrative, but who can use it to gain some sense of the teller's positive sense of self in the world.

But no matter how empowering these strong agentive moves within the discourse of the support group meeting are, it would be a mistake to overestimate the extent to which such personal agency, no matter how intensely and authentically felt, can be effective outside the walls of the support group. They only take their speakers so far before dependence in the real world rears its ugly head to constrain their next steps. After all, positioning oneself as powerful and in charge within a narrated event does not necessarily translate into power in the real world (see Ainsworth-Vaughn, 1998, for a discussion of bases on which power can be claimed). Consider this exchange when the support group facilitator recommends that Max do something to follow up on his reported negative experience with Access-a-Ride:

Excerpt 5 [6. 12:43]

01   Nadine: You gotta call them [Access-a-Ride] and complain.

02   Max: Well, yeah, I'm afraid if you call them and make too much

03   of a fuss they'll drop you as a client.

04   Then what?

05   You gonna come pick me up?

In fact, one can argue that this relative powerlessness expressed by Max in the world outside the support group actually accentuates the therapeutic importance of the *To Whom I May Concern* program. As a script writer, Matthews has the power to transform the personal agency displayed by members in their personal experience narratives into letters directed explicitly (but hypothetically) at selected others represented in the storyworlds. And it is at each step of this transformative process that the keys to the program's therapeutic nature can be found.

- First, through the *shift in text type* (i.e., from personal experience oral narrative to written letter), *speech actions* (from representations of adversity in a narrated event to direct, face-threatening questions addressed to an 'other'), and *in participation framework* (from third person [*he, they*] to second person [*you*]), the agentive stance is amplified beyond the small support group. The hypothetical nature of these letters in *To Whom I May Concern* (i.e., the letter in question will not actually be sent to Access-A-Ride) allows for catharsis with no associated danger of negative real-world consequences for the support group members.
- Second, through this transformation and amplification of fleeting conversational moments and personal experience narratives into scripted letters that will be read aloud by the actors, short-term

memory in the form of script memorization becomes a non-factor to the success of the theatrical performance.

- Third, the letters in the script, along with the associated script rehearsal sessions leading to the live performance, serve as a common focal point of members' attention, providing a rich context for communicative engagement in the form of stylistic editing, personal reflection, and storytelling.
- Fourth, collaboration within the *To Whom I May Concern* process highlights shared knowledge, experiences, and values among group members, and facilitates rapport and group bonding opportunities.
- And, finally, working in a systematic and supportive way toward a future live performance helps members feel enthusiastic and optimistic as they anticipate the fulfillment of their group's common goal.

And, although space constraints in this chapter necessitated our focus on discursive displays of personal agency (as an indicator of participants' control) as the primary way to uncover the therapeutic effects of the *To Whom I May Concern* program, it is clear that the effects are much wider, extending into areas of epistemic stance (as an indicator of participants' knowledge) and affect (as an indicator of participants' emotion). Table 8.6 brings together relevant observations related to the domains of *knowledge, emotion,* and *control* in three contexts of life with dementia (*public fears, individuals' experiences outside the support group,* and *individuals' experiences within the support group*).

In each of the three domains, negativity dominates both the master narrative of dementia as well as experiences reported by group members regarding life outside the support group. As we have reported in this chapter, in terms of control, the negativity refers primarily to a sense of being dependent on others and out of control in one's own life. Beyond this domain, in terms of knowledge, the negativity relates to confusion and memory problems; and in terms of emotion, the negativity is about stigma, anger, frustration, embarrassment, and sadness. The discourse used among participants within the support group could not provide a starker contrast: there, amidst the laughter, the overlapping talk, the co-narration, and, yes, poignant comments, we observed not only linguistic displays of agency both within recounted storyworlds and within the support group interactions, but also strong, epistemic stances that indexed authoritative ways of knowing, and sheer happiness, pride, and a strong sense of belonging among members.

As Basting (2009, p. 155) reports, people clearly are fearful of dementia—specifically, the confusion, memory difficulties, stigma, and lack of control that are associated with the disease. But innovative and

Table 8.6

Knowledge, emotion, and control inside/outside the support group

DOMAINS	Master narrative (public fears about life with dementia; Basting, 2009)	Living life with dementia outside the support group (as portrayed linguistically by group members)	In support group interactions
Knowledge (epistemic stance)	fear of the unknown; confusion, disorientation; difficulty remembering	problems with memory	have epistemic rights and authority; own experiences are validated
Emotion (affect)	stigma, anger, violence	frustration, anger, embarrassment, sadness	happiness, pride, hope, sense of belonging
Control (agency)	being out of control; being a burden; getting lost	dependence and reliance on others to accomplish everyday activities, tasks	take charge of interactions in support group; show agency in represented events

theoretically grounded grassroots attempts to influence these public attitudes and ways of caring in a positive direction may help to shape individuals' experiences of and with dementia now and in the future. It is our hope that our examination of the discourse of one such powerfully creative community-based program may illuminate the positive possibilities at the complex intersection of language use, dementia, institutions, and the arts. We offer these findings as important steps toward improving the everyday lives of people with dementia and close with Amy's uplifting conclusion to the May 10, 2007, performance of *To Whom I May Concern:*

> I live in the tension of remembering and forgetting. Everyday I remember I have a brain disease that isn't going to get better. I exercise my body because they say that is a good treatment for Alzheimer's disease. I exercise my mind because they say *that* is a good treatment for Alzheimer's disease, too. I take the pills and try to keep up with the research. I go to a support group to stay connected to those who understand what it's like to live with this. I guess you could say that's social exercise. So I do all these things because I remember that I have a brain disease that isn't going to get better.

I also try to forget. I know that may sound funny . . . forgetting is at the heart of my problem. But I do try to forget about dementia. I don't want it to define me. I'm more than my memory. Let's have some fun.

And on that note, let me end this letter. Enough about me. How are you these days? Let's get together soon. And thanks for listening and for your concern.

Sincerely yours, Amy

NOTES

1. With the exception of Maureen Matthews, the founder of the interactive theater project *To Whom I May Concern,* all names of individuals and institutions have been changed to pseudonyms. The Greenlake YMCA is a community resource and event space that offers services for a variety of audiences and needs (early childhood care and development, teenage outreach programs, and senior services).

2. The title of the project does not contain a typo, as some readers may assume. The theatrical project seeks to highlight the personal experiences of individuals with Alzheimer's disease and to relate these in the form of letters written to others who could benefit from this perspective; these letters are, therefore, written to others to whom *I* (not *it*) may concern.

3. Scholars interested in Goffman's (1981) deconstruction of speaker in his work on 'footing' may find considerations related to animator, author, and principal to be intriguing throughout this project; unfortunately, space constraints preclude further discussion of this connection.

4. It is a well-known fact about narratives that they need to be about something 'reportable', marked, unexpected (Labov, 1972; Chafe, 1994). It is then perhaps not surprising that negative aspects come up in narrative form, and the more expected experience of competence are reported in other text types. In fact, when Jane did recount a 'very pleasant' Access-A-Ride experience in the first script rehearsal session, responses included "But that's not funny!" and "We can't use that, Jane!" amid knowing laughter.

5. Given the limited temporal scope of the narratives and interactions in our data set, it is not possible for us to explore the relevance of Bamberg's dimension of constancy-change over time.

6. According to Labov (1972, p. 366), evaluation refers to "the means used by the narrator to indicate the point of the narrative, its raison d'être: why it was told, and what the narrator is getting at."

7. The omitted discussion here is about the definition of a Yiddish word Max uses to describe his frustration.

8. The omitted lines are about finding Max a place to sit.

9. The salience of driving to members of the support group cannot be overstated. Note in Table 8.1 (list of addressees of letters) that the two letters read

before the 'Dear Access-a-Ride' letter concern driving/giving up one's driver's license as well ('Dear Department of Motor Vehicles' and 'Dear Chauffeur . . . I mean, loving wife').

10. In these omitted lines, the group members briefly discuss the rehab center that Max attends (e.g., they praise him for going, ask him specifics as to location, etc.).

REFERENCES

Abelson, R. P. (1963). Computer simulation of "hot cognition." In S. S. Tomkins & S. Messick (Eds.), *Computer simulation of personality* (pp. 277–302). New York: Wiley.

Ainsworth-Vaughn, N. (1998). *Claiming power in doctor patient talk.* New York: Oxford University Press.

Bamberg, M. (1997). Positioning between structure and performance. *Journal of Narrative and Life History, 7*, 335–342.

Bamberg, M. (2011). Narrative practice and identity navigation. In J. A. Holstein & J. F. Gubrium (Eds.), *Varieties of narrative analysis* (pp. 99–124). London: Sage Publications.

Basting, A. (2009). *Forget memory: Creating better lives for people with dementia.* Baltimore, MD: Johns Hopkins University Press.

Capps, L., & Ochs, E. (1995). *Constructing panic: The discourse of agoraphobia.* Cambridge, MA: Harvard University Press.

Chafe, W. (1994). *Discourse, consciousness, and time.* Chicago: University of Chicago Press.

Cohen, D., & Eisdorfer, C. (1986). *The loss of self.* New York: Norton.

Davies, B., & Harré, R. (1990). Positioning: The discursive production of selves. *Journal for the Theory of Social Behaviour, 20*(1), 44–63.

Davis, B. H. (Ed.). (2005). *Alzheimer talk, text, and context: Enhancing communication.* New York: Palgrave Macmillan.

De Fina, A. (2003). *Identity in narrative: A study of immigrant discourse.* Philadelphia: John Benjamins.

De Fina, A., Schiffrin, D., & Bamberg, M. (Eds.). (2006). *Discourse and identity.* Cambridge: Cambridge University Press.

Downs, M., Clare, L., & Mackenzie, J. (2006). Understandings of dementia: Exploratory models and their implications for the person with dementia and therapeutic effort. In J. C. Hughes, S. J. Louw, & S. R. Sabat (Eds.), *Dementia: Mind, Meaning and the Person* (pp. 235–258). New York: Oxford University Press.

Goffman, E. (1981). Footing. In E. Goffman (Ed.), *Forms of talk* (pp. 124–159). Philadelphia: University of Pennsylvania Press.

Hamilton, H. E. (1994). *Conversations with an Alzheimer's patient: An interactional sociolinguistic study.* Cambridge: Cambridge University Press.

Hamilton, H. E. (1996). Intratextuality, intertextuality and the construction of identity as patient in Alzheimer's Disease. *Text, 16*(1), 61–90.

Hamilton, H. E. (2011). At the intersection of art, Alzheimer's disease, and discourse: Talk in the surround of paintings. In P. Backhaus (Ed.), *Communication in elderly care: Cross-cultural approaches.* (pp. 166–192). London: Continuum.

Heritage, J. (1997). Conversation analysis and institutional talk: Analyzing data. In D. Silverman (Ed.), *Qualitative research: Theory, method and practice* (pp. 161–182). London: Sage.

Heritage, J., & Clayman, S. E. (2011). *Talk in action: Interactions, identities, and institutions.* Oxford: Blackwell.

Kitwood, T. (1997). *Dementia reconsidered: The person comes first.* Buckingham: Open University Press.

Labov, W. (1972). The transformation of experience in narrative syntax. In *Language in the Inner City* (pp. 354–396). Philadelphia: University of Pennsylvania Press.

Labov, W., & Waletzky, J. (1967). Narrative analysis. In J. Helm (Ed.), *Essays on the Verbal and Visual Arts* (pp. 12–44). Seattle: University of Washington Press.

Lazarus, R. S., & Smith, C. A. (1988). Knowledge and appraisal in the cognition & emotion relationship. *Cognition and Emotion, 2,* 281–300.

Leibing, A. (2006). Divided gazes: Alzheimer's disease, the person within, and death in life. In A. Leibing and L. Cohen (Eds.), *Thinking about Dementia: Culture, Loss, and the Anthropology of Senility* (pp. 240–268). New Brunswick, NJ: Rutgers University Press.

Matthews, M. (2005). *Weaving a life: Five people with early stage dementia share their stories.* Unpublished dissertation. The Steinhardt School of Education, New York University.

Norrick, N. (1997). Twice-told tales: Collaborative narration of familiar stories. *Language in Society, 26,* 199–220.

Ochs, E., Smith, R., & Taylor, C. (1989). Detective stories at dinnertime: Problem-solving through co-narration. *Cultural Dynamics, 2*(2), 238–257.

Polanyi, L. (1985). *Telling the American story: A structural and cultural analysis of conversational storytelling.* Norwood: Ablex Publishing.

Ramanathan, V. (1997). *Alzheimer discourse: Some sociolinguistic dimensions.* New York: Routledge.

Ryan, E. B., Bannister, K. A., & Anas, A. P. (2009). The dementia narrative: Writing to reclaim social identity. *Journal of Aging Studies, 23*(3), 145–157.

Sabat, S. (2001). *The experience of Alzheimer's disease: Life through a tangled veil.* Oxford: Blackwell.

Sabat, S., & Harre, R. (1992). The construction and deconstruction of self in Alzheimer's disease. *Ageing and Society, 12,* 443–461.

Sacks, H. (1992). *Lectures on conversation.* Oxford: Blackwell.

Shenk, D. (2005). There was an old woman: Maintenance of identity by people with Alzheimer's dementia. In B. H. Davis (Ed.), *Alzheimer talk, text, and context* (pp. 3–17). New York: Palgrave.

Schiffrin, D. (1987). *Discourse markers.* Cambridge: Cambridge University Press.

Schiffrin, D. (1990). The management of a cooperative self in argument: The role of opinions and stories. In A. Grimshaw (Ed.), *Conflict talk* (pp. 241–259). Cambridge: Cambridge University Press.

Schiffrin, D. (1996). Narrative as self-portrait: The sociolinguistic construction of identity. *Language in Society, 25*(2), 167–203.

Tannen, D. (1989). *Talking voices.* Cambridge: Cambridge University Press.

Tannen, D. (2005). *Conversational style: Analyzing talk among friends.* New York: Oxford University Press.

9

ALZHEIMER PATHOGRAPHIES

Glimpses into How People with AD and Their Caregivers Text Themselves

Vaidehi Ramanathan

The self is an active agent of its own realization, establishing order among its attitudes and beliefs and giving directions to its actions. It appears to be— how far or how justifiably is not in question now—in some ways self con- stituting or self-made: we are what our attention to ourselves makes us be.

(Seigel, 2005, p. 6)

INTRODUCTION

This chapter focuses on ways in which people with Alzheimer's disease and their caregivers make sense of their everyday living with and around the condition.[1] It does so by closely examining Alzheimer pathographies— diaries and journal entries kept by these people—to call attention how their writing of these texts offers glimpses into ways in which they script a sense of themselves. While previous research on Alzheimer's discourse has called attention to particular discourse features (see Hamilton, 1994; Davis, 2005; Schrauf & Iris, 2011; Ramanathan, 1997), little research has addressed how people with the condition and their caregivers speak or write of the condition themselves. The chapter specifically focuses on issues relating to *repetition* and *intentionality* as they emerge in these di- aries. These perspectives are important to hear, not just for their implica- tions of identity, but for the practical world of caregiving. Incorporating their perspectives into possible policy changes in institutionalized care for seniors is a necessary social change that impacts personnel training and caregiver education.

Building on previous scholarship in the sociolinguistics of Alzheimer's discourse that has called attention to interactional aspects of communication (Hamilton, 1994; Davis, 2005) as well as racial and ethnic concerns around the condition (Schrauf & Iris, 2011), the focus of this chapter is on the diaries and journal entries of Alzheimer patients and their caregivers, and ways in which they write of living with the condition. While scholarship in applied linguistics has explored connections between identities and narratives (Gee, 1990; Pavlenko, 2007; Menard-Warwick, 2004; Ramanathan, 1997), relations between narratives and written selves, especially from the point of view of people with the condition is still a burgeoning area (although, see Hamilton, 2000; Ryan, Bannister, & Anas, 2009). Paying close attention to how people with disabilities and their caregivers write of their coping with their and their loved one's ailments—the changes in their bodies, their wrestling with disabling societal discourses, and lifestyles adjustments they have to make—affords glimpses into contexts where the need to assemble selves through writing becomes both imperative and a crucial mode of survival (Ramanathan & Makoni, 2008). It not only alerts us to the fluidity of identities, but also has implications for policy changes around caregiver education (including family members and nursing personnel). This chapter explores these concerns.

AUTO- AND CAREGIVER ALZHEIMER PATHOGRAPHIES: ISSUES OF SELF AND THE WRITING OF MEMORY LOSS

Phillipe Lejeune (1975) defines autobiography as "retrospective prose narrative written by a real person concerning his own existence, where the focus is his individual life, in particular the story of his personality" (p. 13). This much-cited definition in autobiographical studies seems to characterize the traditional *recit autobiographique,* where a narrative organization marked by linear temporal progression ('this happened, and then this happened . . .') coheres with the essential narrativity of human existence. The genre of autobiography assumes as its focus the value and the singularity of telling an individual lifestory, where oneself becomes both object and subject of one's narrative.[2] The effort to capture who we think we once were is tenuous at best and slippery at worst, and as Lejeune himself points out, even the most orthodox of autobiographies cannot promise absolute referentiality and sincerity (Linde, 2009), since memory is necessarily limited and we always have to have recourse to fictive devices when producing accounts of ourselves. This impossibility that inheres in autobiography helps us to see why individual authors, seduced by the life writing endeavour, build in self-conscious threads that call attention to the form in which they are writing (a point underscored by poststructuralists such as Roland Barthes who contest the formations of a coherent, unified self). The end result, then, is an authorial assemblage that is akin to a textual shadow intended to correspond to "who I am" and "who I think I am."

These points about reaching back into one's past and bringing it forth into some sort of coherent narrative emerge poignantly in the pathographies of those with Alzheimer's disease. Their memories and the interpretations of those memories are 'traces' (in the Derridean sense), with traces being fragments of scenes, images, interactions, and language that our memories store for us. Our sense of who we are also emerges from our stored traces (about who we think we are) as well as traces about what others think of us. Our identities, then, are assembled together with a combination of these traces that together comprise a response to the question: "Who am I?"

In the case of patients suffering from Alzheimer's disease, this point about 'who' or what it is of themselves they are culling into a narrative assumes particular significance because they are doing so in the face of their traces becoming cinders. Languaging memories—writing them into a narrative—then, becomes a way of preserving a sense of themselves they still have (Hamilton, 2000, 2008). At once an effort to keep embers at bay and an effort to retrieve and present a self, their writing of pathographies renders them both subject and hostage of their writing. They are 'subjects' because they are what their diaries are about; they are 'hostages' for the same reason. The writing of an autobiography generally, then, is a genre that is central to identity preservation.

PATHOGRAPHY ENTRIES BY ALZHEIMER PATIENTS AND THEIR CAREGIVERS

The excerpts on which I am basing my discussion are drawn from six pathographies written by patients and caregivers. Some carefully considered criteria went into the selection. First, I wanted to cover an adequate time-span (of about 15–20 years; hence a diary published in 1988 and one in 2007); second, I wanted to include a diary/journal written by an established literary figure to make the pool heterogeneous (hence John Bayley's diary about Iris Murdoch); third, I wanted to address both parent-child concerns (hence a daughter writing about her mother); and fourth, I wanted to include unpublished diaries (hence those shared by my colleague). All of these pathographies, except the unpublished ones, are available as published books and are, on an average, about 150–200 pages each. When selecting excerpts from diaries written by people with the ailment, I focused on those sections where they wrote self-reflectively about their feelings regarding their condition (the diagnoses, their everyday negotiations with living) in a retrospective manner (something they could do if they remembered a part of their immediate past they wanted to text in). Many of these converged around issues of repetition. With caregiver texts, I concentrated on those excerpts that spoke to both capturing aspects of their loved ones' personalities while also speaking to tensions with living with the condition. Many of these selections seemed to have strong concerns with intentionality. Both repetition and intentionality shed light on concerns around preserving a sense of self. While the body of excerpts is quite large, I have picked representative samples that best capture the confluence of issues that inform the present argument.

The diaries are:

1. Kim Zabbia's *Painted Diaries* (entries by both patient and caregiver/daughter); (1996)
2. Rosalie Walsh Honel's *Journey with Grandpa* (1988)
3. Christine Boden's *Who Will I Be When I Die?* (1998)
4. Diana McGowin's *Living in the Labyrinth* (1993)
5. John Bayley's *Iris* (1998)
6. The unpublished diaries of Billie Dotson Vincent, written about her husband, Theodore Vincent (shared with me by their grand-daughter and my colleague Julia Menard-Warwick, personal communication in 2007)

As will be evident, these themes flow into each other; breaking them up as I have done here is more a textual nod at clarity than anything else.

REPETITION AND SELF

The traces that people with Alzheimer's disease pen into place seem to orient heavily around the need to be able to repeat and perform what they once could. Fear of the loss of this ability to repeat seems integrally tied to their sense of who they are. Take for instance the following excerpts from diaries written by two Alzheimer patients: the first by Kim Zabbia's mother, the second by Christine Boden:

Excerpt 1

Journal Entry, November 30, 1985

On October 5, 1985, I went to Dr. Walker for a checkup because I had not been feeling well, and was forgetful and dizzy at times. . .

At this point of my life, I am able to do most things normally. I can hold a normal conversation, although many times a certain word will not come to me. One example is the day I was talking to my son and I said that Alzheimer's was the gradual loss of memory and intellectual skills. I got to the word 'intellectual' and the word would not come to me. I thought about that word all evening. When I woke up the next morning, it was still on my mind. Then I said it immediately.

Some time ago, before I had ever been to a doctor about this condition, I tried to use my typewriter and I was shocked when the letters I typed were all wrong. Unknowingly, I had put my hands on the wrong home keys. I tried over and over to type a sentence and none of them made sense. The same thing happened when I tried to use my sewing machine. I could not remember how to use the machine. I had to change the thread and could not thread the machine properly. I even re-read the instructions and I still couldn't do it right. . . .

(Zabbia, 1996, p. 98)

Excerpt 2

The neurologist with his back towards me, looking at my scans, said, 'Your brain is like that of a much older person, showing signs of marked atrophy, particularly at the front. It's consistent with Alzheimer's.'

He looked away from the scans for a moment, and then said, 'You shouldn't be in any responsible position. You must retire as soon as possible. . .

I must have misheard—he was mistaken—the scans maybe had got mixed up with someone else's . . . 'You're joking—I'm too young to get Alzheimer's!'

I was only forty-six—old by my daughters' reckoning, but surely far too young to get an old people's disease like Alzheimer's. Any rate, I wasn't forgetful, just stressed out—with migraines and getting a little confused every now and then—taking the wrong turn a few times surely didn't mean I was getting senile! (p. 3)

. . .

'Er . . . how long will it be before I . . . er . . . um . . .' I stuttered.

'Until you become demented? Oh, about five years I expect,' answered the specialist, breezily.

. . .

Each patient declines in his or her very own way, losing different abilities at different times. <u>So would I be able to write next week? Would I be able to calculate my finances on next month's bank statement? Would I get lost after taking the girls to school tomorrow? What will it be like to be demented? How are my girls going to cope with my terrible deterioration, and eventual death in maybe 6–8 years' time? All these questions, and more, kept running through my mind, and I had to work through a lot of fear and anxiety.</u>

But 'popular' misunderstandings about Alzheimer's disease didn't help me and my girls much—we were up against more than just the disease itself. (p. 18)

(Boden, 1998)

In both instances, the people with the condition are deeply troubled at not being able to do/repeat what they once could. Zabbia voices anxiety over the ailment impeding everyday actions and Boden anticipates what things will be like as the ailment takes over. Narrating about the (impending) loss of this ability ensures a performative aspect of their abilities. Derrida's term *recit* seems relevant here. He says:

[A recit] is not simply a memory reconstituting a past, a recit is also a promise, it is also something that makes a commitment toward the future. What I dream of is not only the narration of a past that is inaccessible to me, but a narration that would also be a future, that would determine a future. (1976, p. 207)

A *recit* here, then, is not just a memory, but points to the promise of being able to repeat something related to the memory (typing, doing one's finances, dressing oneself). The word reminds us of the English word *recital*, a term that has the performative (and repetition) built into it. A recital, whether of a poem, or of a musical piece or a dance, assumes that the performer is able to repeat what she knows (what partially defines how she sees herself) and that the audience 'reads' her correctly (also informing the performer's self). Recitals of this nature suggest their intent and meaning through repetition of the same words or musical notes or dance gestures. Watching or hearing that repetition gives us not only delight but some deep reassurance that we live in a shared world and that our voicings, movements, and texts echo back—albeit in varied form—what we send forth. What the people with the condition are grieving is the (impending) loss of these repetitions, of being able to re-perform the very acts that they once could and that convey to their caregivers and the world who they are. Their doing so elicits responses from the world that validates their sense of self. When the ability to perform or repeat (or receive the intent of) is lost, a sense of a meaningful shared world recedes, a prospect that is undoubtedly deeply destabilizing for people with the condition.

But herein lie questions we must ask: Why the fear of the loss of being able to repeat? Why is repetition so important? Once again Derrida's views (1976, 1978) resonate here. Derrida's view is that all language is a priori written, whether inscribed or not, in one form or another; writing is the arche-phenomenon of memory and one that calls out for the first recognition (and then for repetition). Memory is what enables us to repeat that first recognition, and without repetition there could be no memory, for the fact of the memory implies that a replica, a repetition of the first thought (what Derrida terms *gramme*) that has been stored. Derrida suggests that we have to leave in the domain of the unthinkable what that a priori signification is—the moment of the birth of meaning. But once it has happened, repetition alone ensures that signification continues through the temporalizing process of difference. The following excerpt captures the importance of being able to repeat, and the fear and pain at not being able to do so:

Excerpt 3

To best understand what this disease can cause, let me tell you some of the things that have happened to me in the last three years. My short-term memory has gotten very bad. I have trouble remembering anything I write down. I continually am asking someone questions and then repeat the question, never remembering that I just asked it. In normal conversations I lose words and names. They will just not come to my mind. It is embarrassing, really. I have trouble following instructions for recipes and medicines, especially medicines with varied dosages at various times. In church, I have found myself not able to keep up with my hymnals or prayers. I can't keep up with the music. Sometimes it seems to be my eyes, but I don't think so. I've recently seen an optomologist and he said I am fine. Anyway, it is annoying, may be it's just my inability to concentrate for any length of time on one thing.

(Zabbia, 1996, p. 100)

Repetition, thus, is crucial in signification, and the fear of not being able to repeat what one could do (one's sure-signs that define oneself) crucially impacts how Zabbia sees herself now. In this sense her pathography, like the others, is a textual shadow that captures her 'sure-signs,' her essences that make up who she is. As Barthes reminds us, sure-signs are signs that point to the undeniability of things. In the present case, the ability to repeat become ways that Alzheimer patients retain a sense of "who they are."

The dread of loosening the grip on meaning for people with Alzheimer's and their caregivers suggests that there is a slow erasure of that initial moment of the signification process, that *gramme* in the arche-memory that enables meaning to be constructed on the basis of difference. What fears is Christine Boden articulating when she wonders: "Would I be able to write next week? Would I be able to calculate my finances on next month's bank statement? Would I get lost after taking the girls to school tomorrow?" (Boden 1998, p. 18). If the *gramme* can be lost, as happens with Alzheimer's patients disease, was its 'founding' equally a matter of brain tissue developing and then decaying? In other words, is the ontology of signification a constructed one? Neurologists and psycholinguists may address this in terms of the storage of information in particular neurons (Eagleman, 2011), some of which become the defining traces by which we communicate who we are. This *gramme,* the very first instantiation of a memory/trace seems to be under erasure, threatening not just memory, but one's very personhood. What appears to be growing, then, is a fear of blankness, no longer the absence of a loved one, or even oneself, but blank nothingness, the Derridean effacement of traces. Zabbia, in the later stages of her ailment notes the following:

Excerpt 4

Journal entry

> Changes since I came home from the last trip to Bethesda term—my short term memory is very bad, I have forgotten if I have eaten or dressed, or eaten. Sometimes forgotten if I have same time it is on the table when we are eating meals.
>
> I know why. I have stopped talking less. This is a complete change in my talking. I have always been able to carry on a conversation on a one to one level or with a group. Probably too vocal.
>
> I cannot decide on anything. Bert gets so outdone with me, and then I cry and he gets mad again. I really try to stop the cycle, but it is hard. It is a vicious cycle. I get depressed because I can't do

things right and there are the tears again. Then Bert is angry again. What a mess!

(Zabbia, 1996, p. 101)

Such a mental disappearance is an analogy of death but far worse, for while the body lives some sense of an "essential self" has gone. This fear of not knowing what there will be in the coming dark, the dread of being abandoned by one's very self and personhood, drives patients and caregivers to writing so as to preserve shreds of that which once lived and moved and had its being in a more than physical presence ('Oh spare me a little that I may recover my strength, before I go hence and be no more seen' as is said in the Book of Common Prayer; Psalm 39). The point here is that a written record gives the illusion that something remains, that something still shines bright caught in the writer's black ink.[3]

INTENTIONALITY AND SELF

Moving away from repetition, I turn now to address the issue of scripting selves in relation to traces and absence. Bataille (1983) speaks of the desert of words in which we are all mired, saying that each grain of sand is a "fold" harboring notions that poetry alone can release. He says, "That sand into which we bury ourselves in order not to see is formed of words and contestation, having to make use of them, causes one to think . . . of the stuck, struggling man whose efforts sink him for certain (p. 14). While language may indeed be and become the noose by which we hang ourselves, it is also the life-line that pulls one out of deep waters into air and light. It is this deliberate, intentional hold on what is fast threatening to become 'absences' as pockets of night creep in that this section explores. In the following series of excerpts, we can discern the anguish of a sense of life-waters flowing away.

Excerpt 5

Journal entry, March 10, 1986

I explained to him [the doctor] how I couldn't remember any medicine when he had asked me. He kept my papers that I had written and told me to keep writing. I also told him about the fact that I have sudden jerks and pulls of my arms. For example, I'll be reading the paper and my arm will jerk suddenly and almost pull the paper out of my hand. Another weird thing is: I will be sitting or standing and

I have this illusion that someone is standing behind me. It's so strong I turn to say something. Now, that's weird!

(Zabbia, 1996, pp. 42–43)

Excerpt 6

Journal entry, August 23, 1986

One think I believe I hate the most is hiding things from myself. I will put something away in a the kitchen and never put it in its original place. Then I have to look everywhere to find it. . . . I think what I hate most is a loss of intellect. My handwriting is horrible; my spelling is worse. I Liquid-Papered this diary to death with my proofreading. Sometimes I repeat what I have said and don't even know it.

(Zabbia, 1996, pp. 42–43)

Excerpt 7

Journal Entry, February 26, 1988

I have been telling myself to perk up and stop getting depressed when everything is lousy and I can't spell well or see well, or remember over and over again . . .

Alright, now comes the time to get dressed. All of these clothes have a front and back, OK? Now we proceed to find out which one is the front, and which one is back. About this time my, husband comes in to see how I am doing. He gives me a tip on finding the right side. By this time I am completely confused . . . Now that is just everyday dressing. Getting ready for a special affair is another story.

(Zabbia, 1996, p. 96)

Excerpt 8

August-September 1988 (Copied by Kim)

I have a problem in my writing and my reading.

. . .

It is hard. I have realized that I cannot read my own writing. I thought that if I could not read it, nobody else could read it.

I really don't have to write. I could live the rest of my life not writing, but I would be very sad . . . I cannot write anymore, It is just a lot of words that don't make sense to me.

. . .

I wish I had more to keep me busy. I really miss not being able to read. I could always pass the time and read. Most of the things I could read and right.

(Zabbia, 1996, p. 102)

What of herself is Kim's mother trying to retain? What traces of her past does she desperately want (us) to remember? The spaces that she wishes to claim are unbearably ordinary—that she could once read and dress herself, that there was a time when she wasn't self-conscious about her handwriting or her body—and yet, in the end, this is what our lives are also about. Her texting of the 'normalcy' she once had affirms both the inalienable human need to claim one's existence, sanity, and balance and the staving off a confrontation with death and abandonment. What people with Alzheimer's are experiencing is a kind of death, their own death even while they live. Under these circumstances what is left to them save to catch the traces of themselves, to write themselves into being? Kim's mother's wrenching worry speaks to anxieties about abandon and about not being able to gather oneself (either in dress or in text).

What we are left with, then, when memory and language are starting to fail, are pieces of ourselves. This is why the gathering of thoughts, memories, images, and sensations into written texts point in some sense to the creating of traces to stall absence of both self and beloved. Following are two very different excerpts from the diaries of caregivers, with each one texting their experiences with the patient very differently:

Excerpt 9

From: Billie Vincent's unpublished diaries

This morning about 5 a.m. while I was writing in my Journal and collecting my thought—drinking tea and reveling in the quiet uninterrupted morning . . . Tad appeared on the scene with you "I have a serious talk I want to have with you. I think we should move to Portland. The folks here are kind but so busy they don't have time for us—and when one of us gets worse we'll really be in trouble."

So calmly I talked to him—but he wasn't listening. "Why don't you call later and talk to the folks in Portland?" I suggested—knowing he would not initiate a call.

"Or better still", he said "I'll write them a letter"—then I relaxed for I knew those promises of letter writing rarely materialize.

After a while I convinced him this was the best place for us—he had Glen to walk with each morning, and play pool with whenever—and we had the family gatherings and the Friends Meeting etc. And it would be difficult finding a more accessible town than Bellingham—I know my way around and we have the world's best doctor, etc. etc.

Later he came in weeping, wondering why we weren't sleeping together, and would I come in and hold him in my bed, and we cried together for a while, then he felt calm enough to return to bed and slept for another couple of hours.

But it was a day when nothing seemed to come out right—even our walk on the beach was not as peaceful as usual and by 7 p.m. my spirit was low, low, low.

(Unpublished diaries of Billie Vincent, pp. 4–5)

Excerpt 10

From Bayley's *Iris*:

Alzheimer sufferers are not always gentle. I know that. But Iris remains her old self in many ways. The power of concentration has gone, along with the ability to form coherent sentences, and to remember where she is, or has been. She does not know she has written twenty-seven remarkable novels, as well as her books on philosophy; received honorary doctorates from the major universities; became a Dame of the British Empire . . . If an admirer or friend asks her to sign a copy of one of her novels she looks at it with pleasure and surprise before laboriously writing her name and, if she can, theirs. 'For Georgiana Smith. For Dear Reggie. . .' It takes her some time, but the letters are formed with care, and resemble, in a surreal way, her old handwriting. She is always anxious to oblige. And the old gentleness remains. *(p. 41)*

Conceivably it is the persons who hug their identity most closely to themselves for whom the condition of Alzheimer's is most dreadful. Iris's own lack of a sense of identity seems to float her more gently into its world of preoccupied emptiness. Placidly every night she insists on laying out quantities of her clothing on my side of the bed and when I quietly remove them, back they come again. She wants to look after me? Is that it? It may be a simpler sort of confusion for when we go to bed she often asks me which side she should be on. Or is it something deeper and fuller and less conscious and less 'caring' than that far too self conscious adjective suggests. (pp. 71–72)

(Bayley, 1998)

In both of these instances, the caregivers are attributing particular intentions to their loved ones, thus creating for them a sense of self (Kramsch, 2000). This attribution of intentionality to the patients—of Billie Vincent writing about Tad's saying that he'd write to the people in Portland, even as she doubts that he will—and of John Bayley writing about Iris Murdoch laying out quantities of her clothing on his side of the bed—emerges from their respective interpretations of their loved ones' acts as still meaningful. The caregivers are in effect attributing consciousness to their loved ones. This is a crucial point. That Tad Vincent and Iris Murdoch emerge as intentional beings with degrees of conscious abilities (writing a letter or gathering clothes by the bedside) is a sense that emerges because these actions have become for their caregivers focal points based on actions performed long ago, foreshadowing outlines traced in advance with repeated, everyday engagements. They are reading what to others might be 'incoherent' acts as ones that are consequential and agentive. They knew their partners intimately over a lifetime, were witness to their glories and successes and pains, and have more recently been on the sidelines caring for their loved ones through more undignified moments and embarrassing situations. No one has a better sense than them of what their partners still retain, and the pockets of darkness that invade their partners' consciousnesses.

This discussion of intentions—what one intends, how we read other's intentions, what intentions we attribute to others—is intimately connected to the texting selves. The reading of what their partner's actions mean to them and their subsequent scripting of their interpretations also points to larger swirls between the potential and actual, the implicit and explicit. All (intentional) experiences (where one willfully sets forth to do something) have rings of potentialities around them that evade our languaging. To intend is to apprehend, to take something up as meaning something, to seize or focus on a way that precludes other foci for the moment. The interpretations that caregivers have texted into place of their loved one's actions is a deliberate attempt at constructing a very particular image of them that presents them as still agentive, still meaningful, so that something 're-cognize-able' of the other remains, an imperative that permits them (the partners) to move on with caring and living. Thus, even while one admits that ones' readings are always uncontained, hovering forever between absence and presence, potential and actual, implicit and explicit, it seems to help in the case of people with Alzheimer's to fix meanings for a little longer.

Derrida was a salutary antidote to those of us who have lived too long with fixed meaning; his ideas seemed to free us into an air that was heady with excitement as we watched philosophical concepts that we had thought immutable and eternal crumble. But in the world inhabited by the Alzheimer patients and their caregivers, fixity of meaning is so very crucial, as Derrida doubtless recognized when he noted that what he dreaded most was the loss of memory. As he said,

> The only loss for which I would never be consoled and that brings together all the others, I would call it loss of memory. The suffering at the origin of memory for me is the suffering from the loss of memory, not only forgetting or amnesia but the effacement of traces. (p. 143)

If there were no fixed traces for him to undo, he would have no task; he could have said nothing about deconstruction. Alzheimer patient caregivers live with the (sometimes slow) erosion of meanings, where will and intention run the risk of counting for nothing. Small wonder then that they keep these diaries to record and fix, to remember their partners' sure-signs.

IMPLICATIONS

Needless to say, these ponderings have all kinds of implications for the training and education of Alzheimer caregivers, be they nursing personnel or family members. It is crucial that we raise awareness of the extent to which language and memory are integrally tied to 'who we are' and to our ability to communicate that. Acts such as retrospectively writing about oneself and one's condition afford us glimpses into 'inner states' and accompanying emotions, and these are important to address as we work with nurses, support staff, and families. Bringing in perspectives from people with the condition and their caregivers into elderly care workshops seems like a necessary first step in sensitizing them to the sense of loss (of self/identity) that is implied in the loss of memory. This exploration raises concerns regarding the self as well. What does repetition and the need for repetition tell us about the self? Where or what is the original trace/memory that is being slowly effaced by the ailment and upon which repetition rests? While these questions do not have straightforward responses—indeed, I have encountered very different responses in family-support workshop—it is worthwhile to dwell on what it is that (auto)biographies manage to communicate both through their forms and content.

Doing an analysis and interpretation of the kind presented here allows us to see why a self or lived life needs to be formed and formed urgently. The need to script oneself and one's partner into place is starkly apparent in the pathographies and makes us aware of how such analyses alert us to ways in which the self-as- 'process' is no longer just one of a self always being in the making, but one of a self that is becoming unmade. 'Process,' then, is not so much about adding on as much as holding on. Such kinds of analyses also show how diary writing becomes an agentive and daring act of texting memories, selves, intentionalities into place, even as they show us how utterly fluid our identities are as memories dim and fade. The caregiver pathographies point to the dissolution of borders between them and their loved ones with the condition. Their partners' stories are theirs and their stories their partners'. The flows into and mergings of each others' stories are reminders that scripting selves may be all we have, and perhaps our last agentive efforts to stall the coming dark. Our actions and movements towards changes and transformations need to emerge from this space of heightened awareness.

NOTES

1. I thank Bob Schrauf and Heidi Hamilton for their nuanced feedback on this writing. This essay is partially based on Ramanathan (2010).
2. As Gusdorf (1980) points out, "Recapitulation of a life lived claims to be valuable for the one who lived it, and yet it reveals no more than a ghostly image of that life, already far distant, and doubtless incomplete, distorted furthermore by the fact that the man who remembers his past has not been for a long time the same being, the child or adolescent, who lived that past" (p. 38).
3. This is worsened by the thought that not even the dignity surrounding death, which has been the inspiration of so many poems ("The Burial of Sir John Moore at Corunna," Marvell's "Ode on the Execution of Charles I," James Shirley's "The Glories of our blood and state," Wordsworth's "A Slumber did my spirit seal," to name a few) or the obliviousness to death is available here. This *is* worse than death. Wordsworth catches the loss powerfully as he remembers the dead Lucy who seemed a thing that could not feel the touch of earthly years:

No motion has she now, no force,
She neither hears nor sees,
Rolled round in earth's diurnal course
With rocks and stones and trees.

If Lucy had been struck by Alzheimer's and Wordsworth had been caregiver (as indeed his wife was caregiver to his 90-year-old Alzheimer-stricken sister Dorothy), he might not have wanted that body to have motion or force but to lie still in earth.

REFERENCES

Bataille, G. (1983). *Inner experience.* Albany, NY: State University Press.
Bayley, J. (1998). *Iris.* London: Abacus.
Boden, C. (1998). *Who will I be when I die?* Sydney, Australia: Harper Collins Press.

Davis, B. (2005). *Alzheimer's talk: text and context.* London: Palgrave.

Derrida, J. (1976). *Of grammatology.* (trans. G. C. Spivak). Baltimore: Johns Hopkins University.

Derrida, J. (1978). *Writing and difference* (trans. A. Bass). Chicago: Chicago University Press.

Eagleman, D. (2011). *Incognitio.* New York: Vintage Books.

Gee, J. (1990). *Social linguistics and literacies: Ideology in discourses.* Philadelphia: Falmer Press.

Gusdorf, G. (1980). Conditions and limits of autobiography. In J. Olney (Ed.), *Autobiography: Essays theoretical and critical* (pp. 25–70). Princeton: Princeton University Press.

Hamilton, H. (1994). *Conversations with an Alzheimer patient.* Cambridge: Cambridge University Press.

Hamilton, H. (2000). Dealing with declining health in old age: Identity construction in the open family letter exchange. In J.K. Peyton, P. Griffin, W. Wolfram, & R. Fasold (Eds.), *Language in action: New studies in language in society in honor of Roger Shuy* (pp. 577–590). Cresskill, NJ: Hampton Press.

Hamilton, H. (2008). Narrative as snapshot: Glimpses into the past in Alzheimer discourse. *Narrative Inquiry, 18*(1), 53–82.

Honel, R.W. (1988). *Journey with Grandpa: Our family's struggle with Alzheimer's disease.* Baltimore, MD: Johns Hopkins University Press.

Kramsch, C. (2000). Social discursive constructions of self in L2 learning. In J. Lantolf (Ed.), *Sociocultural theory and second language learning* (pp. 129–153). London: Longman.

Lejeune, P. (1975). *Le pacte autobiographique.* Paris: Editions du Seuil.

Linde, C. (2009). *Working the past: Narrative and institutional memory.* Oxford: Oxford University Press.

McGowin, D. (1993). *Living in the labyrinth: A personal journey through the maze of Alzheimer's.* San Francisco: Elder Books.

Menard-Warwick, J. (2004). "I have always had the desire to progress a little": Gendered narratives of immigrant language learner. *Journal of Language, Identity and Education, 3*(4), 295–311.

Pavlenko, A. (2007). Autobiographic narratives as data in applied linguistics. *Applied Linguistics, 28*(2), 168–188.

Ramanathan, V. (1997). *Alzheimer discourse: some sociolinguistic dimensions.* Mahwah, NJ: Lawrence Erlbaum, Associates.

Ramanathan, V. (2010). *Bodies and language: Health, ailments, disabilities.* Clevedon, Bristol: Multilingual Matters.

Ramanathan, V., & Makoni, S. (2008). Bringing the body back in body narratives: The (mis)languaging of bodies in bio-medical, societal and post-structuralist discourses on diabetes and epilepsy. *Critical Inquiry in Language Studies, 4*(4), 283–306.

Ryan, E. B., Bannister, K. A., & Anas, A. P. (2009). The dementia narrative: Writing to reclaim social identity. *Journal of Aging Studies, 23*(3), 145–157.

Schrauf, R., & Iris, M. (2011). A direct comparison of popular models of normal memory loss and Alzheimer's disease in samples of African Americans, Mexican Americans, and refugees/immigrants from the Former Soviet Union. *Journal of the American Geriatrics Society, 59*(4), 628–636.

Seigel, J. (2005). *The idea of the self: Thought and experience in western Europe since the seventeenth century*. Cambridge: Cambridge University Press.

Zabbia, K. (1996). *Painted Diaries: A mother and daughter's experience through Alzheimer's*. Minneapolis: Fairview Press.

10

FORMULAIC LANGUAGE AND THREAT
The Challenge of Empathy and Compassion in Alzheimer's Disease Interaction

Alison Wray

INTRODUCTION: THE CHALLENGE OF COMPASSION AND EMPATHY IN DEMENTIA INTERACTION

There is increasing interest in how to bring compassion back into the care services, including care for older people and, in particular, people with dementia. In the UK there has been a focus on dignity in care in recent years, with stories of poor practices brought to light in high-profile reports (e.g., Abraham, 2011; Commission on Dignity in Care for Older People, 2012). Typically, the problems of physical neglect and mental abuse that hit the headlines are attributed to the high demands placed on healthcare systems and limited resources to meet them, exacerbated by competition and market-driven priorities (Goodrich & Cornwell, 2011; Youngson, 2011; Zigmond, 2011). Notwithstanding questions around the personal ethical challenges associated with delivering healthcare under these constraints (see, for example, the discussion group led by philosophers, http://www.thinkabouthealth.net/), poor practice seems to be viewed as endemic and, so far, intransigent at the institutional level, even while individuals are praised for their own approach and level of commitment.

Certainly, within institutional dementia care there are considerable pressures on staff, which can result in a rather perfunctory level of engagement, with low levels of real communication (Alzheimer's Society, 2007, p. v). However, the problems cannot be entirely attributed to the systems of formal care provision, for family members also can find it difficult to sustain a compassionate approach to the care of someone with dementia. Carer forums on the internet often feature personal reports by family members who have coped, or not coped, with the stresses of the carer role. One headed 'Lost it this morning and feeling incredibly guilty' is typical:

> I shouted at him and subsequently broke down in tears in front of him, he knew I was mad at him (I'm not, I'm furious at this awful disease) and exhausted from lack of sleep and his constant need for me.
>
> (http://forum.alzheimers.org.uk/showthread.php?3442, posted 25.05.2011)

In 2013, the Royal College of General Practitioners petitioned for more help for the UK's 7 million family care-givers, 40 percent of whom experience depression or other psychological problems (*Guardian*, 2013). The even higher proportions of 50 percent and 60 percent have been cited by Moore (2005) and Brereton (2012), respectively. The absence of adequate support for care-givers is a time-bomb for the health services since, if there is a crisis of stress, both the care-giver and the cared-for will need professional intervention (Lilly, Robinson, Holtzman, & Bottorff, 2012).

In this chapter it will be suggested that there is a link, through language, between the challenges of compassionate care and the stress experienced by care-givers. For a combination of cognitive and social reasons, people with Alzheimer's disease (AD) need to rely more and more on formulaic language. It will be proposed that this type of language exacerbates an element of a larger problem associated with how care-givers are evolutionarily and culturally primed to approach their role. The argument will be based on the account offered by Gilbert (Cole-King & Gilbert, 2011; Gilbert, 2006, 2009, 2012) of how compassion fits into broader patterns of behaviors that humans have evolved to select. The subsequent section examines the patterns of formulaic language use in normal and disordered communication, and the underlying reasons for them. Following that, the case for why these patterns would create stress for care-givers will be developed, and why there is no easy escape. The final section of this chapter outlines why training care-givers in mindful compassion may offer a way out of the trap.

THE THREAT IMPULSE AND ITS ROLE IN REDUCING THE CAPACITY FOR COMPASSION

Interest in how to train care-givers to behave more compassionately (e.g., Chambers & Ryder, 2011; Cole-King & Gilbert, 2011) often focuses on the capacity for techniques like mindfulness and meditation to reduce stress, where there is some evidence of success (Lavretsky et al., 2013; Oken et al., 2010; Waelde, Thompson, & Gallagher-Thompson, 2004). Gilbert (2006, 2009, 2012) explains the effectiveness of such approaches by locating self-awareness and awareness of others within a model of how humans are evolutionarily primed to behave in different situations. He defines compassion as "a basic kindness, with a deep awareness of the suffering of oneself and of other living things, coupled with the wish and effort to relieve it" (Gilbert, 2009, p. xiii), and observes,

> To be compassionate, a set of abilities (not just a motive or desire to care) are necessary, such as being sensitive to distress, being emotionally moved by distress in others (sympathy), able to tolerate distress (rather than run away or avoid it), develop empathy and understanding for the causes of the distress and to be non-judgemental. (Gilbert, 2006, p. 149)

Gilbert proposes that humans have inherited a system for managing their interaction with the world and each other that is dominated by the response to threat, since assessing risk and avoiding danger are a primitive survival drive across species that must override other impulses such as searching for food. He proposes that even in today's complex society, we continue to evaluate situations for potential threat and deploy strategies for staying safe. Two other system components, a competitive drive for excitement and novelty and a drive to seek reassurance and security, interact with threat and, in the natural world, operate symbiotically to create a balance that enables social bonds and creativity, both of which also offer survival advantages. For instance, risk-taking for gain (the excitement and novelty drive) will be monitored for threat of danger. And at times of perceived threat, humans will seek out comfort and reassurance from others. It follows that those others must be there and able to offer that support. But that will only be possible if they themselves are not experiencing excessive pressure of threat.

Gilbert proposes that certain features of modern (Western) society unseat the natural balance between the three drives by creating and sustaining an environment in which we perceive, and respond to, threat at an abnormally high level. In particular, cultural preoccupations with competition rather than collaboration engender a constant anxiety about how we are performing relative to others. Gilbert (2009, p. xxv) proposes that "[t]he more threat-absorbed we are, the more difficult compassion can be to achieve." This is not just because compassion cannot prevail, but because if the impulse to be competitive is dominant, it will actually be beneficial for the individual to be "relatively *in*sensitive to the distress one causes others . . . [and] . . . *turn off* certain processes that are associated with care-concern, guilt over harming, sympathy and compassion" (Gilbert, 2006, p. 149, original emphasis).

Although Gilbert's model offers an explanation for an endemic reduction of compassion in Western society, it does not directly explain why care-givers should struggle to be compassionate when looking after people with AD. Indeed, on the contrary, one might imagine that such a context would maximize the potential for compassion, both on account of the evident neediness of the person with AD and the likely disposition of the care-giver, whether a professional who has chosen to work in this domain, or as a loving family-member anxious to ensure their loved one is as comfortable as possible.

However, it will be proposed later in this chapter that Gilbert's model does indeed explain the problems that arise in the AD context. First, the patterns of formulaic language used by a person with AD and a care-giver can engender negative responses in the latter, associated with competition and threat. Second, the context of interaction can prevent the caregiver from overriding that impulse, resulting in a conflict between their desired and actual behavior and engendering high levels of personal stress. Insofar as this stress reflects or results in negative feelings about themselves, care-givers will be in a weaker position to enact self-compassion, which is a prerequisite of compassion for others (Hanh, 2001). In order to explain how this situation arises, it is necessary first to outline the main ways in which formulaic language manifests in AD speech, and why it does so.

MANIFESTATIONS OF FORMULAIC LANGUAGE IN NORMAL AND DISORDERED INTERACTION

The Nature of Formulaic Language

Formulaic language is widely recognized as a common characteristic of both normal and abnormal language. It includes, inter alia, routine expressions, fillers and verbatim repetitions, which seem to by-pass full encoding or decoding at the lexical or morphemic level, because some or all of the material is stored in pre-constructed form (Wray, 2002a). Just as it is possible for someone with no knowledge of French to sing a verse of *Frère Jacques* without needing to construct the grammatical forms from scratch, so, it seems, we can reproduce strings of words from our own language without engaging our full encoding capacities—even though we have the knowledge to do so.

Underpinning the theoretical accounts of formulaic language is the assumption that there are more demands on processing than we can comfortably manage, so that saving on processing by relying on pre-fabricated sequences increases our overall capacity for production and comprehension (Kuiper, 1996; Wray, 2002a). Several lines of evidence support this proposal, including simulations in which real communication is facilitated using prefabricated material (e.g., Wray, 2002b, 2004, 2008a), and evidence of faster processing activity for certain kinds of familiar or frequent wordstrings (e.g., Siyanova-Chanturia, Conklin, & Schmitt, 2011; Tremblay & Baayen, 2010).

Wray (2002a) proposes that formulaic language performs a set of interrelated functions, all focused on promoting the survival and well-being of the speaker. The human's drive to survive is primary, and language is deployed to support it. As listeners we aim to glean information from others that may be beneficial to our capacity to fulfill physical, psychological and emotional needs—where to find food, how to achieve something important, what our loved ones will most reward us for doing for them, and so on. As speakers, we attempt to manipulate others in order to control our physical, mental and emotional world. Although there are inherent processing advantages in selecting previously used wordstrings, the main value to the speaker is that they are easy for the hearer to process. Speakers select the wordstrings that others are most likely to understand with least processing since this is the most reliable way to ensure they are appropriately decoded and responded to.

Of course, speakers cannot expect to deliver novel information if they only draw on what their addressee has previously said. Thus, much of the resource is partly underspecified—frames with gaps for content words. And it also means that output will tend to consist of a patchwork of formulaic and non-formulaic material or, in the terms of construction grammar (e.g., Goldberg, 2003, 2006), fully lexicalized and partially lexicalized constructions. A very clear example of this combination is provided by Kuiper (1996), who shows how auctioneers and sports commentators sustain fluent fast speech by producing a great many preconstructed expressions and frames, between and into which they can slot the new information. Listeners can easily spot the formulaic material because of its familiarity from past experience in the same context and its classic phonological features (e.g., faster, more assimilation and vowel reduction; Lin, 2010). They can assign a global meaning or function to such material that obviates the need to unpack it further, leaving their processing resources free to engage with the new information.

In other words, speakers signal to hearers how much attention to pay to different parts of what is said: how to foreground and background, what is given and what is new, and what is up for questioning and negotiation. Thus, hearers can direct their own limited cognitive capacities towards the elements most likely to be of joint relevance. A hearer will be able to tell the difference between the four instances of *you know* in Example 1 and recognize that only the last of them actually requires attention to the proposition 'you know'. (The first is a topic marker, the second a filler, the third marks given, agreed information.)

Example 1:

'You know' (constructed)

you know that woman in flat 3, you know, the one you know from college, well, did you know her son died

Since speakers learn which wordstrings to use by attending to and reproducing the ones they have heard others use, in due course members of a speech community come to share the same ways of expressing common and important ideas. This process has some important consequences. Through repeated use without full analysis, formulaic language typically accumulates lexical, grammatical and phonological features that make it difficult to decode if you don't already know what it means (Bybee, 2010; Bybee & Torres Cacoullos, 2009; Lin, 2010). As a result, it will be difficult for outsiders to understand, and thus it creates a protective marker of identity around the community, much as jargon does in the more localized communities of specialized work and leisure. Accordingly, Wray and Grace (2007) suggest that different levels of formulaicity will naturally be found in different types of cultural context—the more inward-looking and exclusive a group, the more formulaic their language can be since they share a lot of contextual information. Conversely, groups that often interact with outsiders will tend to reduce the overall level of formulaicity since it is a barrier to communication (see also Trudgill, 2011).

It follows that formulaic language acquires a set of rather subtle roles in communication that contribute to cohesion in society. As hearers, we become well-attuned to the social and psychological significance of others' linguistic choices—such as a teenager using the expressions of his peers, and the dynamics of inclusion and exclusion when 'in-group' language is used.

However, formulaic language contributes to a further layer of social meaning making, too. If language is a toolbox that contains devices for conveying many different types of information (e.g., meaning, function, attitude, identity), there is also information encoded in the *manner* in which the tools themselves are deployed—that is, subtle features are encoded in the ways we use language as a whole. For instance, not speaking, when one could, can carry more meaning than words themselves.

In the present context of AD interaction, two such features of deployment are particularly relevant. The first is the way our use of language signals the level of attention we are paying to a situation or an interlocutor. As will be outlined next, the presence and absence of formulaic language is highly significant in this regard. The second is the way in which the tools in the language toolbox can be assigned new functions if the normal tool for the job is unavailable—as if the wrench is called upon to hammer in a nail because the hammer cannot be found. The loss of language in AD can make it difficult to achieve previously simple communicative tasks in the customary way, but the speaker may nevertheless be able to patch the problem using language that is still to hand—and a primary resource will be formulaic language.

Formulaic Language in Language Disorders

In language disorders, formulaic language can become, or at least seem to become, more prominent (Wray, 2008b). In a context where fluency is diminished overall, whether on account of aphasia, AD or something else, the successful production of multiword strings will be striking and may lead to inaccurate assumptions on the part of the observer about the overall capacity of the speaker to construct strings of grammatical output (Wray, 2002a). It has long been recognized that in dysfluent aphasias a small number of formulaic expressions may be available for production, even though the words within them cannot be separately used (Van Lancker, 1987). As indicated previously, this phenomenon is normally explained in terms of a separate lexical representation for the expression, which can therefore be produced whole without reference to its components.

If we take it that formulaic expressions are lexical entries just like words, then explanations for their use should be based on the relative availability of words and wordstrings. In this case, all other things being equal (e.g., there could be constraints on access that are related purely to length), all lexical entries will be subject to the same parameters affecting access. One such parameter might be that it is easier and more useful to produce a lexical item that represents a complete function (e.g., *yes, thanks; see you later*) or meaning (e.g., *John; here; over there*) rather than one that is incomplete on its own (e.g., *more; latest; in order to*). If so, the tendency for functional messages to be carried by multiword strings, and for formulaic expressions to carry a large portion of the entire proposition (e.g., *if I were you*)—and often all of it (e.g., *there's no time like the present*)—will make them particularly useful. Single words, even if successfully produced to express the desired meaning, will tend to reinforce the impression of inadequate communication since we use utterance length as an informal gauge of fluency.

Nevertheless there are many puzzles about the nature and distribution of formulaic material in language disorders that remain unexplained. One of them turns the customary approach on its head and, instead of asking why formulaic expressions are so common in otherwise disordered language, asks why so many of them are *not* apparently available. Among the enormous set of multiword strings in a native speaker's lexicon (Pawley & Syder, 1983), what is special about the small subset that remains accessible?

One possible answer relates to the generally held view that among the multiword entries in the lexicon are many incomplete frames, or constructions, that require an additional operation, usually the insertion of another item, to complete them (Goldberg, 2003, 2006). If we suppose, as before, that all lexical entries are equally likely to be available or unavailable for retrieval, then we would hypothesize that both lexically complete (e.g., *Thank you very much; I wouldn't do that if I were you*) and incomplete items (e.g., *Could you* VERB *for me? It's* DAY *today. I've been watching* TV PROGRAM) could be produced. But the latter, requiring additional processing, might not be completed successfully, and thus could be perceived primarily in terms of their *failure* as utterances, rather than their partial success, since the missing information is the very part that delivers the bespoke meaning. Indeed, other than when collected by linguists with an interest in usage-based linguistic knowledge and production, such frames might not be recognized as formulaic at all. As a result, it may be that rather more formulaic lexical entries are accessed and available in acquired dysfluent language conditions than customarily thought. And if so, there may be more resources available for communication than is often assumed.

Formulaic Language in Alzheimer's Disease

Turning specifically to the linguistic challenges of people with AD, there are particular ways in which formulaic language might be triggered, over and above the uses associated with language disorders more generally. In order to understand why, it is important to see how uses of language reflect the core problems arising from AD. Alzheimer's disease affects different parts of the brain—some directly associated with language functions but others indirectly affecting language. For instance, damage to the hippocampus and entorhinal cortex, which can occur quite early, depletes the transfer of short term memories to longer term storage (Hampel et al., 2008). Difficulties with memory will impact on how a person understands and produces language quite independently of any problems arising from damage to the language areas themselves. In particular, it will be difficult to sustain the thread of a conversation and to plan complex utterances.

Furthermore, virtually any kind of functional problem, whether linguistic or not, can affect confidence, attitude and interactional behavior. Individual variation in the extent and impact of AD (Prince & Jackson, 2009) may be partly attributable to differences in how people cope with the arising problems. Someone who has an effective strategy for covering up their difficulties may not only feel better, but also elicit a more supportive response from others (e.g., Maureen Littlejohn in Davis & Maclagan's chapter, this volume; Joan in Wray, 2010, described in the following section). Formulaic language is one mechanism for coping with the communication problems that AD brings.

The Patching Role of Formulaic Language in AD Communication

Interpreting the ways that formulaic language is deployed to accommodate problems in AD communication relies on understanding its roles in normal communication. The most parsimonious explanation will be one in which formulaic language is not reinvented as a communication tool—that is, is not called upon to do something new—but rather continues to do what it has always done, but to a greater and lesser extent than previously, as the triggers for its use change. In particular, as memory problems increase the pressures on cognitive processing, formulaic language will be called upon to work harder than it previously did in reducing processing pressure.

The effect can be illustrated by considering how lapses in lexical access are handled. Problems with retrieving lexical items can arise for anyone, and formulaic language, in the form of fillers such as *you know, what do you call it*, and so on, are customarily used as placeholders in lieu of the intended item. Although many such expressions contain more words than the target item, their presence in the lexicon as a single entry means they are no more troublesome to retrieve than a single word, and indeed they are presumably easier to retrieve than the target because they are so frequently used for that function. The more problems there are with lexical retrieval, the more fillers there will need to be if the output is not to break down. The following examples are taken from a case study of 'Joan', a singing teacher with AD symptoms, who used place fillers to complete her sentences.

Example 2a:

Joan's fillers (Wray, 2010, p. 523)

a) So that you do that, darling.

b) It makes it go on like that all the time.

c) It's that kind of feeling, you know, of doing it.

d) So you've got to do there, darling.

e) You've got to watch the high note that's got the feel of it, this business.

Example 2b:

Joan's fillers (unpublished data from the same study)

Polly   It's hard when you're holding the copy.

Joan   Yes, holding the copy, that's right, hold it up. Send it to me, send it to me like that, up up up, don't forget people are, and things are down there, but up there yes.

Here, as in the subsequent discussion, it should be kept in mind that formulaic language is simply one of a set of tools and so is not the only potential way of patching a problem. Another solution to the loss of a word is circumlocution or the selection of a synonym, which may be so successful that the original difficulty is not detectable. Alternatively, the speaker may effect a self-repair that changes the structure so that the failure to supply the missing word no longer appears relevant. In Example 3, the interviewer (IV) has asked the patient (P) to recount an incident from that morning in which he got lost. The extract here begins after eight turns. In both of P's utterances he comes to a place where he needs to supply content information (in the form, presumably, of a lengthy memorized string constituting his address). In the first case he patches with a circumlocution, and in the second he 'repairs' the utterance by using a new sentence to comment on the failure to complete the previous one.

Example 3:

Getting lost (Asp & de Villiers, 2010, pp. 143–144)

IV   Do you know your address off by heart?

P   Uh it's at uh # well # the one I'm staying at that's at her her uh her place here

IV   Can you tell me what the address is?

P   Well that's uh # I I should have been able to

Cognitive processing problems will also potentially impact on the discourse as a whole. If the thread of the discourse is lost, a conversation will either break down or go off track. For unimpaired speakers, such problems tend to arise through lack of attention, competing processing activities, or reduced processing capacity (e.g., due to tiredness). In AD, the impairment to short term memory can make it difficult to hold onto the thread of a conversation. In Example 4, from Jones (2012), May is talking to Natalie on the telephone about her room in her care home. In the course of the conversation, she forgets what they are talking about. She simply asks for clarification, and if her turn is formulaic (e.g., QUESTION again?), it is no more so than other lexis that she uses.

Example 4:

May's room (Jones, 2012, pp. 188–189)[1]

124	May	I will go and find it. And stay there
125	Nat	Al:ri:ight
126	(.)	
127	May	Okay,
...	...	...
152	Nat	.hh Well your room's lovely the:re
153	(1.5)	
154	Nat	I [don-] if you could just remember it you'd–well =
155	May	[( )]
156	Nat	= go and find it. You'll find how nice it is.

157		(0.2)

157   (0.2)

158 May Where am I going again.

159 Nat Your room n that (0.2) pla:ce where you're

160   staying.

In Example 5, from Asp and de Villiers (2010), P similarly uses a direct question to restore the topic, but the preceding turns feature a number of formulaic expressions that seem to be an attempt to hold onto and work with the receding topic. P is talking with two caregivers (CG) about the risks of getting scalded in the shower. The entire quoted text is 20 lines long of which the following quoted section begins at line 10.

Example 5:

Scalding water (Asp & de Villiers, 2010, pp. 182–183)[2]

P: My Mom my Mom used to have a: people used to say she doesn't even put her you know [if] she doesn't even bother to put the this here and that there

P: I don't know

P: she is always taking care of herself

P: she's always you know

P: and then she'd turn right around and disconnect what I had been talking about

P: and I mean she's everybody used to think you know I I'll be lucky if I'm doing that or I'll be lucky

P: if I you're not lucky girl you've had it

P: and ah # I don't know #

P: what have we got to now?

CG1: scalding scalding in the hot water

P: no no

Asp and de Villiers speculate about whether P is talking about scalding or not, and note the impossibility of being sure, because the frequency of incomplete utterances, false starts, indefinite reference and reference without antecedent, together with limited lexicalization and marked modalization are features which make it difficult to identify topic of even a coherent relationship between the predications that are actually complete. (p. 183)

P seems to hold in mind the basic idea of the risk of being scalded in the shower. And she seems to have generated a related, new idea regarding her mother. But she struggles to bring the ideas together into coherent linguistic output, and her output is characterized by linking expressions (e.g., *I don't know; people use to say X; I'll be lucky*). Elsewhere, the vital lexical item of reference is missing (lines 2, 5, 7, 10). Although this could indicate simple word-finding difficulties, rather than loss of the thread of meaning, certainly her question in line 11 is interpreted by the caregiver as an indication that she has forgotten the main idea of the conversation.

It is not only pressure on processing that a person with AD has to navigate. As the world becomes more troublesome to manage single-handedly, formulaic language will play an ever greater role in manipulating others to meet the speaker's needs. This may include repeated questions to fill gaps in short term memory. And as AD gradually robs the person of her sense of normality and identity and her capacity to understand where she and others fit in the immediate situation, formulaic language will be used for anchoring routines and a sense of self. In the former case, repetition may itself be part of the routine. In Brown and Clegg (2007, p. 135; also available at http://www.trebusprojects.org/read/stories-in-extremis/lily), Lily, whom they describe as having "more progressed dementia," recites a lengthy account of what she does each morning, itemizing her routine activities, from getting out of bed, through feeding the cats and taking her tablets, to getting ready to go out. This narrative, which she repeats over and over in almost identical words, may be a means for her to ensure she remembers to do the various important things that she is describing.

Repetition of statements that anchor identity, on the other hand, may reflect anxiety. Joan, in Wray's (2010) study, delivered on three different occasions what was almost certainly a much more longstanding autobiographical phrase, about having played a certain operatic role a large number of times at a particular opera house. On the first occasion she stood on the stairs, announcing her achievement to the group below, and on the third she cupped her hands round her mouth like a megaphone, again marking her utterance as a speech act.

If such repetitions, and other formulaic language, play a significant role for a person with AD in helping them rescue communication or elements of self that feel unsafe, they also have an impact on those who receive them, and not necessarily a positive one.

THE ROLE OF FORMULAIC LANGUAGE IN CREATING STRESS AND REDUCING COMPASSION IN CARE-GIVERS

As pointed out earlier, formulaic language is a core part of a contract between speaker and hearer. The uses of it are subtly managed within normal interaction—neither too much nor too little must be produced—with high sensitivity to the knowledge and expectations of the interlocutor. In AD, these balances are upset by the huge increase in the amount of formulaic language. In this section, we will examine different aspects of this disruption, which jointly explain why it is difficult for care-givers to make the necessary adjustments. That is, one might ask why care-givers do not simply rewrite the contract to allow for more formulaicity. We shall see that there are particular reasons why it is difficult for them to do so, and that they relate directly to the question of why compassionate care is challenging, and why caring is so stressful.

Ways of Interpreting Excessive Formulaic Language

We have seen earlier in this chapter that there are a number of legitimate reasons why the amount of formulaic language produced by a person with AD might increase. Formulaic language is a tool that we learn to deploy in a number of ways to facilitate effective communication, exploiting the fact that it requires less processing. In situations where we are under more cognitive strain, we will naturally resort to a greater use of formulaic language. It is a means of coping. The problem is that formulaic language is not a neutral package. It already has a set of functions, and they are fine-tuned for normal interaction. Therefore, it is easy for the changes in formulaic language use in AD to be misconstrued.

Table 10.1 shows how a care-giver could be drawn into a negative reaction to formulaic language, by interpreting it from the standpoint of normal communication: it will seem excessive and in breach of the customary rules of use. In order to avoid this happening, a care-giver needs to be able to recognize which elements of the formulaic language use are normal and which are not. It is normal to solve the problems listed in the final column using formulaic language. A person who is very tired or distracted might solve them in the same way. The issue is not that the person with AD is using language inappropriately, but rather that it appears inappropriate when construed as having been created on the basis of normal processing capacities. We shall see presently *why* it is not a simple matter for a care-giver to remove the expectation of normal language use when interacting with a person with AD. First, however, we will consider the impact of not being able to do so.

As the third column of Table 10.1 indicates, a care-giver who receives the formulaic language of a person with AD as if it were part of normal communication is at risk of feeling insulted, undervalued, ignored and patronized. Under such conditions, which might constitute an element of 'threat' in Gilbert's terms, it would not be unreasonable for the care-giver to respond defensively, whether with aggressive counter-attacks or by taking steps to reduce the level of threat. Many could entail formulaic language, e.g., aggressive parroting of questions and statements, the use of formulaic commands or comments, and so on (Wray, 2011). A powerful means of achieving protection against apparent rejection of one's extensive personal effort is to reduce the level of engagement: if

Table 10.1
Ways of construing formulaic language use

Type of formulaic language	Significance when used in:		
	Normal quantities	Excessive quantities	AD language
Manipulative requests or statements	Fast track to appropriate action. Not worth unpacking. Not intended to be rude.	Rude	Reduced sense of agency and increased anxiety → increased need to control things. Unable to formulate more subtle alternatives
Repetition	Marked. But there must be a reason why you repeated this (apply Grice's Maxims)	You have not been listening/engaging	Previous iterations or their outcomes forgotten. Repetition is easier than a new configuration
Express identity or feelings (e.g., swearing)	Signal of belonging or distancing	Showing off; making a point; being offensive	Need to constantly reinforce diminishing sense of own identity
Back-channelling and background discourse marking	Appropriate low level engagement, so as not to detract from big ideas	You're not paying attention to me	Struggling to follow discourse; bootstrapping to hold ideas together
Fillers	Expressing difficult ideas or tired. Sympathetic	Irritated; hard to follow	Word finding difficulties; patching as best can

not much is put in, then that becomes the reason why not much is given back. A care-giver who reduces his cognitive engagement during inter-action with a person with AD will draw on the same resource that saves on cognitive processing in AD: formulaic language. Thus, the care-giver may produce repetitive, superficial or off-pat responses to statements and questions.

Wray (2011, 2012) discusses this pattern in some depth, showing how it can lead to a vicious circle of formulaicity, with little cognitive engage-ment for either party. Example 6 illustrates the case. Daisy's statements are ones that she very often makes, so they can be regarded as formu-laic for her—manipulative requests for confirmation of her identity. The nurse's responses are both appropriate and relevant, but the way they mirror Daisy's words, and are produced without turning round, suggest she is engaging cognitively only at a minimum level.

Example 6

Daisy (Clegg, 2010, p. xxiii)

1	Daisy:	Are you my mother
2	Nurse:	(without turning round): No Daisy I'm not your mother
3	Daisy:	I'm your daughter (.) say I'm pretty
4	Nurse:	You're pretty

The Double-Bind of a Care-giver's Response to Formulaic Language

If, as has been suggested, care-givers experience hurt and frustration as a result of interpreting AD formulaic language as a version of nor-mal language, why do they not simply recategorize it as abnormal? To understand why, we need to consider how very strong the drive is to interpret language input as comprehensible and relevant. Wilson and Sperber (2002) propose that humans have evolved to seek relevance in the stimuli in their environment. Grice (1975) proposed that humans are bound to assume that their interlocutor is attempting to apply core maxims relating to the quantity, quality, relevance and manner.

To abandon the interpretation of AD language as normal would be to abandon the applicability of these maxims. And since the maxims are taken by speakers and hearers to be universal, if one excuses a speaker from adhering to them, one is undercutting a core element of what makes them human. Wray (in press) explores this paradox in more depth and proposes that it creates a quandary for a care-giver. On the one hand, to treat the language of the person with AD as normal means that what is being said is hurtful, and this, as we have just seen, may be an incentive for the care-giver to respond defensively, in ways that are less than compassionate. On the other hand, to treat the language of the person with AD as abnormal because it breaches the basic terms by which pragmatics operate between humans in communication, is to challenge the person's capacity to behave like a human being, and this might change the ground rules for how the person is treated. Wray proposes that neither of these scenarios is morally acceptable for most care-givers so that they reject their own responses and they experience uncomfortable dissonances between their reactions to caring and their aspirations for being a compassionate care-giver. It is this double-bind that causes the stress.

WHY EMPATHY AND COMPASSION TRAINING MIGHT HELP

It was noted earlier that increasing attention is being paid to ways of teaching care-givers to be more compassionate, something that is achieved by means of empathy-training (Blane & Mercer, 2011), mindfulness and spirituality (Gilbert, 2009, 2012; Lavretsky et al., 2013; Oken et al., 2010; Waelde et al., 2004). In this final section, we will consider how these approaches might break down the impasse created by the response of care-givers to the language of people with AD.

Escaping the double-bind must entail untangling the two elements, which between them place the care-giver in a position where it is acceptable neither to view the person with AD as a normal interactant nor an abnormal one. To do this, some underpinning assumptions must be re-evaluated. The AD intervention literature often invites care-givers to re-evaluate their assumptions as a mechanism for finding choices in their own behaviors. To give one example, there is considerable discussion in advice literature and web forums about the question of lying to a person with AD in order to avoid creating or exacerbating stress.[3] Typically, family members only slowly accept the possibility that it might be less distressing to enter the 'alternative reality' of a person with AD, who may believe their child to be their parent, or a deceased spouse still to be alive. Some therapies, such as Validation Therapy (Feil, 1993), aim to navigate a path between directly agreeing with a person's distorted view, which "can become detrimental when the person truly believes that something bad is happening" (Krauthamer, 2010, p. xv), and "accepting and validating the feelings of the demented old person; to acknowledge their reminiscences, losses and the human needs that underlie their behaviours without trying to insert or force new insights" (Feil, 1993, p. 200).

What the recommended approaches towards lying and distorted reality are doing is suggesting that care-givers create a distinction between their own reality and that of the person with AD, and that they then tolerate and manage the discrepancies in a sensitive manner. A care-giver may have to accept that in the alternative reality of the person with AD, they have rather little importance, and can expect little. This diminution of their status is stressful for as long as it appears to be a version of their own reality (e.g., what their mother *really* thinks of them). Managing the discrepancies entails simultaneously and independently working with their own beliefs and those of the person with AD.

Compassion training, particularly if through mindfulness, encourages trainees to become fully aware of their own thoughts and feelings, and then to challenge the assumption that they are the only reality. As a result, they are able to recognize that their own perspective is neither the only nor necessarily the most important one in a given situation. One of the characteristics of empathy is the capacity to "understand [another person's] situation, perspective, and feelings (and their attached meanings)" (Mercer & Reynolds, 2002, p. S9). This entails disentangling one's own beliefs and motives from those of others and examining their relationship.

A care-giver who is able to juxtapose two different experiences of the world is in a strong position to escape the double-bind of AD communication. This escape will be achieved by recognizing that, by default, the pragmatics of communication entail our interpreting what others do in terms of what we would mean if we were doing it ourselves. For instance, when we infer that an interlocutor is bored with us because they have used excessive formulaic language, we are drawing on how we ourselves would respond linguistically if bored, and assuming that others are like us. In normal circumstances, we may well be right in our interpretation, though not necessarily right about its motivation—if our interlocutor is distracted because of a significant worry that we are not aware of, we may misinterpret their behavior as simply dismissive of our importance to them.

But when our interlocutor has very different reasons for using that amount of formulaic language than we would have, the default assumption that speaker and hearer are applying the linguistic rules in the same way is inappropriate. Escaping the double bind will involve recognizing that not all humans are exactly like me. It means not jumping to conclusions about what a particular linguistic action signifies and looking for more subtle ways to navigate the similarities and differences between self and another.

Although interpreting formulaic language according to its normal pragmatic principles remains possible, a second option thus opens up because of the capacity for heightened awareness of parallel ways of see-ing and dealing with the world. In a nutshell, it becomes easier to won-der, when hearing a person with AD use formulaic language, what jobs that language might be doing, rather than assuming one already knows.

Recognizing that the very language that can be annoying and offen-sive can also be the lifeline of continuing communication, because it is a major tool for patching difficulties, will generate a different interpreta-tive space for care-givers. They can aim to understand what the speaker is trying to achieve by using this language, and use empathy as a means of understanding the challenges and imperatives that underpin the sur-face behavior.

Viewing formulaic language as a 'rescue remedy', that is, a significant communicative resource with enhanced functionality, does not entail complex engagement with linguistic principles because the underlying pattern is very simple. Formulaic language is a 'Swiss Army knife', capable of doing several things by virtue of a single characteristic: it requires less processing.

- It can ensure fluency and continuity of the interaction without over-burdening the weakened cognitive processing system. This enables the person with AD to manage her limited resources better. Using easily produced formulaic expressions deals with the linguistic pro-duction without detracting from the speaker's real focus of attention. So the question for the care-giver ceases to be, 'Why are you being so annoying?' and becomes, 'Where is the important new information that you are wanting to convey?'
- It can bundle up important affective information using little or no novel packaging. So the care-giver may ask, 'What is the *real* message underlying this formulaic expression?' For instance, is a repeated question actually a way of asking for reassurance? Is a repeated state-ment about the self an attempt to anchor the failing sense of identity?
- When cognition is compromised, formulaic language may not be a marker of *lack* of attention, as it would be in normal circumstances. Rather, it may be the very evidence of attention. Formulaic language may become the carrier of the main message, rather than back-ground information. Thus, it needs to be taken seriously, not neces-sarily for its *direct* content meaning, but for its functional purpose in the discourse. For example, Meg, in Clegg's (2010) study, responds to his help in untangling her fingers from the strings of an apron with a succession of her most common formulas, not all of which are directly relevant to the context, but all of which convey positive acknowledgement:

Example 7:

Meg saying thank you (Clegg, 2010, pp. xix-xx)[4]

Meg   Thank you . . . thank you . . . for helping me . . . one thousand times thank you . . . you're a nice lady . . . I'll write to you privately. You're my brother! Will you see me home now? . . .

CONCLUSION

It has been proposed in this chapter that part of the reason why care-givers struggle to behave with compassion and why they become so stressed is that the linguistic environment in which they operate puts them in a double bind. They naturally bring to the activity of care-giving a lifetime of linguistic experience that is difficult to set aside. Their default approach to understanding interaction offers them two ways of interpreting the significance of the formulaic language used by the person with AD. But neither of itself leads to a charitable interpretation of the nature of the communication, and thus both can tend to engender negative responses. This situation is morally and emotionally uncomfortable for care-givers, and the resulting dissonance leads to high levels of stress.

Approaches to compassion using mindfulness and empathy create a basis for releasing the care-giver from the traps created by customary receptions of formulaic language, which are inevitably informed by a personal view of their significance. They create a route for by-passing the care-giver's preoccupation with the 'curse of the self' (Leary, 2004): the persistent pursuance of attention, which Derber (2000) sees as creating the modern malaises of normal Western culture: stress, self-doubt, depression and anxiety. The double-bind is escaped by learning to recognize one's own perceptions of the interaction simply as perceptions, for which there may be more than one interpretation; and to hold and work with more than one such interpretation at once so that the underlying messages of the person with AD can be accessed more effectively.

If this explanation of the evidence for the effectiveness of mindful compassion as an approach to care-giving is right, then there are significant implications for society. Rather simple processes of training and awareness-raising could radically improve the day to day experiences of both people with AD and those who care for them.

NOTES

1. The numbers in the left hand column are the original transcript lines. The layout and punctuation are reproduced as in the original.

2. Transcription conventions are as the original (p. x).: is 'extension of previous vowel'; [if] is 'uncertain'; # is 'noticeable pause, unmeasured'.
3. See, for example, 'My dad has Alzheimer's. Is it ever okay to lie to him if it calms him down?' http://alzheimers.about.com/od/caregiving/f/lying. htm; 'Alzheimer's world and the art of lying' http://www.alzheimersread ingroom.com/2011/09/alzheimers-world-and-art-of-lying.html; 'Do you think it's okay to lie to a dementia patient?' http://caring-for-alzheimers. com/do-you-think-it-is-ok-to-lie-to-a-dementia-patient.php
4. In Clegg's transcription, dots signify only that the utterances are disjointed.

REFERENCES

Abraham, A. (2011). *Care and compassion? Report of the Health Service Ombudsman on ten investigations into NHS care of older people.* London: Her Majesty's Stationery Office.

Alzheimer's Society. (2007). *Home from home: A report highlighting the opportunities for improving standards of dementia care in care homes.* London: Alzheimer's Society.

Asp, E. D., & de Villiers, J. (2010). *When language breaks down.* Cambridge: Cambridge University Press.

Blane, D., & Mercer, S. W. (2011). Compassionate healthcare: Is empathy the key? *Journal of Holistic Healthcare, 8*(3), 18–21.

Brereton, D. (2012). Caring for carers: Supporting the wellbeing of Britain's hidden vulnerable. *Improving care, Improving Lives Conference.* Manchester, December 5th.

Brown, M., & Clegg, D. (Eds.). (2007). *Ancient mysteries.* London: Trebus Project. Available online at http://www.trebusprojects.org.

Bybee, J. (2010). *Language, usage and cognition.* Cambridge: Cambridge University Press.

Bybee, J., & Torres Cacoullos, R. (2009). The role of prefabs in grammaticization: How the particular and the general interact in language change. In R. Corrigan, E. Moravcsik, H. Ouali, & K. Wheatley (Eds.), *Formulaic language: Vol 1: Structure, distribution and historical change* (pp. 187–217). Amsterdam: John Benjamins.

Chambers, C., & Ryder, E. (2011). Excellence in compassionate nursing care: Leading the change. *Journal of Holistic Healthcare, 8*(3), 46–49.

Clegg, D. (Ed.). (2010). *Tell Mrs Mill her husband is still dead*: Trebus Project. Available online at http://www.trebusprojects.org.

Cole-King, A., & Gilbert, P. (2011). Compassionate care: The theory and the reality. *Journal of Holistic Healthcare, 8*(3), 29–37.

Commission on Dignity in Care for Older People. (2012). *Delivering dignity.* London: NHS Confederation.

Derber, C. (2000). *The pursuit of attention: Power and ego in everyday life* (2nd edition). Oxford: Oxford University Press.

Feil, N. (1993). Validation therapy with late-onset dementia populations. In G.M.M. Jones & B.M.L. Miesen (Eds.), *Care-giving in dementia: Research and applications, Vol 1* (pp. 199–218). New York: Routledge.

Gilbert, P. (2006). Old and new ideas on the evolution of mind and psychotherapy. *Clinical Neuropsychiatry, 3*(2), 139–153.

Gilbert, P. (2009). *The compassionate mind: Coping with the challenges of living.* London: Constable Robinson.

Gilbert, P. (2012). The conditions for a compassionate society. *Empathy and compassion in society: A conference for professionals in education, health and social care.* London, November 23–24.

Goldberg, A. E. (2003). Constructions: A new theoretical approach to language. *Trends in Cognitive Sciences, 7*(5), 219–224.

Goldberg, A. E. (2006). *Constructions at work.* Oxford: Oxford University Press.

Goodrich, J., & Cornwell, J. (2011). Seeing the person in the patient: The King's Fund Point of Care programme. *Journal of Holistic Healthcare, 8*(3), 10–12.

Grice, H. P. (1975). Logic and conversation. In P. Cole & J. L. Morgan (Eds.), *Syntax and Semantics, vol. 3* (pp. 41–58). New York: Academic Press.

Guardian (2013). Carers should be monitored for mental health problems, warn doctors. *The Guardian* on line, Saturday 11 May 2013, http://www.guardian.co.uk/society/2013/may/11/carers-monitored-mental-health-problems

Hampel, H., Bürger, K., Teipel, S. J., Bokde, A. L. W., Zetterberg, H., & Blennow, K. (2008). Core candidate neurochemical and imaging biomarkers of Alzheimer's disease. *Alzheimer's and Dementia, 4*(1), 38–48.

Hanh, T. N. (2001). *Anger: Buddhist wisdom for cooling the flames.* London: Rider.

Jones, D. (2012). *Family conversations with an Alzheimer's sufferer: A conversation analytic study.* Unpublished D. Phil thesis, University of York, UK.

Krauthamer, M. (2010). *Walking in their shoes: Communicating with loved ones who have Alzheimer's disease.* Bloomington, IN: Authorhouse.

Kuiper, K. (1996). *Smooth talkers: The linguistic performance of auctioneers and sportscasters.* Mahwah, NJ.: Lawrence Erlbaum.

Lavretsky, H., Spel, E., Siddarth, P., Nazarian, N., St Cyr, N., Khalsa, D., . . . Irwin, M. R. (2013). A pilot study of yogic meditation for family dementia caregivers with depressive symptoms: Effects on mental health, cognition and telomerase activity. *International Journal of Geriatric Psychiatry, 28*(1), 57–65.

Leary, M. R. (2004). *The curse of the self: Self-awareness, egotism and the quality of human life.* New York: Oxford University Press.

Lilly, M., Robinson, C., Holtzman, S., & Bottorff, J. (2012). Can we move beyond burden and burnout to support the health and wellness of family caregivers to persons with dementia? Evidence from British Columbia, Canada. *Health & Social Care in the Community, 20*(1), 103–112.

Lin, P.M.S. (2010). The phonology of formulaic sequences: A review. In D. Wood (Ed.), *Perspectives on formulaic language: Acquisition and communication* (pp. 174–193). London: Continuum.

Mercer, S. W., & Reynolds, W. J. (2002). Empathy and quality of care. *British Journal of General Practice, 52*(Supplement), S9–13.

Moore, W. (2005). *Carers and stress.* http://www.channel4.com/health/microsites//0-9/4health/stress/cws_carers.html

Oken, B., Fonareva, I., Hass, M., Wahbeh, H., Lane, J., Zajdel, D., & Amen, A. (2010). Pilot controlled trial of mindfulness meditation and education for dementia caregivers. *Journal of Alternative and Complementary Medicine, 16*(10), 1031–1038.

Pawley, A., & Syder, F. H. (1983). Two puzzles for linguistic theory: Nativelike selection and nativelike fluency. In J. C. Richards & R. W. Schmidt (Eds.), *Language and communication* (pp. 191–226). New York: Longman.

Prince, M., & Jackson, J. (2009). *World Alzheimer's report.* http://www.alz.co.uk/research/worldreport/.

Siyanova-Chanturia, A., Conklin, K., & Schmitt, N. (2011). Adding more fuel to the fire: An eye-tracking study of idiom processing by native and non-native speakers. *Second Language Research, 27*(2): 251–272.

Tremblay, A., & Baayen, H. (2010). Holistic processing of regular four-word sequences: A behavioural and ERP study of the effects of structure, frequency, and probability on immediate free recall. In D. Wood (Ed.), *Perspectives on formulaic language* (pp. 151–173). London: Continuum.

Trudgill, P. (2011). *Sociolinguistic typology: Social determinants of linguistic complexity.* Oxford: Oxford University Press.

Van Lancker, D. (1987). Nonpropositional speech: Neurolinguistic studies. In A. W. Ellis (Ed.), *Progress in the psychology of language, vol 3* (pp. 49–118). Hillsdale, NJ: Lawrence Erlbaum.

Waelde, L., Thompson, L., & Gallagher-Thompson, D. (2004). A pilot study of a yoga and meditation intervention for dementia caregiver stress. *Journal of Clinical Psychology, 60*(6), 677–687.

Wilson, D., & Sperber, D. (2002). Relevance theory. *UCL Working Papers in Linguistics, 14,* 249–290.

Wray, A. (2002a). *Formulaic language and the lexicon.* Cambridge: Cambridge University Press.

Wray, A. (2002b). Formulaic language in computer-supported communication: Theory meets reality. *Language Awareness, 11*(2), 114–131.

Wray, A. (2004). 'Here's one I prepared earlier': Formulaic language learning on television. In N. Schmitt (Ed.), *Formulaic sequences: Acquisition, processing and use* (pp. 249–268). Amsterdam: John Benjamins.

Wray, A. (2008a). *Formulaic language: Pushing the boundaries.* Oxford: Oxford University Press.

Wray, A. (2008b). Formulaic sequences and language disorders. In M. Ball, M. Perkins, N. Müller, & S. Howard (Eds.), *Handbook of clinical linguistics* (pp. 184–197). Oxford: Blackwell.

Wray, A. (2010). We've had a wonderful, wonderful thing: Formulaic interaction when an expert has dementia. *Dementia: The International Journal of Social Research and Practice, 9*(4), 517–534.

Wray, A. (2011). Formulaic language as a barrier to effective communication with people with Alzheimer's disease. *Canadian Modern Language Review, 67*(4), 429–458.

Wray, A. (2012). Patterns of formulaic language in Alzheimer's disease: Implications for quality of life. *Quality in Ageing and Older Adults, 13*(3), 168–175.

Wray, A. (in press). Mislaying compassion: Linguistic triggers for inadequate care-giving in Alzheimer's disease care. In B. Davis & J. Guendouzi (Eds.), *Pragmatics in dementia discourse.* Newcastle-Upon-Tyne: Cambridge Scholars Publishing.

Wray, A., & Grace, G. W. (2007). The consequences of talking to strangers: evolutionary corollaries of socio-cultural influences on linguistic form. *Lingua, 117*(3), 543–578.

Youngson, R. (2011). Compassion in healthcare: The missing dimension of healthcare reform? *Journal of Holistic Healthcare, 8*(3), 6–9.

Zigmond, D. (2011). Five executive follies: How commodification imperils compassion in personal healthcare. *Journal of Holistic Healthcare, 8*(3), 13–17.

AUTHOR INDEX

SUBJECT INDEX

acknowledging speaker involvement 127
activation: of semantic information
131–3; spreading 134, 138, 141, 143
affiliation 89
agency 215, 226, 239; interactional 220
alignment 16, 22, 87, 89, 90–1, 96, 111,
115, 151, 215
Alzheimer's Association 14
Alzheimer's Disease: co-construction
50–4; social history 13–14; see
frontotemporal dementia, compared to
Alzheimer's disease
American Psychiatric Association (APA)
7, 10
assessment: emotional / evaluative 115;
emotive / affective 92–3, 95, 97
attention 6, 11, 21, 40, 73, 121, 131, 141,
159, 173, 197, 200, 268–9, 273, 277,
281–2
attunement 16

brain: degeneration, areas of 147

CANCAD 104
Caregiving/caregivers: awareness
164–5; burden 161, 167, 174–7;
communication ; experiences 154–55,
174–7; responses 160–61
Carolina Conversations Collection 88
Central Surround Mechanism 132–33
chunk, chunking 98, 99, 109, 110, 116,
117
claims, displays, demonstrations of
understanding 17, 149, 150, 151–3,
156–7, 161, 163, 165, 167–8, 171–2,
174

cognition: "cognition in the wild" 64,
70, 80; cognitive schema 82, 132,
137–8, 140–4; definition 6–10, 62;
discursivist paradigm 13–22; ecological
validity 173–4 executive functioning
147–9 executive impairment 153,
159–60, 171–174 extended and
distributed 4, 6–8, 15, 17–18, 23,
62–4 frontotemporal dementia and
147–149 measures of 147–8; 153, 173
neurocognitive perspective 3–6,
16, 23
cognitive: deficits 122, 142; mechanisms
143–4; preserved skills 159, 171–4
processing load 130; resources 15,
121–3, 138, 142, 144, 153, 163
colloquialism(s) 97–8, 100–1, 116
common ground 65, 70, 82, 90
communication: environment 184–86
Communication Predicament of Aging
18, 184–88
compassion 21, 263–266, 276, 279–80,
282
compensatory strategies 16, 123, 133, 134,
141–42
continuer(s) 90, 91, 197, 222
conversation: adjacency pairs 35, 36,
40–41, 48, 53, 159, 160, 163, 173;
casual 63–4, 66; cooperative principle
16, 17, 124, 133, 138, 142; hypothesis
testing in c. 62, 71–3, 83; management
87–88, 103; modified repeats 157–8,
164 rehearsing information in c. 15,
64, 75–6, 79, 81; sequence(s) 149
sequential organization 155 *see also*
storytelling; writing